P9-BJW-171

POWER and PETROLEUM

VENEZUELA,

CUBA and COLOMBIA,

A TROIKA ?

by

EMMA BROSSARD, Ph.D.

Copyright 2001 by E.B.Brossard

Library of Congress Cataloging-in-Publication Data

All rights reserved, including the right of reproduction

Maps by Briant Peterson

Power and Petroleum: Venezuela, Cuba and Colombia,
A Troika?
by Emma Brossard

Includes index
1. Venezuelan government – Hugo Chavez – Petroleum
    Industry (PDVSA)
2. Cuba – Fidel Castro – History
3. Colombia – guerrilleros – History
4. China – Great Leap Forward - History

ISBN 0-9632261-6-9
Canaima Press

Printed on acid free paper
Manufactured in the United States of America

CONTENTS

Introduction   vi
Chapter I   AMERICA'S ENEMY: HUGO CHAVEZ   1
            The Floods
            Bolivarian Republic of Venezuela
            Enter Fidel Castro – and a "sea of happiness"
            Petroleos de Chavez
            Gran Colombia
Chapter II ELECTED DICTATOR –
            RICH GOVERNMENT, POOR PEOPLE   14
            Chavez's Incessant Voice, and Campaigns
            Venezuela's Constitutions and Presidents
            Constitutional Government
            The Chavez Government
            The Unions
            The Military
            Ceresole
            Education and Decree No. 1011
            Venezuela's Military History
            Narco Traffic
            Sovereignty
            Black Friday 1983 and the Bolivar
            The Venezuelan Economy
            The Airwaves
            The Church
            The Sao Paulo Forum
            Conclusion
Chapter III A HISTORIC TRAGEDY: PDVSA   51
            President Giusti
            Oil Industry as Provider (Cornucopia/Govt.)
            Apertura
            Cristobal Colon
            Strategic Associations
            First Round – Mature Fields
            Second Round – Mature Fields
            Profit Sharing Exploration
            The Lemmings Rush Off the Cliff

The New Realities
Restructuring: "the task of pulling down"
The Mystery of the Price of Oil
Venezuelan Oil Industry Data

Chapter IV COOKED and DEVOURED GOOSE   **85**
1998 Oil Price Collapse
Roberto Mandini
Hector Ciavaldini
General Guaicaipuro Lameda
PDVSA Gas
Veba Oel – Ruhr Oel
Citgo Petroleum Corporation
Saudi Arabia, Kuwait and Foreign Integration
Petroleos de Chavez

Chapter V CUBA and FIDEL CASTRO   **110**
Kennedy Abandons the Cubans
Cuban History
U.S. Pushes Batista Out of Cuba
Castro Gets Cuba
Castro's Executions
Out with Religion
Communism Arrives
Castro's First Invasion: Venezuela
Exodus from Castro's Hell
Cuban Adjustment Act of 1966
The Floridas – Captaincy-General of Cuba
The Trade Embargo
1996 Helms-Burton Act – LIBERTAD
Castro and His Destruction of a Pearl
Fall of the Soviet Union
The Deceit of Castro
First the Cubans, Now the Venezuelans

Chapter VI CHAVEZ: CUBA and CHINA   **148**
Betancourt and Chavez
Chavez and Castro
Fidel Castro
Hugo Chavez
Venezuelan Indian Tribes
Baseball

Travel
Castro's Visits to Venezuela
Caracas Energy Cooperation Accord
San Jose Pact
United: Chavez and Castro
Che Guevara
Grenada
Angola
DGI – Espionage
China
  Chavez and Mao
  Accounts of Chinese Terror
  U.S. Abandonment of Nationalist China
  South Korea
  Taiwan
  Chinese Ballistic Missiles
  Panama Canal
  Chavez's Protector

Chapter VII VENEZUELA's POPULATION   **195**
          and BOUNDARY PROBLEM
The Colombians
The Communists & the Nazis in Colombia
The Guerrilleros
Cuban Protection and Aid
Colombian Penetration of Venezuela
Chavez versus Pastrana
Panama
The Flight of Colombians
Xenophobia in Venezuela
Simon Bolivar and Gran Colombia
Venezuela's Boundaries
  Amazonas
  Three New States
  Trinidad – Tobago
  The Guayana Esequibo (Essequibo)

Epilogue   **229**
Selected Bibliography   **234**
Index   **236**

INTRODUCTION

The happiness of the people was the <u>purpose</u> of government, and that happiness derived from virtue. All good government was republican, and the true idea of a republic was "an empire of laws and not of men." These are the thoughts of John Adams from the remarkable new book on <u>John Adams</u> by David McCullough. I read this book as I was finishing this manuscript on Chavez, and I found the contrasts between Adams and Chavez to be stark, a difference between good and evil.

John Adams was superbly capable of pulling down a government (British rule in the American colonies), but he was equally gifted at constructing a new, superior government. Whereas Chavez has successfully pulled down a Venezuelan government, he has been incapable of constructing a new one. Adams set out to preserve, not destroy, while Chavez set out only to destroy.

There is an apt joke told in Venezuela in 2001. "In the U.S., people in the morning turn on their televisions to see what the weather report is for the day. In Venezuela, people turn on the TV each morning to see if Venezuela is still a country."

And while the nation of Venezuela is under such devastating stress, Hugo Chavez goes from country to country and around the world, trying to stir up trouble for the United States, and dogging his many crises at home. He speaks of a "unipolar world," when he attacks the United States, just as Russia and China never fail to denounce the unipolarity of the current world structure. In 1962, it was Charles de Gaulle, who after loosing Algeria, came up with the term "Third World." France, always the leader in anti-American dialogue, in order to achieve its "rightful place" in the concert of nations would organize a Third World in foreign affairs between the power groupings of the United States and the Soviet Union. Fidel Castro was next in seeking leadership among the "undeveloped countries" in various "Groups," against the United States. Now Hugo Chavez has picked up this mantle.

The United States remains the preeminent economic and military power on a scale not seen since the Roman Empire. And here is Hugo Chavez trying to line up forces against the United States, as his own country skids downward.

John Adams once explained why the citizens of the United States of America referred to themselves as "Americans." It was because there was no other convenient adjective. However, the effect was to seem to annex the entire continent, claiming the part for the whole. "To their neighbors it was one more example of Yankee [Yanqui] expansionism." [The term Yankee was derisively used by the British for New Englanders and after the Battle of Lexington in 1775, New Englanders dignified the name. Southerners first gave the term to Northerners in 1817. It was thus not an appropriate name for the citizens of the new nation.] "North America" obliterates the Canadians and Mexicans. I grew up conscious of the fact that South Americans were also Americans. For this reason, I have adopted "US-Americans" in my writing. It identifies us, and does not vex the other inhabitants of the Western Hemisphere.

When I started writing this manuscript in the last decade of the 20th century, it was to be another book on the Venezuelan oil industry, the industry into which I was born. However Hugo Chavez focused my mind on his disastrous regime. For years, I taught university courses on Latin American revolutions, Simon Bolivar's and Fidel Castro's in particular, and now along comes Hugo Chavez claiming to follow Bolivar and having Castro as his mentor, with his first goal to take over Colombia and form La Gran Colombia.

In writing this book, I had two goals. First, to inform the Bush Administration and other decision makers of a serious danger in the Caribbean – the Chavez/Castro partnership with their sights set first on Colombia, then Panama, with other countries to follow. Second, to remind the Venezuelans of what is still to come in Venezuela under Chavez – by describing the Cuban experience under Fidel Castro. It was a most difficult book to write, about a nation I've been closely tied to, watching its destruction, with a government in Castro's image. The most important difference between the two regimes is that Chavez after gaining power controls Venezuela's huge petroleum resources, which are now at the disposal of Castro.

July 4, 2001
Palm Beach, Florida

To my three sons, Todd, Dane and Briant

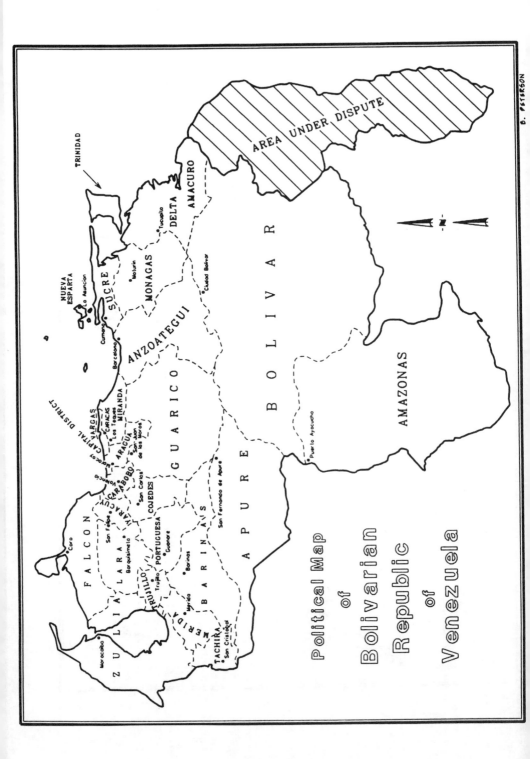

Political Map of Bolivarian Republic of Venezuela

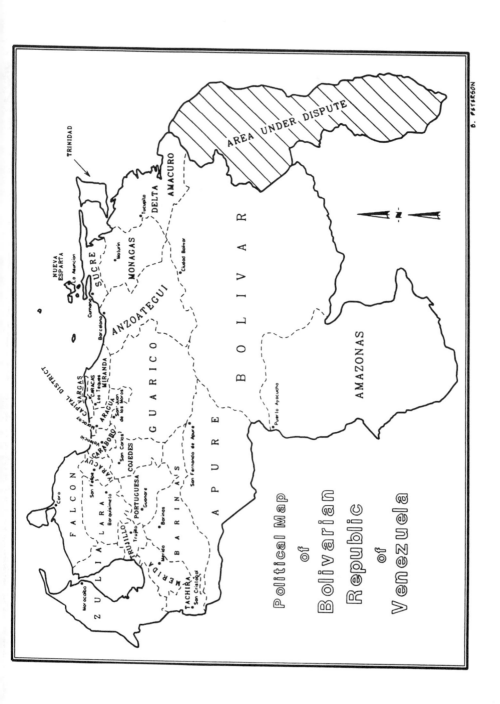

Political Map of Bolivarian Republic of Venezuela

AREA UNDER DISPUTE

B. PETERSON

TRINIDAD

DELTA AMACURO

MONAGAS

SUCRE

NUEVA ESPARTA

ANZOATEGUI

BOLIVAR

CAPITAL DISTRICT

VARGAS

CARACAS

MIRANDA

ARAGUA

GUARICO

AMAZONAS

FALCON

CARABOBO

YARACUY

COJEDES

PORTUGUESA

APURE

ZULIA

LARA

TRUJILLO

BARINAS

MERIDA

TACHIRA

CHAPTER 1

AMERICA'S ENEMY: HUGO CHAVEZ

Once Hugo Chavez Frias achieved the presidency of Venezuela in 1999, his quest for power was achieved with unending elections, using the airwaves for his incessant harangues against his enemies, and he did this with the revenues of Petroleos de Venezuela. The destructive alteration of Petroleos de Venezuela, S.A. (PDVSA) under Chavez, in 1999 and 2000, has rendered the Venezuelan oil industry less important as an international oil company. PDVSA no longer has the status of number second or third largest oil company in the world. This book reflects that change, for there are only two chapters devoted to the petroleum industry.

Of special concern for the United States is Venezuela's change from a long time ally and reliable supplier of petroleum since 1928, to a very unfriendly government with reduced oil production. It was the United States' and Venezuela's oil exports that helped the Allies fuel and win World War II. Venezuela opened its ports and airfields to U.S. and Allied naval vessels and aircraft. Venezuela supplied oil to the U.S. during the Korean War and the Vietnam War, and during the Arab Oil Embargo in 1973-74. The close relationship between the United States and Venezuela is in danger! This is evident, not only from Hugo Chavez's harangues, but apparent from his government (former guerrillas and Communists), and circle of foreign friends, i.e., Fidel Castro, Mu'amar Qadhafi, Saddam Hussein, and Carlos the Jackal (Carlos Ilich Ramirez Sanchez) who is in jail in France; and those now deceased whom he admired, like Mao Zedong and Che Guevara. All murders of their own people, and all enemies of the United States. And of growing concern is Hugo Chavez's enormous aid to Fidel Castro and Cuba, and his apparent aid to the Colombian guerrilleros – the FARC and ELN.

Hugo Chavez not only became the President of Venezuela in February 1999, but the acting President of PDVSA, as well. This became clear when Chavez sat at the first Board meeting of PDVSA in 1999, and held it at Miraflores, the presidential palace.

1

Never before in Venezuela had a president of the country interjected himself so blatantly into the operations of the oil industry. PDVSA was turned into a company full of fear – if you were not a "Chavista" you were in danger of losing your job. Those who could, took the retirement package and PDVSA lost much of its institutional memory with the retirement of these dedicated, experienced executives. These executives could not be replaced from the lower ranks of employees, particularly from the ranks in exploration and production operations.

Chavez declared that PDVSA must be reshaped into "a lever for the sustainable development" of Venezuela. In a TV address, in late February 2000, Chavez stated that the "old rentist model" of the oil industry is a thing of the past. He was shifting PDVSA's focus away from the United States, and toward markets in the Caribbean (Cuba), Latin America, and China.

China could act as Venezuela's protector when and if Chavez makes his final break with the United States. Chavez could then cancel Venezuela's multi-million dollar foreign debt ($35 billion in 1999), and interest payments that amount to one-third of the annual federal budget. But before he can do this, he must sell Citgo Petroleum Co., PDVSA's multi-billion dollar refining and marketing company in the United States – for obvious reasons.

The Floods

The December 1999 mud floods were a defining moment in the new Chavez regime. On December 14, intoxicated with his power and aware of the possible catastrophe, Chavez repeated Simon Bolivar's famous words, "If Nature oppose us we shall fight it. And we shall force it to our will." Bolivar uttered these words after the terrible earthquake of March 26, 1812, that ushered in the physical and moral collapse of the First Republic of Venezuela, only ten days after the Congress had convened in Valencia, on March 16. (J.D. Diaz, Recuerdos de la rebelion de Caracas, Madrid, 1829, pp.38-39) Chavez shocked many Venezuelans, by using Bolivar's famous quote, at this moment. The heavens did indeed rain down and kill many thousands of Venezuelans, just as the earthquake of 1812 had in Caracas before Bolivar said this. Chavez often quotes Simon Bolivar, however, the intent of this quote at this time was horrifying. Not even God would be allowed

2

to stop his Constitution: a blueprint for a Cuban-style dictatorial regime, with all power concentrated in Chavez's hands.

Chavez can never live down the suspicion that he downplayed the danger of the torrential rain, so that the people would vote in the December 15 plebiscite, and approve his Magna Carta, as he called his new Constitution (which he now refers to as "la bicha") for the Fifth Republic. The new Constitution provides for the president's longer term, and re-election, i.e., to remain in power for 12 more years. Why didn't Chavez declare a national emergency before the voting, after two weeks of steady, heavy rainfall? And, why were people not told to prepare for possible floods and mudslides? What took priority: the voting, or the thousands of people in harm's way?

Where was Chavez after the vote was counted on the evening of December 15, and day of December 16? He had flown to the Venezuelan island of La Orchila, to celebrate with his friend, Fidel Castro. Chavez has denied this, but there were too many people there, to be able to cover up this drinking celebration. It cannot be denied that the man who speaks all the time was no where to be seen on television, until 11 PM on Thursday, the 16th, when he scarcely recognized the magnitude of the tragedy.

Finally, in the days immediately after the floods, while Venezuelans and the world at large were coping with Venezuela's worst human and natural disaster, Chavez was tightening his grip on power and legal dictatorship, by appointing allies to key public institutions. Without the publication of the new Constitution in the Gaceta Oficial (which is when a Venezuelan law goes into effect), Chavez named judges on a new Supreme Court (Tribunal of Justice), a new Comptroller General, and Public Prosecutor. And most important, he named members of his Constitutional Assembly, that just wrote his Constitution, as the new mini-Congress (a 21 member Legislative Commission known as the "Congresillo"), and once more headed by Luis Miquilena (85 years old). This was all done on December 22; and on December 23, he named a new Electoral Commission, which was to supervise his *mega-elections* in May 2000, when he would run again for a full 6-year term. While the shock of the devastation and recovery diverted everyone's attention, Chavez took complete control of the Venezuelan government. Once more!

3

US-Americans should not forget the events of January 12, 2000, when President Chavez announced that "U.S. troops" would not be permitted to land in Venezuela. Those "U.S. troops" were two Navy ships loaded with 450 Marine engineers, tractors, bulldozers, and machinery sent to remove mud and boulders and rebuild highways and roads along the Venezuelan coast. Also aboard were water purification plants, food, medicine and medical personnel, to help the Venezuelans who had suffered the devastating mud floods of December 15 and 16. The loss of 30,000 or more lives (the number may never be determined), and billions of dollars of damage (compounded by considerable looting) on Venezuela's northern coast, impelled the Venezuelan Minister of Defense, General Raul Salazar to ask the U.S. on December 24, 1999, for further help. Some help from the U.S. and other countries had arrived immediately after the flood occurred. However, when the U.S. ships were loaded and on their way, Chavez was urged by his pro-Cuban, Minister of Foreign Affairs, Jose Vicente Rangel, to prevent their landing! (In February 2001, Chavez named Rangel as Minister of Defense, much to the chagrin of the Venezuelan Armed Forces.)

Thus, the help that the Venezuelans desperately needed was denied by their President. An editorial in *El Nacional* (16 January 2000) stated "this is the last in a series of revealing incidents of a policy that in this case, besides being absurd and criminal, is inhuman." Right after the disaster occurred in December, the United States offered 30 helicopters from their Puerto Rican base. However, Minister Rangel rebuffed the offer and said three or four helicopters were enough. They were not enough! And hundreds on the coast who should have been evacuated were not evacuated. Members of my family, in the small coastal state of Vargas, were among the lucky ones to be evacuated by one of the eight U.S. helicopters that were permitted into Venezuela.

The tragedy in the state of Vargas allowed the defacto militarization of Venezuela. Not only was Congress dissolved, but both political opponents and independent journalists were warned – there was to be no opposition voice. Freedom of expression is allowed – for President Chavez who never stops talking, attacking the United States, the upper and middle classes, the Catholic Church, the newsmedia, and spreading his class hatred. The new

Ministry of Truth under the new Constitution obliges the media to provide only "timely, truthful and impartial" information. How do you guarantee the transparency of the Chavez regime, if he has complete control over every branch of the Venezuelan government and there is no opposition party, or group, to challenge his absolute power?

Bolivarian Republic of Venezuela

"Democracy" in Venezuela has scant resemblance to democracy in the United States of America. The 2 million voters (out of 11 million eligible) who voted on December 15 during the deluge, did so on a Constitution that they had not seen. Chavez wanted to avoid opposition to his Magna Carta, which he had dictated to the Constitutional Assembly by telephone from Miraflores, during the three months they were in session. He even changed the name of Venezuela. It is now the Bolivarian Republic of Venezuela, a tongue twister.

Alexis de Tocqueville, in Democracy in America (1835), tried to show men how they might be both equal and free. The real driving force of democracy, i.e., the passion for equality, is compatible with tyranny, as well as with liberty. Tocqueville understood that the democratic principle was susceptible to a terrible despotism. In other words, the people could vote for a despot, and destroy democracy. This would be easy to do if the uneducated were given the vote. The majority who are poor could thus vote for tyranny, because they have little understanding of what they are giving up, that others in the minority who came before them struggled to obtain. The poor thus choose their own masters! And as the saying goes, "you get the government that you deserve."

Without a strong middle class that possesses property and defend property rights, democracy is always in danger. In Venezuela, I witnessed the rise of a middle class after World War II, and then watched its demise in the 1990s, under one corrupt government after another.

When I contemplate Venezuela in 2001, I cannot help but remember Friedrich Hayek and his perceptive book, The Road to Serfdom (1944). Hayek argued that socialism would produce tyranny in practice. He pointed out that *fascism* and *communism* are merely varients of the same totalitarianism. Utopian dreams

5

turn into police state nightmares. This power over the lives of the people *attracts leaders without scruples.* In 1973, Hayek wrote: "The important point is that all coercive action of government must be unambiguously determined by a permanent legal framework which enables the individual to plan with a degree of confidence and which reduces human uncertainty as much as possible." (*Wall Street Journal*, April 8, 1992, "Hayek's Road from Serfdom ...." By L.Gordon Crovitz)

How did Venezuela enter the year 2000 as one of the poorest and most corrupt countries in the Western Hemisphere? This country, the size of Texas and Oklahoma combined, with incredible natural resources: the largest petroleum reserves in the Western Hemisphere; huge deposits of iron ore, bauxite, and coal; gold, and diamond mines; fertile agricultural lands; hydroelectric power; its flora rich in lumber and plant species, a magnificent coastline and great fishing; majestic mountains; and the Orinoco River; has greater riches than one could ever imagine in one country. As the old Venezuelan joke goes, after God bestowed all of these wondrous gifts on this Land of Grace (as Columbus called it in 1498), with the other hand He gave it to the Venezuelans!

There is one explanation for 80% of the 23 million Venezuelans being poor. (Another reason for Venezuela's poor is discussed in Chapter VII.) Venezuela has incredible government corruption, which they have had for the past 30 years – ever since the petrodollars started pouring into Venezuela in the 1970s, soon followed by drug laundering money from Colombia. Chavez said that he represented the poor and was going to clean up corruption. Robin Hood? He appeared as a demagogue, a savior. It is now apparent that Hugo Chavez has brought the worst kind of corruption that Venezuela has ever seen.

The social contract has surely unraveled. Venezuela has become a country where people think that they should enjoy unearned oil income just like the state. In the 1940s, Arturo Uslar Pietri repeatedly said that Venezuela should "sow the oil," but Venezuela did not! Venezuelans have seen the creation of several generations of millionaires, while 80% of the population sank into poverty. This was done through the corrupt power and spending of the government that supposedly had the opposite intention.

While the rest of South America has dealt with the conflict between state socialism and global markets in the last two decades, Venezuela has not. Venezuela's gross domestic product has remained flat and now is rapidly declining (in 1999 it shrank 7.2%)

Enter Fidel Castro – and a "sea of happiness"

It is Chavez's personal relationship with Fidel Castro that is of greatest concern. It is ironic that the first country that Castro tried to take over in 1960, was Venezuela. The first constitutionally elected President of Venezuela was Romulo Betancourt (December 1958) and he was able to defeat Castro's attempt to overthrow his government. Now Castro has succeeded in Venezuela without his guerrillas, through his protegee Hugo Chavez and the ballot! Anyone who has followed the communist revolutionary life of Fidel Castro can see and understand what Chavez has done in Venezuela, chapter and verse, down to the Circulos Bolivarianos. These are like the *Cuban Vigilance Committees*, in every street, to spy on the neighbors and organized under the MBR-200, Chavez's formerly clandestine military organization.

Chavez was inaugurated February 2, 1999, and as President started traveling the world. In China, Chavez proclaimed (on October 11, 1999) that he had always been a Maoist. Chavez compared China's revolution to his country's resurrection after decades of corruption and bad government. While visiting Mao's tomb, he wrote in a guest book: "To the great strategist, to the great soldier, to the great statesman and to the great revolutionary." On his last day in China, Chavez called for a "multi-polar world" free of U.S. domination (October 13).

His trip to China came after a trip to the United States in September, where he tried to reassure the United Nations, the U.S. Government, and Wall Street that he was not solidifying a dictatorship. After these two trips, first to the United States in September (he went the first time June 8th to reassure Wall Street), and then to China and Asia in October, Chavez went to Havana for the IX Ibero-American Summit, on November 14. A number of Latin countries were not represented by their presidents, e.g. Argentina, Chile, Costa Rica, Nicaragua, and El Salvador.

In Cuba, Chavez proclaimed that "we [Cuba and Venezuela] are navigating towards a perfect future," and called

Fidel "his brother." He referred to the Cuban revolution as a "sea of happiness, of true social justice, of peace." And when, he returned to Venezuela, he asked the Constitutional Assembly to strike some of the more moderate clauses that had crept into the text of the proposed Constitution in his absence.

After the disastrous floods of December 15 occurred, Chavez welcomed 450 Cuban medical personnel into Venezuela, while preventing hundreds of Venezuelan doctors and medical personnel who volunteered, from attending the victims from the state of Vargas. On March 8, 2000, during a farewell ceremony honoring some of these Cuban doctors, Chavez had a lot more to say about Cuba and his friend Fidel.

1. Venezuelans and Cubans are "navigating in the same sea." (This is one of Chavez's favorite expressions.) "It is necessary that the peoples of this continent march toward that sea of happiness, of equality and justice."
2. Chavez lauded Cuba's achievements in health and education [the Venezuelan doctors who witnessed their medical methods thought they were primitive], and said Venezuela should follow the communist island's example.
3. To the Cuban doctors: "Go tell Fidel that we love him."

On the same day, March 8th, Venezuelan Foreign Minister, Jose Vicente Rangel said that Venezuela opposes two anti-drug monitoring centers the United States had set up on the islands of Curacao and Aruba after loosing its Panama bases. Chavez stated that his policy toward the U.S. was based on "demanding respect for sovereignty." Another favorite word, "sovereignty." Chavez refused to permit U.S. airplanes from those staging centers, to fly over Venezuelan territory en route to Colombia, hindering the anti-drug efforts. Furthermore, Chavez stated that since Venezuela and Cuba face the same foes, "The fact that our opponents liken us to the Cuban revolution is an honor for us."

Let me introduce you to the new Cuba!

Venezuela is now a predatory jungle with no social contract. Venezuela is the 6th most violent country, and becoming much more violent under Chavez, causing a serious emigration of citizens.

Assaults, murders and thefts, particularly of cars, increase daily under Chavez's class hatred warfare that concludes, if you have more, then you took it from others, and not that you earned it working. For Venezuela, theft is the principal motivating factor of economic behavior. It was the reckless spending and borrowing in the 1970s which started with Carlos Andres Perez's government, and led to a system of corruption, now rampant. This was when oil looked like it would rise forever, to $100 a barrel, and it was when Venezuela lost its moral compass. Theft then became institutionalized in "a culture of theft."

Unfortunately, many of the people who voted for Chavez thought, "its my turn now." Chavez promised the end of theft, but he is already producing much more of it. Much of Venezuelan government officials' theft winds up in foreign countries in the form of capital flight. Venezuelans are believed to have over $100 billion overseas. Many also left with their funds, fleeing a country without hope, in deep trouble.

What was causing the greatest alarm in Venezuela in 2001 was Decree 1011 published in the <u>Gaceta Oficial</u> in October 2000, which affects all families with school age children. The Chavez decree gives traveling inspectors sweeping powers to intervene in the running of any school, public or private and replace its administration. Chavez denounced private educators, many of whom work in Catholic schools, as "education salesmen" charging high admission fees. He said he would inspect private schools from kindergarten through high school, and could withdraw state funding that some private schools receive. In his harangues against those who oppose his decree, he called them "egotists" and "possessed by the Devil." Those possessed would include the 20% of the population with children in private schools, who had not left Venezuela.

Petroleos de Chavez

PDVSA's role is to provide the government with as much money as possible. However, under Chavez, who is trying to maintain the world price of oil as high as possible through OPEC quotas, PDVSA's task becomes more difficult because its investments and maintenance in its oil production have been seriously curtailed by the government. Furthermore, the company has been *publicly attacked* and *downsized*. As Michael Rowan wrote in one of his articles, "For Chavez, nobody on his team stands taller than the colonel's shoe tops." (7/16/99, "Venezuela Onward to the Past?") Between February 2, 1999 and October 15. 2000, Chavez appointed three new Presidents of PDVSA (Mandini, Ciavaldini, and Lameda), and with each new purge more employees departed.

Venezuela has lost a significant amount of production capacity due to lack of investments, and this surely will continue with Chavez's demands on PDVSA's revenues; and the October 2000 collective contract with the oil workers unions, for 60% raises, for 40,000 workers. The raises amounted to a $320,000/day increase in salaries for PDVSA. When the price of oil drops, it will be difficult for PDVSA to manage these raises. Furthermore, how will private operators who are obliged to pay their employees in accordance with PDVSA's collective contract, but were not party to the contract negotiations, pay their workers? It makes new foreign investments in Venezuela that much more expensive, therefore less attractive. This was apparent in June 2001, when the Ministry of Energy offered the first natural gas fields, and U.S. petroleum companies were absent from the bidding.

Gran Colombia

When, and if, Hugo Chavez is militarily and politically able, he will launch his Gran Colombia. He has been conferring with the Colombian Marxist guerrillas, and helping the FARC and ELN, that now effectively control half of Colombia. Thanks to the narco traffic money, along with the millions they extort from oil companies in Colombia, Colombian rebel forces may have enough power to fatally undermine President Andres Pastrana and his democratically elected government. From Colombia, the rebels would move into undefended Panama, which has no army. Thus, Chavez's plan is to reunite Venezuela with Colombia and Panama (which was once part of Colombia), and Ecuador, and form "la Gran Colombia."

Will the U.S.'s "Plan Colombia," the aid program to transform the Colombian military into a more effective drug-fighting force, succeed in better preparing the military to fight the guerrilleros and protect citizens – and save Colombia?

Simon Bolivar, in liberating five countries, or half the southern continent, endured the greatest deprivations. The break-up of Gran Colombia was Bolivar' greatest disappointment. He wrote to Santander, "I fear my beloved fatherland more than all the rest of America. I believe myself more capable of ruling the New World than of ruling Venezuela." A Colombian saying at the time: "Venezuela was a barracks, Colombia a university, and Ecuador, a monastery." In Caracas the soldier was important, in Bogota the lawyer, and in Quito the priest. How prophetic!

Does anyone remember Fidel Castro's adventures in South and Central America? This was the period of the Cold War, and the Soviet Union was Castro's arms supplier and banker. Now it will be China's turn – to help Hugo Chavez in his grand design for the Western Hemisphere. Chavez has huge Venezuelan oil reserves, location, location, south of the United States and on the northern coast of South America—and a perfect fit for China. Just as China plans to push the United States out of the Pacific, Chavez plans to push the U.S. out of Latin America and the Caribbean. He has openly stated that "Puerto Rico is and will always be independent," and part of Latin America.

From the Venezuelan coast, 353 miles to the island of Isla de Aves (5.3 ha big, at longitude 63 degrees, latitude 15 degrees) in the Caribbean, Chavez was flag waving at the 15-nation Caribbean Community (Caricom), in July 2001. Chavez defiantly claimed sovereignty over the wee island, stating it was "as Venezuelan was Caracas," and he was going to defend Venezuela's sovereignty "in the sky and in the sea." Dominica has a claim to the wee island, which is located 70 miles west of Dominica, arguing that a submarine sandbank, the Aves Ridge, directly connects it geographically to the Isla de Aves.

It should have been clear at the end of 2000, that Hugo Chavez and his leftist government were engaged in efforts to harm Venezuela's economic partners, the United States and Colombia. Chavez is in pursuit of less prosperous or reliable partners. Key positions of government are in the hands of people or groups with a history of totalitarian and communist beliefs. Among Chavez's grandiose goals is an alignment with Saddam Hussein to supplant Saudi Arabia as the dominant force in OPEC. This goal ties in with his plans to fortify relations with Russia. These efforts with Iraq and Russia will become more important as Chavez becomes more isolated in Latin America.

There is a rapidly developing problem for the United States, i.e., China has replaced the Soviet Union in supplying Cuba with arms, and Cuba is a surrogate power for Chavez's Venezuela. The United States is once more going to be forced to look south of its border – to the Caribbean!

Trying to research Hugo Chavez was an exercise into the illogical, irrational, absurd, preposterous and shocking. However, the first step was to recognize reality. Reality became clearer after a friend gave me a file on the *Sao Paulo Forum*, organized in 1990, by Fidel Castro. This Forum has brought together all the leftist movements in Latin America, including the armed guerrilleros of Colombia. The clear purpose of the Forum is to spread the Cuban Revolution across Latin America, and Hugo Chavez is their new leader.

Since the end of the Cold War, we have a hard time recognizing our enemies. Lest U.S. politicians in the future say they had little warning, as they were wont to do with Fidel Castro, the following chapters are a loud wake-up alarm – that the United States has a clear and present danger in Hugo Chavez Frias, the new "elected" dictator of Venezuela!

The Venezuelan oil industry has supplied Chavez with the financial means to wage his takeover of the Venezuelan government, as well as prop up Fidel Castro's government in Cuba, and now to follow through on his anti-U.S. plans. Eventually, U.S. oil companies operating in Venezuela will have to decide whether they can remain, and facilitate the operations of an enemy of the United States.

My intent is to give the background of important Venezuelan events and the consequences of President Chavez's power grab. Chavez has been moving at such rapid speed in transforming Venezuela into the "new Cuba" that few in the United States have been able to follow his "achievements." Subsequent chapters deal with: Chavez's elections and government; PDVSA and the oil industry Chavez controls; Fidel Castro and Cuba; Chavez and his friend Fidel, together with China; and Venezuela's population problem that is closely tied to Colombia and its guerrilleros, and boundary problems which are predominantly with Colombia and Guyana. Hugo Chavez ricochets through these pages trying to change Venezuela and Latin America, as he demonizes the United States.

Chavez states his goal clearly, as he did on October 26, 2000, in welcoming Fidel Castro on a state visit. Chavez said that cultivating Venezuelan ties with Cuba was part of an effort to counter-balance the economic clout of the United States and the European Union, in Latin America. "We have no alternative but to form an axis of power." To form an axis with Cuba (Castro), Libya (Qadhafi), and China, against the USA has been Chavez's primary goal. On September 7, 2001, Venezuela and Cuba signed an agreement (Acuerdo de Facilitacion) removing the need for visas for Cubans entering Venezuela, and vice versa. Chavez, thus, moved integration with Cuba even closer.

Arturo Uslar Pietri once said that Venezuela had become a society of accomplices, where some misguided sense of solidarity covered up and excused crimes in many different institutions. Thus, today, many are fighting from a weakened position because of their own past tolerance toward all sorts of misdeeds. The government does not depend on the private sector; it is the private sector that depends on the government, for it is the Venezuelan government that decides who gets rich, and who does not. This corrupt system has created a subservient, deal making business community, with the exception of a group of principled local entrepreneurs. And, the international business community is helping to keep the Venezuelan economy from collapse, and Chavez in power!

CHAPTER II

ELECTED DICTATOR –
RICH GOVERNMENT, POOR PEOPLE

"Only those opinions in which the moral ingredient of the laws of nature and of nature's God is given due weight can have a role in creating legitimate government." Harry V. Jaffa, <u>Equality and Liberty</u>, 1965 (p17)

On Sunday, December 6, 1998, Hugo Chavez Frias was elected President of Venezuela, with 56% of the vote. He won a country in ruins, with high unemployment, rampant crime, a fiscal deficit of 9% of Gross National Product (GNP), 30% of the government's budget going to pay the foreign debt – and the price of Venezuelan crude oil at $7 per barrel. Government oil revenues were only $4.8 billion, in 1998. He campaigned as the antiestablishment candidate against the corrupt political parties that had bankrupted this rich nation. With the drop in oil prices in 1998, the Accion Democratica (AD) and COPEI parties were left without enough money to buy votes, and Chavez was able to win the presidency by appealing to the many poor. Chavez was inaugurated on February 2, 1999, taking an unusual oath, in the gold domed Capitol, before his invited guests, including a beaming Fidel Castro. His first order of business was to sign a Decree calling for a referendum for a constitutional assembly to replace "this moribund constitution" on which he had just taken his oath of office.

Antonio Herrera-Vaillant, Editor of *Business Venezuela,* published by VenAmCham, in the April 2000 edition, wrote:

"The Chavez avalanche of 1998 and 1999 is in many ways comparable to the cataclysm that befell Vargas State and other regions last December: It has been tremendously effective in destruction and notoriously incompetent in construction. Like the inanimate yet accelerated rocks that fell upon Macuto and Caraballeda, it has destroyed everything in its path. In similar fashion, not much of substance has been done towards rebuilding."

"Mismanagement and ineptitude in government have reached epic, unprecedented depths. Some positions of great responsibility have been placed in the hands of people no more effective or competent than Caligula's horse."

While Venezuela faced the worst depression in its history, the Chavez government collected the highest oil revenues ever: $7.2 billion in 1999; and estimated $16.5 billion in 2000, on PDVSA's total estimated accrued income of $46.5 billion for all its affiliates (including Citgo, etc.).

In spite of this largesse, the Government in 2000 faced a $4 billion deficit, or 4% of gross domestic product. Venezuela's Treasury received a $1.7 billion transfer from the Central Bank in August 2000. To give the Treasury these funds, the Central Bank would have to *print money*. The move violated the new Bolivarian Constitution, which stipulates that the Central Bank cannot be subordinate to the Executive branch and must not support or finance fiscal deficits. (Article 320)

The Venezuelans voted on the Bolivarian Constitution on December 15, 1999. But the mother of all ironies, after Chavez got his Bolivarian Constitution, his government started ignoring it, uncomfortable with the provisions they had written. Not only did they ignore their own constitution, they made changes in the wording before it was officially published in the Gaceta Oficial, on December 30, 1999. One of the members of the Constitutional Assembly, Allan Brewer Carias, who is also a constitutional lawyer, discovered **74** textual differences. After Allan Brewer's discovery, several new Constitutions appeared. And a year after the Constitution was voted on, El Universal, on December 10, 2000, had a banner headline, "They Changed the Constitution." The Attorney General's office (Fiscalia de la Republica) detected 179 articles [out of 350] that were changed in the Constitution.

El Nacional on December 15, ran a picture of Chavez holding the Constitution, with a caption under the picture, "Constitutional Confusion." The article went on to explain that it was a psychiatric constitution that was said to have "three personalities," and "eternally in transit." The three personalities are for the three texts: the one presented to the voters on December 15, 1999; the second one that was supposedly corrected for errors, and was published in the Gaceta Oficial on December

30; and a third one that was published on March 24, 2000 with additional corrections. Chavez's so-called Magna Carta is a floating Constitution and there is no rule of law in Venezuela. And in June 2001, Chavez suddenly started calling his little Blue Book (which he often carried and pulled out) – *"la bicha."* Allan Brewer Carias and others protested that Chavez was disrespectful in referring to the Bolivarian Constitution as <u>la bicha</u> (whore).

Under the Bolivarian Constitution, the inauguration of the President is to be held on January 10. Chavez was sworn in August 19, 2000 (the third time), thus extending his 6-year term by *5 months.* What some of us had suspected became obvious. The only reason for getting rid of the "moribund" 1961 Constitution was to lengthen the 5-year single presidential term, to *6-year double terms*, and make Chavez dictator legally!

Chavez told voters in his last campaign for re-election in July 2000, that it was his decision to cut oil production that had pushed OPEC to cut production. However, his claim that he almost single-handedly engineered the world rise in oil prices, further raised expectations among the poor that he would deliver prosperity and entitlements. These Venezuelans believe that the main function of government is to share the wealth – oil, that is! One of the ways of doing this was in subsidized gasoline, the lowest price per gallon in the world, presently some 24 cents per gallon, cheaper than bottled water. This, however, does not affect the poor that have no vehicles. Chavez promised to give the poor: land, cars, homes, education, and health care services, if he became president and got his new constitution. He must now deliver or risk a civil war. Venezuela has forgotten how to create wealth, it only knows how to distribute it – unevenly!

Hugo Chavez in one year, succeeded in returning Venezuela 65 years backwards, to the end of the Gomez dictatorship. General Juan Vicente Gomez ruled Venezuela as a plantation owner for 27 years, from 1908, until his death, December 17, 1935. Actually, Chavez has not been compared much to Gomez, but rather to Papa Doc Duvalier of Haiti, and Fidel Castro, both far worse than Gomez. Gomez did not foster hatred between the classes of people, as Papa Doc, Castro and Chavez did, maintaining their power by turning the poor against those who had more. With slums housing a third of Caracas' 4 million inhabitants, and 80% of Venezuelans now classified as poor, Venezuela was ripe for a demagogue. And that demagogue accuses those who have money, of having stolen it, and those who leave Venezuela as thieves fleeing with their stolen money!

Chavez's Incessant Voice and Campaigns

Chavez started **three** new media avenues to communicate his rambling thoughts on class hatred to the populace. He took to the air waves to continue campaigning via radio, "Hello President" (Alo Presidente), and television, "Face to Face with the President;" and his very own government funded newspaper as editor-in-chief, "The President's Mail."

After becoming president, Chavez first held a Referendum on having a Constitutional Assembly on Sunday, April 25, 1999, which he won. Next, he held the actual election of the 131-member Assembly, on July 25, 1999. The third election in 1999 was the Referendum on the Chavez Constitution, held on December 15, when the heavens opened up. Finally, on July 30, 2000, under the new Constitution, Chavez had his 2nd election as President, for a 6-year term; along with the new one-house National Assembly, for 5-year terms; and the governors of the 23 states, for 4-year terms. Chavez was still in constant campaign mode for the first two years of his presidency (actually for the first three years, with the December 3, 2000 referendum to create a single government dominated union).

His media appearances were used for stinging diatribes against opponents whom he labeled *corrupt cliques, putrid elites, nests of vipers, dupes of the adecos, destroyers of the nation, vampires*, the very words reminiscent of genocide and ethnic cleansing and warfare. This is not the language culturally or historically fitting for Venezuela. Venezuelans have been bombarded by the incessant "unsheathing my sword;" "I am at war;" "I'm putting on my boots;" "plans to launch a massive and intensive counter-attack;" and on and on! It is not only the vile speech, *it never ceases*, as with a mad man. Those leading the "no" campaign in voting against his constitution, he labeled *"a truckload of pigs."* Everyone, but everyone, who would disagree with Chavez is attacked, whether he is a priest or Cardinal (*"he has a problem with God, and needs an exorcism,"* or *"degenerate priests"*), a business leader (*"he is a traitor out to destroy the nation"*) will afterwards be followed by the police. As the Venezuelan Cardinal said: "Chavez speaks with great verbal violence, trying to annihilate all the dissidents."

Some of the poor are no longer convinced. Graffiti against Chavez appears, e.g. "He feeds us rhetoric to fill our minds, but our stomachs are empty." And in October 1999, when Chavez was traveling in China, government workers marched against Chavez with placards: "Hugo Chavez Frias las neveras estan vacias" (HCF the refrigerators are empty).

Chavez attacked the rule of law and the separation of powers, all of which created fear among the educated. This is a dictator who can even change the name of his country, to the **Bolivarian Republic of Venezuela**, from the official name of the Republic of Venezuela. (Actually, Venezuela has been a republic in name only.) He is on a mission, first, to eliminate his local enemies: business men, the Church, private education, the news media; and then to eliminate the United States! "The dominance of the imperialists must be left behind," Chavez said, after returning to Caracas from an Andean Community (Bolivia, Colombia, Ecuador, Peru, and Venezuela) meeting in Lima, in June 2000. He stressed that opposing a "unipolar" world dominated by a single superpower will benefit the Andean nations. Chavez's purpose is a *national, regional,* and *continental revolution!* He will be the 2nd Bolivar, creating a Gran Colombia, which Bolivar did not succeed in doing. Chavez quotes Bolivar and uses his image to enhance his actions, but he does not comprehend Bolivar. Simon Bolivar, the Liberator of Venezuela and four other South American Republics was a nobleman, a warrior, statesman, writer, genius and hero. Chavez is none of these, therefore, it is impossible for him to be a second Bolivar.

Venezuela's Constitutions and Presidents

Chavez, after taking office in February 1999, insisted on the election of a 131-seat National Constitutional Assembly (ANC) on July 25, to write a new Constitution in six months. When he took his oath of office on the 1961 Constitution, he swore to replace "**this moribund constitution**" with a new one. And, he announced that he would sign a decree later that day (February 2) calling for a referendum for a constitutional assembly. Forget the rule of law, or Congress! "Que nos importa que el decreto de la

Constituyente no cumple con no se que cosa de la ley ..." (What does it matter to us that the decree for the Constitutional Assembly does not comply with whatever thing in the law.) This was his opening battle with Congress, to destroy it!

Writing constitutions is a pastime with Venezuelan governments. The first one was written in 1811. Venezuela is South America's champion with 26 separate charters. The first three constitutions, 1811, 1819 and 1821 were written during the War of Independence. The longest lasting constitution was Betancourt's 1961 Constitution, which ended with Chavez's 1999 Constitution. Venezuela's other constitutions were: 1830, 1857, 1858, 1864, 1874, 1881, 1891, 1893, 1901, 1904, 1909, 1914, 1922, 1925, 1928, 1929, 1931, 1936, 1945, 1947, and 1953. One man, Juan Vicente Gomez accounted for seven of these constitutions (from the 1909 to the 1931). The amending process was difficult, therefore, it was easier to write a supposedly new constitution. The basic structure of government (until the 1999 Constitution) continued to be the same, with only a few articles changed. The Executive is dominant in the Venezuelan government, thus the provisions which would permit Congress to enact amendments were of little value. The personal wishes of the dictators motivate change – not a subservient Congress or the states.

Simon Bolivar joined New Granada (present day Colombia) and Venezuela to from Gran Colombia, and win independence from Spain, in 1821. Following the separation from the Gran Colombia in 1830, Venezuela had 20 years of peace before it plunged into the Federal War (1858 to 1863) when fighting among rival classes reached a high point of destructiveness. The Liberals, who championed federalism, formed the **United States of Venezuela**, under the **1864** Constitution, and established a union of 20 states. The word "state" was used for the first time in this Constitution. From 1870 to 1888, Guzman Blanco dominated Venezuela, and he and other Liberal party presidents were Masons (in a Catholic country). All the Venezuelan Presidents from 1899 to 1945 came from the State of Tachira; and once again in 1952-1958, when Perez Jimenez was President, as well as Carlos Andres Perez, who was twice elected, in 1973, and 1988.

Two presidents followed each other twice, Carlos Andres Perez followed Rafael Caldera in 1974, and Caldera followed Perez in 1994 – thus covering nearly 20 years in the presidency between the two. (CAP did not finish his last presidency, as he was impeached in 1993.)

It was Perez Jimenez who, in his 1953 Constitution, changed the name of the country from the United States of Venezuela, to the **Republic of Venezuela**, which Betancourt retained in his 1961 Constitution. Large territory, scarce population, a lack of qualified men agreeing to serve, have been detrimental factors for federalism in Venezuela.

Simon Bolivar thought federalism was a mistake for Venezuela. He acknowledged the U.S. success with federalism, but believed that laws should conform with the habits of the people, whom he knew were not ready for a truly representative system. The existence of a strong personal government is a tradition in Venezuela, and not that of a federal government, nor a democracy. From 1936 to 1945, under the Lopez Contreras and Medina governments, a genuine attempt was made to establish a more representative government. It was President Eleazar Lopez Contreras who shortened the term of president from seven to four years. This was still the period when the states had presidents, not governors, and Lopez Contreras on March 3, 1941, sent them a document requesting a similar shorter term. Political chaos followed the overthrow of Medina in 1945, until another caudillo, Perez Jimenez was able to consolidate his power in the 1950s. One of the reasons for Medina's overthrow was his distancing himself from Lopez Contreras after becoming President in 1941. Medina's departure ended 46 years of rule by Andinos (the men from Tachira).

The history of Venezuela reveals that real material progress was made almost entirely under Marcos Perez Jimenez. Venezuela became a showpiece of what US-American funds and U.S. technology can do where foreign capital is welcomed, and where there are exciting investment opportunities. Everywhere there was construction. And, as the oil industry increased production and filled the government treasury, the government put on a huge public works program. The largest single project in Caracas was the new Central University with 28 modern buildings, including a medical center. (University City was actually started under President Medina.) Workers housing, modern airports, roads, highways, harbour development, new schools, hospitals and clinics were built. During this period, 1950 to 1957, Venezuela was probably the fastest developing country in the world. I was still living in Venezuela during this period and witnessed this incredible progress. Such stability and growth was achieved at the expense of individual freedom. This was the "New National Ideal," and political liberty would "interfere" with economic planning. Large foreign investments in new companies contributed to this growth, along with a large American colony.

As a result of these huge public works program, the government of P.J. needed additional funds for the National Treasury and they granted new oil concessions covering over 2 million acres, to Creole, Shell, Mene Grande, Sun, Signal, Superior, etc.. The Venezuelan government collected $684,776,000 for these new concessions, and the **last** ever granted. U.S. independents gained concessions in Venezuela, and it was their new production that helped drive up world oil production, causing a series of boomerangs: a drop in world oil prices, the U.S. Mandatory Oil Import Program of 1959, and the creation of OPEC, in 1960.

Constitutional Government

James Madison, father of the United States Constitution of 1787, searched through the writings of the great philosophers for an explanation of how a government for the people could be established "by the people." Madison's answer was the invention of the constitutional convention. The U.S. Constitutional Convention was comprised of the capable few, who convened for prudent political deliberations. Their combined effort was then ratified by representatives of the population at large. The result was a stable and effective government that has endured for over 200 years.

How truly rare was the United States founding. Republican government and strict constructionist reading of the Constitution would check the ambitions of the few. The United States Constitution was a mix of principles: partly national, and partly federal. It has enumerated powers, as well as implied powers. It promised majority rule, with the rights of a minority protected. It was short and flexible: only seven articles, with Article V allowing for amendments (26 in all have been ratified, including the 10 Bill of Rights in 1791). It begins: "We the People of the United States, in Order to form a more perfect Union, establish Justice, insure domestic Tranquility, provide for the common defence, promote the general Welfare, and secure the Blessings of Liberty . . ."

Now compare Venezuela's 26 constitutions since its first one in 1811, adopted after Venezuela declared her independence from Spain, July 5. The clearest irony in Venezuela's many constitutions is their devotion to liberty alongside their willingness to submit to a dictator. The states, 23 in 1999, have little sovereignty, therefore, there has been little experience with local self-government. It wasn't until December 6, **1992**, that Venezuela first elected state governors, town mayors, municipal councils, and parish boards, by name, "uninominal" balloting. The following year, 1993, the voto uninominal, direct-vote system was first used for Congressional elections, but only for **50%** of the seats, the other half was by *party slates*. In other words, the President and his party had control of the selection of government officials **and** supplied their budget with needed revenues, for they had little or no means of taxing. There was no representative government, for the governors and the Congress were *beholden* to the President. To displease the President of Venezuela was to have your funds cut off, as Chavez did in 1999 to a number of important states (e.g. Zulia and Carabobo).

Venezuela for 40 years was not a democracy, as it has been called, but a party ruling government, i.e., ruled by one party or the other. In 1958, the three principal parties (AD, COPEI, and URD) led by Romulo Betancourt (AD) and Rafael Caldera (COPEI), tried to unite for the first presidential elections after the fall of the Perez Jimenez government. They signed on October 31, the Unity Pact (later known as the Pacto de Punto Fijo.) It was an agreement to refrain from attacking one another – united in principle to carry out a government of political integration. Whoever won the presidency promised not to load the Cabinet or high administrative posts with his party members. Unfortunately, this pact led to a labyrinth of corruption with the number of government employees growing from 484,000 in the last 25 years, to over 1.2 million, partly because it was too expensive to fire anyone. Salaries were financed by inflating the bolivar, over 14,000%; from Bs 4.30 to the dollar (between 1964 and 1983), to over Bs 700 to the dollar in 2001. It was this system of Punto Fijo that Chavez destroyed, in order to rule as a dictator.

Venezuela's elder statesman and author, Arturo Uslar Pietri, stated that Venezuela "has no institutions" and "has **never** had democracy." And, those men that have sat in Congress during the past 20 or 30 years cannot say who they represent, "because they do not represent anyone." Venezuela has never had majority rule, i.e., a democracy. What Venezuela has had is a series of civil caudillos, or "a government of personalities." And now, Venezuela has a new caudillo, Hugo Chavez, with enormous messianic power, but without a program for governing. "He imagines that by his mere presence, problems will be solved." And Venezuela's problems are enormous: it has become a country that "redistributed a wealth which Venezuelans did not produce;" and a country with a monstrous sized national government that is "one of the most interventionist, powerful, and bothersome in the world." "It is a government outside of reality." (Taken from a long interview of Uslar Pietri by Roberto Giusti, in *El Universal*, July 4, 1999.) Uslar Pietri died at the age of 95, on February 26, 2001.

After the Constitutional Assembly was elected in Venezuela, on July 25, 1999, the usual Venezuelan humour began to dry up. Reasonable people became progressively more worried, even scared, as they watched the power Chavez was gathering, by using the Assembly to grant him total power over every Venezuelan arm of government. And after he had his new Constitution and Congress (now called the National Assembly, having discarded the Senate) in place, in August 2000, and with his group in control, Chavez still wanted another Enabling Law (Ley Habilitante) so he could write his own laws. He wanted to write **36 laws** in three areas: Tributary finance, Social-Economic, and modernization of Public Administration. In other words, Chavez was going to completely rewrite the legal system of Venezuela! The 36 general codes included everything, from land reform through electronic data, banking, to national planning. The obvious question is why did Chavez need a Congress if he was going to write all the laws?

Hugo Chavez likes to speak about his new constitution as the Magna Carta. It can be assumed that Chavez likes the name, but knows little about the actual Great Charter of June 15, 1215. The English Magna Carta dealt with grievances of the time in a practical way. It provided the language to set down the guarantee of freedom under the law. It was the English barons who made demands against King John, when they met at Runnymede, in 1215. It was the English colonists that settled in Virginia who introduced the principles of the Great Charter, to the New World, and gave us the roots of freedom under the law, and later the Constitution of the United States. Spain gave Venezuela no heritage in self-government, or freedom under the law. It is ironic that Chavez used the name of this great document to try to legitimize his long (**350 articles**) authoritarian constitution.

There is a particularly troubling aspect to Chavez's use of the term Magna Carta in writing his constitution. King John was forced to agree to this declaration of <u>rights</u> and <u>liberties</u> for his barons and people. Therefore, future kings like the Stuarts found it difficult to invoke the doctrine of Divine Right. It is Chavez who essentially wrote his 1999 Constitution, not the Venezuelan barons or the people, although he has the façade of an elected Constitutional Assembly. He demanded this constitution in order to enormously <u>increase</u> <u>his</u> <u>presidential</u> <u>powers,</u> at the expense of the people and all the other Venezuelan branches of government and institutions, **and** to extend his term from 5 years to 12 (two terms of 6 years).

The final irony with Chavez's efforts to use a venerable English document for his dictatorial purposes is that the English have no constitution! The English rule of law and its Common Law is a living constitution in constant change, but so gradual that they hardly perceive it. The English have had what they call Reform Acts, e.g. of 1832, and of 1867. As the great Walter Bagehot wrote in 1872, in <u>The English Constitution</u>: "No one can approach to understanding of the English institutions . . . unless he divide them into two classes." First, the <u>dignified</u> parts, which preserve the reverence of the population, and second, the <u>efficient</u> parts, which works and rules, are essential to every constitution to be successful. "Every constitution must first **gain** authority, and then **use** authority; it must first win the loyalty and confidence of mankind and then employ that homage in the work of government." (p63-64)

With Chavez, ironies are unending. After carrying around a Blue pocket-size copy of his "Bolivarian Constitution" (a reminder of Mao's little Red Book) and thumbing through it on his weekly television appearances, in June 2001, Chavez suddenly started calling his Constitution, "*la bicha*." This crude expression can be translated as snake, insect or whore. It neatly sums up Chavez's verbal corruption lavished on the Venezuelan people.

The Chavez Government

Chavez has no idea of how to govern, or how a country's economy functions, no understanding of the marketplace. In his first year in office, the price of Venezuela's oil exports more than tripled, however, the Venezuelan economy *contracted by more than 7 percent.* How could billions of dollars, a bonanza, simply be unaccounted for in improving the Venezuelan economy? With so much in government revenues, how could the country sink deeper in a hole? With such complete power in the hands of one man there is no transparency – no accountability, therefore, the result is the worst form of corruption. The term for this form of government is totalitarianism!

We need look no further than our own Hemisphere to see past examples of this form of government, starting with Juan and Eva Peron in the Argentine, and Fidel Castro in Cuba. The Argentine was the breadbasket of the southern Continent, exporting grain and beef to Europe; and Cuba was the world's leading sugar exporter. The Argentine 50 years later is still recovering from the Perons, and Cuba is still going downhill with Castro in control. In other words, Venezuela's fate seems abysmal for decades to come. As for the hope some Venezuelans have that the United States is going to step in and save them, I think not. The people voted 5 times for Chavez and his constitution. So the Venezuelans can either leave if they have the means, or stay until the end of Chavezuela. An agonizing decision!

Chavez's presidency may survive because he has effectively eliminated the opposition. The opposition's last gasp was the candidacy of Francisco Arias Cardenas in the July 30,

2000 Presidential and National Assembly elections. It was then that I changed the analysis of this book and started over, because after Chavez won in July, although it was a stolen election, he had his dictatorship assured. Jimmy Carter, who led one of the two observer groups, pronounced the balloting "clean and fair," even though the fraud in the tabulation of votes was easily observed. The ballots were so difficult to decipher that only with very careful previous study could you possibly know whom you were voting for. The uneducated (the many) had their ballots filled out for them by the Chavistas. Friends sent me samples of these ballots and I could not figure them out. They were meant to confuse, totally!

Curiously, it was an act of God, the great floods of December 15 and 16, that caused a delay in the mega-elections under the new Constitution. Chavez's actions after the floods brought forth the candidacy of Francisco Arias Cardenas. Without the floods that forced the delay of the elections, originally set for March, and moved to May 28, and then to July 30, there probably would not have been an opposition candidate, certainly not a strong candidate like the governor of Zulia, former Lt. Colonel and Chavez partner in the attempted coup in February 1992. Elections were not to be held until 6 months after ratification of Chavez's Constitution. Nevertheless, Chavez does things when he wants to, regardless of his own laws. A former candidate for the presidency, Oswaldo Alvarez Paz, stated (*El Universal*, 24-8-00) "In this democracy without real democrats, Hugo Chavez goes from victory to victory constructing the total downfall of Venezuela."

Chavez's Cabinet is composed of men who were Marxist guerrillas and on the outside of Venezuelan political power. Two men have the strongest influence on Chavez and are the most powerful. Luis Miquilena, the old communist, 86 years old, was Chavez's first Minister of Interior and Justice (Chavez united the two powerful ministries), then President of Chavez's Constitutional Convention, then President of the Congresillo, and back as Minister of the Interior and Justice, in February 2001. Jose Vicente Rangel, the other strong influence on Chavez, was Minister of Foreign Affairs (February 1999 to February 2001) until Chavez made the strangest appointment by naming Rangel the Minister of Defense. (It probably was part of the Sao Paolo Forum plans.) With all the military officers he had appointed in his government, in PDVSA, and in state agencies and companies, this was considered a slap to the Armed Forces. This strong pro-Fidelista is a man that the military despise as thoroughly corrupt. (In November 2000 Rangel's wife, Ana Avalos, a sculptress, was able to have an exhibit of her work in Paris under the sponsorship of the French Foreign Minister. The opening coincided with Minister Rangel's trip to Paris, which was no surprise in Venezuela where he has promoted the sale of her work.) And Rangel is the one who got Chavez to stop the two U.S. ships from going to help Venezuelans after the December floods, and also got the Minister of Defense fired, General Raul Salazar, who had requested the U.S. aid.

Equally strange was the appointment of Colonel Luis Alfonzo Davila, who had been a disaster at Interior, to take Rangel's place at Foreign Affairs. (Davila had been Chavez's traveling companion, even used his car to escort Chavez across Venezuela when he campaigned for President.) Chavez recycles mediocrity in his Cabinet, as one of my Venezuelan friends pointed out.

In December 2000, Chavez changed his Vice-President, from Isaias Rodriguez, to a woman, Adina Bastidas. This announcement was made on his Sunday morning radio show, "Alo President," where he now makes all of his appointments. He maintains a large audience, for one has to tune in to see if you have a job or are fired, and who's in and who's out of the government.

The Unions

With the collapse of the political parties as political opposition to Chavez, the only possible opposition remaining were the unions. And Chavez set out to destroy them in the **December 3, 2000 referendum**. (Another referendum!) The week before the referendum, Chavez received two warnings regarding his referendum from two important foreign organizations: OPIC and ICFTU.

The Overseas Private Investment Corp (OPIC) said it would review how the referendum affected workers rights. OPIC, a U.S. Government Agency, has either financed or insured private investments totaling $1.3 billion in Venezuela, and was studying similar participation in $1.5 billion of additional investments over the next year. George Munoz, President of OPIC, said that Venezuela's case was not as severe as the 1989 Tiananmen Square massacre in China when OPIC suspended all investment assistance, but OPIC would see "if there is an interruption of workers' rights." (*Wall Street Journal*, 11-00)

The second warning came from the Brussels-based International Confederation of Free Trade Unions (ICFTU) with 123 million members, that stated it would not recognize new unions emerging from the referendum. Both the ICFTU and the Geneva-based International Labor Organization (ILO) warned Venezuela that it could face trade sanctions. With this warning, Chavez replied: "I'm sorry for the workers of the world, because if these are the gentlemen that claim to defend their rights, its no wonder that the world's working class is so oppressed."

For the first time in Venezuelan elections, there was 78% vote abstention. Some went to the polls and tore up their ballots in front of reporters, to condemn Chavez's efforts to get rid of the unions. Actually of the 2.2 million (out of 11 million registered voters) that voted, **96.5% refused** to cast ballots in the referendum, merely voting for the town councils and neighborhood committees. This meant that the 2 million union members did not vote! The referendum passed with only 1½ % of the vote! It was a huge defeat for Chavez.

The battle with the Venezuelan unions commenced with the oil workers unions' collective contract for 40,000 workers. The president of Fedepetrol, Carlos Ortega (who, before Chavez, used to sit on the PDVSA Board) claimed 90% of Venezuela's oil workers heeded the call to strike, which lasted 5 days. Chavez called the union leaders "corrupt bandits," and said he would not negotiate with them. He threatened the unions up to Friday, October 13, then he gave in, completely, blaming Hector Ciavaldini, whom he fired as President of PDVSA, on Sunday morning on his radio program "Alo Presidente." The reason for the sudden change: Chavez was flying to Houston late Sunday to have breakfast and lunch with hundreds of oilmen on Monday, and introduce his new president of Citgo, General Contreras, and as it turned out also taking his new president of PDVSA, General Lameda. How could he make the trip with his oil industry shut down, and speak to U.S. oil companies about investments in

Venezuela? So Chavez caved and gave the oil workers 60% raises! This also affected the service companies and the foreign oil companies in Venezuela, as their contracts with PDVSA obligate these companies to pay the same wages. It added an estimated $.90 to the cost of producing a barrel of oil in Venezuela, or about $1 billion per year.

On Friday the 13th, during the oil workers' strike, Chavez made an amazing threat in Carupano. "If this strike continues, if you shut down the petroleum industry, then **I** will shut down the country!" Who has the power, who commands, and dominates is me. I can do what I want, and when I want. There is no one above me on earth! However, four hours later, at 8 PM, everything changed and Chavez agreed to the oil workers demands. It was the first time since 1936 that an oil strike succeeded in Venezuela.

There was another problem Chavez was facing Friday the 13th, i.e., the largest federation of public sector workers with a million members, the **CTV** (Venezuelan Workers' Confederation) said it would lead a nationwide strike the week of October 16, to support the oil workers. Chavez was now prepared "to demolish the CTV." Chavez had proposed a referendum to be held along with local elections in December, to establish a single government dominated union, thus destroying the more than 9,000 unions in Venezuela. Some Venezuelans compare this effort to destroy private unions and form a single government union, to Mussolini's, the Soviet Union's, the Nazis', and Franco's government unions. Actually, the referendum violates Chavez's own Constitution. Article 95 guarantees the right to freely establish "such union organizations as they may deem right to join or not to join."

What few remember is that the unions were formed after the death of Juan Vicente Gomez in December 1935 and the end of his 27-year dictatorship. They were effectively destroyed 64 years later, by a new Venezuelan dictator through his referendum. In February 1936, the oil laborers started to organize in unions. In July 1936, the Labor Law (largely the work of a young lawyer, Rafael Caldera) was promulgated, adopting modern social principles; and in December, the new oil unions held their first strike. Thus, the union movement that commenced in 1936, and grew to 9,000 unions, was shot down in December 2000.

The Military

Venezuela lacks bold leadership to challenge Chavez. No one can challenge that his ends cannot be achieved by his means. His means are the military, what Fausto Maso (*El Universal*, 16-9-00) called *"militarism with vaseline."* By October 2000, Chavez had *35 generals* in-place, administering Cabinet Ministries, the National Assembly, and key industries: CVG (iron), PDVSA (petroleum), even Citgo Petroleum in the United States. There were six governors of the 23 states who were military men! With a sense of dark humour Rodolfo Schmidt (24-10-00) pointed out that there was also General Unemployment, and General Insecurity, and corruption was Generalized. To keep the military happy, besides giving raises in pay, and fancy new uniforms, Chavez gave out many promotions. The FAN now has 300% more Generals and Admirals than under the previous government. There are now the same number of Generals and Admirals as there are colonels navy captains, doubling the number for available posts (which did not change). With their ascension, their pay went up, too. Hugo Chavez has established his own Praetorian Guard like the Emperors of old.

At the same time that Chavez was moving the military into controlling all aspects of civil society, there was a negative effect on the defense capability of the National Armed Forces (**FAN**). Of the 90,000 Armed Forces, 70,000 soldiers were assigned to work on public works. This was resented, as soldiers consider their mission to defend Venezuela. It was his *Plan Bolivar 2000,* to use tens of thousands of the troops, to paint schools, repair hospitals, and run bargain food markets that caused the most unrest in the ranks. It diverted resources away from essential training and was viewed as a tiresome chore by the soldiers.

This military domination of a country is not seen in any other country in Latin America. Chavez campaigned on this concept of a uniformed population with the Armed Forces as the *re-distributor of wealth* under his *Plan Bolivar 2000* and *Fondo Unico Social (FUS).* His aim is to turn the military into his political arm.

But there are those in the military who oppose Chavez. The officers who staged the February 4, 1992 revolt against Carlos Andres Perez (CAP) are now divided into two groups, with one group opposed to Chavez. They oppose the concentration of power in one man and his "sea of happiness with Cuba." At a ceremony, in July 2000, to award 93 retiring officers with one of the military's highest honours, **42 officers** due to be decorated stayed away rather than receive the award from Chavez's hands. The same month, an Air Force colonel (Silvino Bustillos) was arrested after accusing Chavez of illegally using patriotic symbols in his re-election bid. He was the second active military officer to publicly denounce Chavez in less than a month. Captain Luis Garcia Morales was kicked out of the National Guard for publicly calling for Chavez's resignation. As of June 14, 2000, Chavez ordered the Armed Forces to address him as, "*mi comandante en jefe*," which translates as "my commander in chief." This order was not well received, as it was thought to be an abuse of authority and another aberration for the military. This title had not been previously used in the Venezuelan Armed Forces.

No one has elected the military that are now governing Venezuela. The military is an expensive institution to maintain. They must be fed, housed, and armed at the expense of the citizenry, and for this reason they should have a restricted mission and be subordinate to the civil authority. In a democracy the military exists to serve society, but in Latin America, society exists to serve the military. Thus, the vote was denied to military personnel, until Chavez included it in his 1999 Constitution. Before Chavez, the general intent was to reduce the importance of the military by making them more professional, and better educated. Romulo Betancourt over 40 years ago introduced the subordination of the military to civil government and made it work, as he fought off Fidel Castro's inspired **FALN** (Fuerzas Armadas de Liberacion Nacional).

Without the perception of the government, the citizenry or the media, the revolutionary left *infiltrated* the Venezuelan military. In 1957, Teodoro Petkoff, Elroy Torres and Douglas Bravo meeting in the home of then Colonel Arraez Morles in El Paraiso, organized the Frente Militar de Carrera (**FMC**), in the bosom of the FAN. From then to now, there have been Marxists operating within the FAN, with hatred toward the U.S. and for those governing Venezuela. This penetration by the Communists of the Venezuelan Armed Forces only came to light in late 1999, with the publication of Alberto Garrido's book, Guerrilla y Conspiracion Militar en Venezuela, with the testimonies of the leaders of the guerrillas of the 1960s. We now know that the Chavez February 4, 1992 revolt, thought to be against the corruption of CAP's Government, was actually a derivation of the Marxists battles of the 1960s.

These guerrilla/military groups evolved and changed, went by different code names, e.g. Partido de la Revolucion Venezolana (PRV) started in Merida, in 1957; the FMC in 1957; the FALN in 1962; and Alianza Revolucionaria de Militares Activos (ARMA), in 1983. Chavez was associated with some and formed his own groups like the MBR-200 and the most important one, the **MVR** (Movimiento Quinta Republica), which would be his Fifth Republic.

During his two years in prison in Yare, his visitors became his advisors in gaining *control of Venezuela*. It was then that the Grupo Garibaldi (commanded by Jorge Giordani) was formed; and Norberto Ceresole's ideas discussed. The old communist Luis Miquilena, and Jose Vicente Rangel become key advisors; and Hector Ciavaldini (to become president of PDVSA), along with Isaias Rodriguez (whom Chavez would appoint as his Vice-President) joined the team. Not only was the plan hatched by these men as to how to take over Venezuela, but also the anti-USA program would be disguised as anti-imperialism, anti-globilazation, anti-neoliberalism, and savage capitalism. Chavez would, later break ranks with the other three Lt. Colonels that staged the February 4 coup attempt with him, as he would drop others too, or they would turn against him.

There was no doubt that Chavez admired Fidel Castro, Che Guevara, and Mao Zedong when he was in prison, before he was in prison, and after he got out of prison. On September 29, 1994, in the Argentine newspaper *Pagina 12*, Chavez declared Fidel Castro to be "the symbol of dignity for Latin America." And earlier, from the Yare prison, in an interview with Jose Vicente Rangel, who was then a newspaper writer, Chavez said his model for his political strategy was that of the anti-Catholic, communist Antonio Gramsci (founder of the Italian Communist Party). Gramsci's strategy is to attack all established institutions: religion, the armed forces, education, the private sector, political system, even the manner of thinking of the population; and substitute these established institutions with a new totalitarian order. This has been Chavez's road map – carefully planned and announced from Yare. Rangel would be Chavez's constant helper in accomplishing his totalitarian takeover of Venezuela. And Fidel was helping, too, in setting up his intelligence and spy system, and in reeducating Venezuelan children.

Ceresole

Not clear is how great an influence the Argentine sociologist writer, Norberto Ceresole, and his racist teachings along with his *caudillo, military, masses* troika formula for taking over a country, had on Chavez. Votes or political parties are not considered important in a political victory, rather it is the prominence of the military along with its strategic intelligence. *"The only disciplined party is the military."* By strategic intelligence in the military, Ceresole means the search for fractures in the political world to give Venezuela a role, i.e., to insert Venezuela in an entente with Iran, Iraq, Lydia, Cuba and Russia. Thus, the emphasis in joining the Arabs (OPEC), along with Cuba and Russia. At one time, Ceresole worked in the Academy of Sciences in the USSR, and presently works with German historian revisionists, who deny the existence of the Holocaust, claiming that there were no more than 400,000 deaths. "If there was no Holocaust there would be no state of Israel. Israel signifies the expulsion and death of a populace that lived there." (*El Nacional*, 28-2-99) In the matter of the Jews, Ceresole is opposed by Chavez's Foreign Minister, Jose Vicente Rangel, who also denies that Ceresole in an adviser to Chavez. Ceresole, in turn, in news interviews warns Chavez not to take Rangel on his trips to visit the Arab countries (OPEC).

It was Ceresole who urged Chavez to dissolve Congress, the Supreme Court, etc., and Chavez did. Ceresole claims that democracies do not work, and that they bring poverty – all over Latin America. In an interview with *El Nacional*, Siete Dias (28-2-99), Ceresole stated that he traveled across Venezuela with Chavez between 1994 and 1995, town by town. "My attraction for Chavez is that he represents the political model that I designed since the 1960s." "There is in the rest of Hispano America no one

compared to Hugo Chavez. Everything else is excrement."
Ceresole since 1968, has written 30 books on the military.

Chavez and Ceresole met in Buenos Aires in 1994, when
Chavez went to Argentina with Colonel Luis Alfonzo Davila and
Manuel Quijada. Ceresole later, took Chavez to Brazil and
Argentina. He has been in and out of Venezuela, returning on
January 1, 1999, a month prior to Chavez's inauguration, on a 6-
month visa. Not only J.V. Rangel has attacked Ceresole, Jorge
Olavarria has been one of his strongest critics.

But it was Nicomedes Zuloaga Pocaterra, from a
distinguished Venezuelan family and former Ambassador to the
Argentine, who best nailed Ceresole in an article he wrote for *El
Universal* (13-4-00). Mr. Zuloaga points out the differences
between Ceresole's Argentina, and Venezuela. The whites in the
Argentine eliminated the Indians, and Argentina remains a white
European country, without negroes, zambos and very few
mestizos. Much of their immigrations took place after the World
Wars ended, they include both Jews and Nazis. In contrast,
Venezuela has a population of Carib Indians and furious Negroes,
the last ones to get off the slave ships after they let off the tame
ones in Central America. You then mix in the ferocious Whites,
the soldiers of fortune, and the Basques, and you understand why
the Venezuelans led the Wars for Independence from Spain.
"Thank God, Venezuela is an ungovernable country." "Here, Mr.
Ceresole we are all philosophers. The fisherman in Margarita and
our campesinos every afternoon drink their beers and sit and
philosophize." Venezuelans dislike all that you, Ceresole, like.
"We are a furious populace, we seek peace."

Education and Decree 1011

That is definitely not what Chavez and Ceresole have in
mind, as they plan the re-education of the Venezuelan children.
Starting in the Fall of 2000, Venezuelan schools were ordered to
have one day a week of military training, in uniform, with a
military teacher. And this has, indeed, terrified parents – another
reason for leaving Venezuela! Furthermore, in November, Chavez
issued **Decree No 1011** creating "itinerant supervisors" whose
function was to intervene in any school in Venezuela, public **or**
private, and remove the administrators with no guidelines for
taking this action. The conception is Cuban, to indoctrinate the

children. In Venezuela there are some 400,000 teachers and school employees and they, along with thousands of parents and students, demonstrated against this assault by the Chavez Government. At the same time, the Hotel El Tama in San Cristobal, Tachira had been completely rented by the Chavez Government to serve as a training center for young people, with the Cuban militia acting as the teachers. Will the mothers of school children organize to challenge Chavez's indoctrination of their children, the way the Chilean women did to get rid of Allende in 1973? No, because the Venezuelan people are no longer disposed to make sacrifices, nor unite and fight. Commodious living has changed educated Venezuelans.

Strange isn't it – Fidel Castro had his Argentine in the person of Che Guevara, and Hugo Chavez has his in the person of Norberto Ceresole. Che advocated taking over Latin America and Africa. Ceresole is working on a multi-polar world with Chavez at the head of one of the poles. Chavez was to first start with the formation of a South Atlantic Military Organization (a NATO) for Latin American nations. If Chavez is going to oppose the United States then he needs a big military, which Venezuela does not have. There can be no other reason for Chavez's grandiose plans, "a la Ceresoliana," since there is no hegemony in the southern continent. And while Chavez was planning his grand southern Alliance, he had his own soldiers selling vegetables in the market place and giving children haircuts. This picture is absurd.

Venezuela's Military History

Military history in Venezuela begins in 1830. Between 1830 and 1999, of the **52 presidents** that Venezuela had in these 169 years, 17 were civilian presidents during 53 years; and 35 presidents were military men during 116 years. However, up to 1945, not one of these presidents who had been in the military, qualified as a militarist when he was President. If they achieved the presidency as a military man, it was leading their own troops and under their own flag. Which explains why Venezuela did not have a professional or permanent army, until the 20th century.

Venezuela was torn by civil wars until 1903, when General Juan Vicente Gomez defeated Nicolas Rolando in Ciudad Bolivar. Then, President Cipriano Castro began the foundations of a military and Juan Vicente Gomez inaugurated the new institution in 1910. Thus, when Gomez died in 1935, Venezuela had had 27 years of peace, had a healthy Treasury, no foreign debt, and a disciplined military. Supposedly, there would no longer be honorary generals, as there had been in the Andean states and earlier in the Llanos.

The young officers who studied in the Military Academy and then went abroad to take advanced courses would change the Venezuelan military. The Air Force became the most prestigious arm of the FAN, after the arrival of the Saber jets in the 1950s, and in the 1980s, the F16s. Venezuela has compulsory military service, but wealthy families pay others to serve in their son's place. The composition of the Venezuelan military traditionally has been different than Chile, Argentina and Colombia, where the officers more often come from the upper classes, particularly in the Navies of Chile and Argentina. The Castro regime in Cuba disbanded the traditional Army, as well as Castro's own Rebel Army, entrusting military functions largely to a party-controlled militia. For the Venezuelan lower class, military schooling and training has been a means of personal improvement, and for a few a means to power!

Under Romulo Betancourt in 1959, the professional period of the Venezuelan military commenced. It was the Armed Forces that successfully fought Fidel Castro's guerrillas and the communists' attempt to take over Venezuela in the 1960s, e.g. the naval insurrections at Carupano, in May 1962, and at Puerto Cabello, Venezuela's largest naval base, in June. Casualties amounted to several thousand, as Army units and civilians supported the government in crushing the mutineers. That was the beginning of the FALN in 1962, with urban terrorism and guerrilla warfare. The FAN was being infiltrated, and it was happening undetected.

And because the FAN is mainly drawn from the lower classes, it has been easier for the Communists and revolutionaries to penetrate, since 1957. With the upper classes engaged elsewhere in industry and commerce, the military became less supportive of the government, which was also being drawn form the lower classes through their political parties (AD and COPEI, and the minority parties). However, when the parties were in the government they were able to skim off the revenues, and this came about through the Punto Fijo agreement in 1958 between the three parties to share power. It is also the result of Venezuela having over 1.2 million government employees, out of a population of 23 million. Only top officers in the FAN received any of this largesse – through commissions on new arms and equipment, etc.

Within this undetected infiltration of the FAN, there were changes occurring in the thinking of the participants, i.e., moving from Soviet Communist orthodoxy to a Marxist-Leninist-Bolivariano nationalism, and in the middle was Hugo Chavez! But a curious opportunity to meet, exchange ideas, and plot often occurred when these young men were in jail, either in the Cuartel of San Carlos, or Yare!

There was an important historical event that occurred on May 13, 1958, on the occasion of the visit of the Vice President of the United States, Richard Nixon. The Communist Party did not know its strength until that day. They were able to carry out a large demonstration, not only down at the airport at Maiquetia, but through the streets of Caracas until Nixon was safely delivered to the U.S. Embassy. Pat and Dick Nixon and their party were spat upon at the airport, and had their cars stormed and rocked by frenzied mobs. People everywhere along the route were waving red flags. Those of us living in Caracas at the time will never forget these frightening hours. Venezuela had just gone through a revolution in January, forcing out the government of Marcos Perez Jimenez, and now had a Junta Government that was unable to control the rioting mobs, that had been led to believe that they had caused the government to fall. Caracas did not settle down until Betancourt became President in 1959. But the country was soon to be in for an even longer siege, one more terrifying, the work of Fidel Castro and the Communists.

And in 2000, Venezuela had a Lt. Colonel as president, who often wore his new white uniform with a new chest full of medals, and his specially made in Spain presidential sash, across his chest. More often, and less formal, he wore army fatigues and his paratrooper red beret. And when Chavez went out on the "People's Balcony" at Miraflores to greet his cheering crowds, as he did on his re-election, July 31, we heard him say, *"You really love me, don't you?"* and then he pledged *"Everything I have in life, I give to you."* Within a couple of months, however, there

37

were no more crowds showing up. The adulation was gone and reality was setting in

But it is not his clothes or speeches from the Peoples' Balcony that are of concern, it is his inability to listen to good advise, for he does not tolerate other opinions or a contrary view. This is why Chavez is so dangerous with the absolute power he has. His habit of abandoning those he had conspired with became evident even before he gained power. Chavez's popularity with the poor populace began to sharply decline in January 2001, and some Venezuelans began to hope that his departure was drawing near. There were more and more student demonstrations and rock throwing, and major thoroughfares shut down by strikers. Is he so incompetent with no knowledge of governing, or as some suspect, he seeks anarchy and disorder, in order to clamp down and justify totalitarian government like Castro's Cuba? Venezuelans have a new verb, "cubanizar," for what Chavez is doing to Venezuela.

Narco Traffic

Then there is the big problem of drugs, so often forgotten. But in Venezuela, narco-traffic is a very big problem, since it is next to Colombia with its huge cocaine production. The Orinoco River has been converted into a major commercial route for drugs in the southern continent. And there has been increasing penetration in Venezuelan airspace by international drug criminals. The U.S. wanted to over fly Venezuela and send spotter planes to visually identify suspected aircraft that are detected by radar leaving Colombia, and set up a sting operation at its destination. After the loss of their Panama air base in 1999, under the 1977 Treaty with Panama, the United States began to fall behind in the fight against Latin American drug trafficking. Chavez, arguing that U.S. surveillance flights would compromise Venezuela's sovereignty, has denied U.S. requests. Thus, Venezuela has become one of the safest narco routes to Europe and the United States, with some 110 tons of cocaine transported through, annually.

Sovereignty

Sovereignty is a red herring. Chavez uses the term "Venezuelan sovereignty" whenever he speaks of the United States. Once more he does not know of what he speaks. All countries surrender some sovereignty when they agree to enter international agreements. There is no better example for Venezuela than the Organization of Petroleum Exporting Countries (**OPEC**) which Venezuela under the Romulo Betancourt Government was the founding father. What kind of sovereignty did Venezuela lose when in 1982, they first agreed to OPEC oil production quotas? There have been no new members of OPEC since the organization agreed to apply quotas in 1982 (actually two members dropped out, Ecuador in November 1992, and Gabon in June 1996). Venezuela not only lost oil production they lost market to Mexico!

And what about the **Andean Pact**? Venezuela in 1973, was dragged by Rafael Caldera into this 1969 creation by Colombia, Ecuador, Peru, Bolivia and Chile. Venezuela had few restrictions on foreign investments until it joined the Pact. The Pact included Decision 24, which laid down strict rules for foreigners, e.g. limited profits they could repatriate; gave foreign companies in the region 15 years to sell off 51% of their Andean operations to local buyers. Needless to say, foreign investment in these countries dwindled, and Chile quit the Pact in 1976. Venezuela, as the richest member was expected to make all of the concessions, and get little in return. Venezuela's Fedecamaras (Federation of Chambers of Commerce) lobbied openly to keep Venezuela out of the pact. This was an obvious case of a government giving up sovereignty to other countries. Obviously, Chavez's use of the word "sovereignty" is merely a code word against the United States.

In 2000, Hugo Chavez assumed the rotating post as President of the Andean Pact, now named Andean Community of Nations (**CAN**). However, after the first meeting he chaired, he was unable to get the other Presidents to attend meetings he called.

In April 1999, Venezuela was odd man out because the other members of CAN had opened their markets and eliminated import tariffs on CAN products. Chavez's response was to temporarily prohibit the import of beef, rice and white corn (used in arepas), a measure aimed at protecting Venezuelan agricultural and live stock producers. Plunging consumption in CAN countries depressed their economies in 1999, and these nations have a great mass of population existing outside the consumer economy. Furthermore, differences in real bilateral exchange rates made some countries do better and some do worse. Ecuadorian production was favored in all countries of CAN, and Venezuela lost competitiveness in all Andean markets. On September 9, 2000, Ecuador completed its adoption of the U.S. dollar as its currency (and retired the sucre), a decision made by then-President Jamil Mahuad on January 9. (Panama officially dollarized in 1904, a year after declaring independence from Colombia.) This, while the Venezuelan **bolivar** (Bs) continues to be slowly devalued – a speed which is less than inflation is rising, i.e., inflation is twice the devaluation, making exports overpriced.

"Slow devaluation has harmed exports of Venezuelan products," said Roger Boulton (*Business Venezuela*, April 2000, p36). However, if the bolivar were abruptly devalued as it was in 1983, it would cost so much more to buy dollars, for the thousands of Venezuelans who continue to get their money out of the country. Today, the biggest export of Venezuela's private sector is *itself*. The managers and scientists who have global skills are leaving, frightened by the rising crime wake and Chavez's attacks on the successful. Venezuela has become in the past 25 years a very corrupt country. According to Transparency International, a small independent organization that does surveys of surveys on how the public and international businesses view corruption worldwide, Venezuela is at the bottom of the scale, along with Cameroon, Paraguay, Honduras, Nigeria, Indonesia and Colombia. Its rate of violent crime is the highest in the region.

Black Friday 1983 and the Bolivar

The middle class has been the most effected by the devaluation of the bolivar, beginning with a 78% devaluation on Black Friday, February 18, 1983. The Venezuelan economy runs on the monetary bolivar, but all Venezuelans equate the value of the bolivar to the U.S. dollar. The United States is a second country for Venezuelans, where they sent their children to learn English and to college, where they traveled widely and vacationed, did their shopping, and where some had their second homes. Venezuela for 19 years, since 1964, had a fixed exchange rate of Bs 4.30 per dollar. On December 29, 2000, the Central Bank set the rate at Bs 700 to the dollar, with the expectation that it would reach Bs 750 at the end of 2001.

In 1983, the Luis Herrera Government established a three-tier exchange rate system along with a foreign exchange agency, called Recadi, that approved the sale of U.S. dollars, causing immeasurable problems for every Venezuelan using dollars for imports, travel, or with foreign debt to repay. Nearly every Venezuelan was delayed or rejected by Recadi for some reason. Of course, if they were desperate for dollars they could go to the free market and pay three times the subsidized rate. It is assumed that out of $40 billion authorized for payment by Recadi, over the 6-years of its existence (discontinued in early 1989 by Perez), as much as $8 billion was illegally skimmed. Arturo Uslar Pietri sarcastically proposed a new medal (Venezuelan presidents give out countless medal awards), "The Order of the Fool," to be bestowed on honest citizens. Thousands marched in the Parade of Fools to protest government corruption. This was the beginning of the most pernicious form of corruption and the destruction of the middle class!

Another irony: this all came about because Luis Herrera in 1980, inherited a bankrupted country from Carlos Andres Perez, whose government ravished the largess of the Petrodollars in the 1970s, when Venezuela's annual oil export revenues jumped from $2.3 billion to $18 billion with oil production over 2 million barrels/day. The spending was so grand by the Perez Government, that a new phrase was coined, *pharaohism*. The money supply in the 1970s tripled in four years, and Venezuelans were hit by the first double-digit inflation in memory. It was a government and society out of control. Not only did the Perez Government spend on big projects, the middle class and the lower class became South America's biggest spenders, and most frequent travelers to Miami, to go "shopping." They were known in Miami as the "tabaratos tribe" (dame dos porque estan tan barratos) "give me two because they are so cheap."

President Herrera simply did not know how to handle this new external Venezuelan debt that amounted to **$35 billion**, the first foreign deficits in 50 years. And there was the further problem of illegal aliens, from the other Andean countries, so great as to raise the 13 million Venezuelan population by another 4 million. (see Chapter VII)

Incredibly generous at the time, Luis Herrera sponsored an aid program, unlike any Venezuela ever had, the San Jose Pact, of energy assistance to Central American and Caribbean countries, in August 1980. With the U.S. Government (Jimmy Carter) unwilling to step in and help El Salvador and the Contras in Nicaragua fighting a Cuban/Marxist takeover in Central America, President Herrera stepped up aid to $500 million in 1980, alone.

A few months before Black Friday, the Herrera Government let the ax fall on Petroleos de Venezuela, which with only 5 years in existence had accumulated **$6 billion** in its foreign dollar accounts. The government was in a deep economic crisis as the price of oil was dropping, and the Herrera Government's principal concern was renegotiating the foreign debt it had inherited from the previous government, and which it was also now increasing. Herrera simply transferred PDVSA's dollar account to the Central Bank, on October 28, 1982, to bolster Venezuela's foreign currency reserves. It was the beginning of PDVSA's loss of independence.

The Venezuelan Economy

Chavez has failed to formulate a plan for Venezuela's economic recovery. In 1999, the government spent 20% of GNP and the country had the worst economic performance in decades, with a 7% shrinking of the economy. Capital flight grew 1000% in the first half of 2000, over the same period in 1999. With so many businesses closing and so many industries laying off workers, there were 1.5 million out of work. There were 90,000 university graduates and 26,000 executives unemployed, a result of the largest companies reducing personnel, like the oil industry, food companies and hotels, as well as a general reduction in the manufacturing industries in Venezuela.

The country is in a Depression. However, one area of the economy is prospering: high cost imports; as well as the low cost Chinese **imports.** In the first three trimesters of 2000, Venezuelan imports grew 12 percent. The new government and their entourage are the new rich and were buying costly imports. The poor were buying the cheap imports. Venezuela has greatly reduced its manufacturing capacity. Foreign investment in 1999, was $560 million compared to $1.20 billion in 1998. The sum of this depression is: unemployment caused by businesses closing, foreign investment dropping, and capital flight of around $10 billion in 2000. Furthermore, **54%** of the economically active population is working in the informal economy, i.e., 5,130,000 people. Really alarming is that approximately 10% of the unemployed belong to the upper-middle and top management – something new to Venezuela.

Orlando Ochoa, economist, estimates that the Venezuelan economy will have to grow a minimum average of 5.5% during coming years, in order not to worsen the levels of employment and real income per capita. Since Venezuela cannot generate enough internal savings to meet the $30 billion per year public and private investment total that Ochoa says is necessary to fight unemployment with an 8% growth, foreign investments are necessary. This means opening the economy in traditional sectors (petroleum) and non-traditional sectors (telecommunications). And this Chavez is not about to do.

Any rise in Venezuela's GNP in 2000 was a result of government spending and of imports (manufactured goods, communications and commercial goods). Public consumption was 4 times private consumption. There was an increase of 70% in public spending between January and July of 2000, compared to the same period in 1999. This was done while the Government had a 4% deficit in GNP, and with high revenues coming from PDVSA's oil exports, averaging $26/barrel.

On October 1, 2000, Chavez introduced his draft budget for 2001, which called for an increase in public spending of 28.3% over the 2000 Budget. However, since the Chavez Government introduced numerous budget increases, spending in 2000 was 65% higher than budgeted. The actual 2001 Budget, thus, represents a 16.6% reduction in real terms. More than half of the 2001 Budget of **$33.2 billion** was dedicated to social initiatives. Education was allotted $6.1 billion, infrastructure $2.2 billion, health and social development $2.2 billion, security and defense $2 billion (primarily for the judiciary), and employment programs $1.7 billion. The 2001 Budget also includes $7.7 billion for debt servicing (23.2% of total budget). It also includes $60 million for 10 trips abroad for Chavez. Edgar Angulo in an article about Summit meetings, in *El Universal* (25-10-00), concludes with, "Mr. President, you are right, we Venezuelans go from Abyss to

Abyss, while you go from Summit to Summit, and for this you will
have a lot of money from the 2001 budget."

Since PDVSA, customs, and income taxes cannot supply
all the revenues Chavez needs, the Government will raise $9.7
billion through public borrowing. This budget and Chavez's
spending plans were dependent on the price of oil – a drop in
world oil prices and the Venezuelan economy slips deeper into
recession.

In 1999, the price of Venezuela's exported oil rose from
$8/barrel to $23/barrel – not seen in Venezuela since the Arab Oil
Embargo in 1973-74, and the Iranian Crisis in 1979, and the
Persian War in 1990. The average price for Venezuelan oil in
1999 was $16/barrel, amounting to $16.6 billion in revenues. But
the question for Chavez's first year in power was where are those
funds?

The Airwaves

One of the areas of Chavez's abuse of power is his
usurpation of the airwaves. The owners of television and radio
stations have lost their rights to Chavez. When Chavez speaks he
demands that all the stations form a chain (en cadena) and carry his
speeches, and he speaks for hours, sometimes on a daily basis.
The private stations are losing money at a rapid rate. Why should
the Venezuelans have to listen to a president who likes to hear
himself speak and ramble on and on for hours, with what could be
said in a mere 10 minutes. He thinks he is teaching the ignorant
Venezuelans, and this is one way of silencing dissident voices.
This abuse by Chavez became unbearable during Fidel Castro's
trip to Venezuela in October 2000. Television and radio
transmissions were interrupted more than once a day, and for
hours, to cover Chavez and Castro's every move across Venezuela.
Juan Jose Caldera (Rafael Caldera's son) on November 1, said that
his party, Convergencia would present an anti-chain bill to the
National Assembly to put a stop to these constant presidential
speeches en cadena. But first he was going directly to the people
for support, because he knew the Assembly was controlled by
Chavistas. Nothing came of this attempt. Nothing stops Chavez,
e.g. on June 15, 2001, he talked past midnight until 1:10 AM in the
morning, and said from now on he'd talk when ever convenient

and without any time limit. He sometimes comes on television with a replica or the real sword of Simon Bolivar.

The Church

Hugo Chavez's battle with the Catholic Church became full blown after the Archbishop of Merida, Baltazar Porras, who was also President of the Venezuelan Episcopal Conference (CEV), published an Open Letter to President Chavez, on April 25, 2000.

Archbishop Baltazar was responding to Chavez's many attacks against the Church and its priests. "You said in Havana last November that the Catholic Church in Venezuela was an accomplice in the corruption of the past 40 years. A few days ago, from the same place, and upon your return you expressed this again." He continued for 6 pages and ended asking for an audience with the President "to advance a constructive dialogue ... based on the truth and mutual respect."

Chavez responded on May 17, with his own Open Letter to the Episcopal Conference and the Bishops that had signed the April 25 letter. Chavez's letter was 20 pages long. He signs off with "Imploring the Apostolic blessing, Bolivariamente, Hugo Chavez," after writing an irreverent, offensive and threatening letter.

Why this battle with the Catholic Church? The Church every Sunday has well over a million Venezuelans gathered in the Churches attending Mass. The Church is a powerful social force with potential for mobilization, because it is the one institution that Venezuelans esteem. There are more religious in the barrios (slums) than there are Bolivarianos whom Chavez supposedly represents. Therefore, Chavez has attempted to destroy the head of the Church in Venezuela, by destroying the reputation of Baltazar Porras, in order to separate him from the other 40 Venezuelan bishops, and thereby take over the Church. Chavez's strategy is to divide and conquer. If the bishops do not all support Monsignor Baltazar Porras and the Episcopal Conference, they will be picked off one by one – and Chavez will have his Bolivarian Church. Finally, the battle exists with the Church because Chavez has stated that he is not a Christian. "I do not know Christian doctrine and do not practice it." (Habla el Comandante, by Agustin Blanco Munoz, p398)

The Sao Paulo Forum

The Foro de Sao Paulo, and in English the Sao Paulo Forum, is an organization created in July 1990 by Fidel Castro, to gather together all the leftist movements in Latin America, including the armed guerrilleros like the Colombian FARC and ELN. The Forum is the new International for Latin American Marxists, and Chavez is their new leader in extending the Cuban Revolution.

After the fall of the Berlin Wall in 1989, followed by the downfall of the Soviet communists, Fidel Castro convened a meeting with Luis Ignacio "Lula" Da Silva, in July 1990, in Sao Paolo. They gathered together all the Latin American guerrillero groups. The groups that joined included: the Workers Party (PT) in Brazil, the Cuban Communist Party, the FARC, the ELN, the Sandinistas, the Democratic Revolutionary Party (PRD) of Mexico, etc. There were 68 groups from 22 IberioAmerican and Caribbean countries at the founding meeting, along with observers from the United States, Canada, Spain, France, Italy, and the former Soviet Union. Since then, the Forum has grown to 112 groups and holds annual meetings in different cities, i.e., in Mexico City, Managua, Havana, Montevideo, etc.

At the Sao Paolo meeting, they set their objective to take power in all of Latin America – through the ballot or with arms. Since then other guerrillero groups have joined, like the Zapatistas (EZLN) of Mexico. The Forum created both a civil staff and a military staff headed by Fidel. Prominent in leadership roles were Sandinista Daniel Ortega, and Argentine Enrique Gorriaran Merlo.

The Forum has a permanent system of communication, and even publishes a magazine titled, America Libre. They have strong financial backing through kidnappings, bank robberies, pirating, and protection money, etc. And since Marxism had fallen into disfavor, the Forum decided to mask their true intent in several ways, by promoting the rights of Indians (Zapatistas); the promotion of separation of tribal lands; radical environmentalism to stop road building or electric power; divide the Catholic Church and justify violence with presumed Christian arguments.

Chavez joined the Forum on May 20, 1995, in Montevideo, along with his Bolivariano Revolutionary Movement 200. After becoming President of Venezuela, Chavez first declared his neutrality in the guerrillero attempt to take over Colombia and offered them refuge in Venezuela. On October 8, 1999, he invited the ELN to have their national convention in Venezuela. Chavez's Foreign Minister Jose Vicente Rangel maintained ties with the FARC and ELN, and opposition to the Pastrana Government. On June 13, 2000, the ex-Director of the DISIP (Direccion de los Servicios de Inteligencia y Prevencion), Col. Jesus Urdaneta Hernandez (one of Chavez's partners in the February 1992 revolt) accused the Chavez Government of ordering him to supply the Colombian guerrilleros with $300 million worth of arms. Col. Urdaneta also accused Chavez of always wanting to give arms to the guerrilleros. In Colombia there are many who understand that Chavez has been supplying the FARC and ELN with arms. In December 2000, ex-President Alfonso Lopez Michelsen, gave a long interview in Bogota, accusing Chavez of being Fidel Castro's successor and the disruptive effect he is capable of having on the Hemisphere. Chavez's interventionism in Colombia, by giving arms and aid to the guerrilleros, has denied Pastrana the ability to govern Colombia.

It was Alejandro Pena, former candidate for President, who in November 1998 documented and published information on the Forum for the first time in Venezuela. In The Plan of the Forum of Sao Paolo to Conquer Venezuela, he accused Hugo Chavez of being a member of the Forum. The Forum planned to use Venezuela's resources to bring down the Pastrana Government in Colombia, and next the Noboa Government in Ecuador.

Conclusion

The sum of the first 200 days of Chavez's government were perhaps "the worst 200 days in the lives, possibilities and hopes of the population," wrote Michael Rowan in the Caracas, *Daily Journal*, August 19, 1999.

The end of **August 1999** was Venezuela's *watershed* in destroying democracy, and PDVSA! Both were the work of Hugo Chavez.

A. On Monday, August 30, 1999, the 40 years of what was known as democracy in Venezuela ended, when Chavez's Constitutional Assembly stripped the Venezuelan Congress of its remaining powers. The National Constitutional Assembly (ANC) with 131 seats, elected July 25, with 121 Chavez supporters, including his wife, brother, and five of his most trusted cabinet members who resigned in order to be able to control the ANC, was to write a new constitution. Instead, its first acts, after taking power early in August, was to limit Congress' duties by declaring on August 12, a "state of emergency" and prohibiting Congress from passing laws or even convening as a full body! Finally, at the end of the month, the Assembly usurped Congress' few remaining powers, including the right to approve presidential trips abroad, and *budget outlays*! The Assembly, led by Luis Miquilena, former guerrillero in Castro's efforts to take over Venezuela, and former Minister of the Interior (most powerful post) in Chavez's Cabinet, also gave itself sweeping powers to fire judges and overhaul the justice system. It was in this way that Hugo Chavez achieved his coup and declared himself the supreme power in Venezuela, by eliminating the other two branches of government. And, one of those branches, the Congress, was elected in November 1998, a month ahead of the presidential election when Chavez was elected, and both were elected by the same populace.

B. The second part of Venezuela's *watershed*, on August 30, was the forced resignation of Roberto Mandini and the Chavez takeover of PDVSA, with the appointment of Hector Ciavaldini as President of PDVSA. It was one grand sweep of taking over the entire country – and truly breathtaking in its audacity. And, the next day, August 31, Chavez flew off to Panama to attend Mireya Moscoso's inauguration as President, taking along with him his new President of PDVSA, Ciavaldini.

Venezuela's flag – was designed by Francisco Miranda, independence hero, and the flag symbolizes the fight for independence:

The red band is for the blood spilled in the many bloody battles.
The top band of yellow stands for Venezuela's riches.
The middle band of blue represents the ocean separating Venezuela from Spain.

The seven white stars in the blue stripe represent the seven united states, which proclaimed their independence July 5, 1811.

A flag is a symbol of what a nation stands for, and what our forefathers bequeathed to us – our political traditions. Venezuela's political traditions are centered around Simon Bolivar. Chavez has

48

cleverly used the name of Venezuela's most respected hero in his efforts to tear down its political institutions. After the second year he did not mention Bolivar as often, Bolivar having served Chavez's purpose of using him as a protective shield.

Venezuelans are numb from the constant assaults to their way of life in the land of Chavez – Chavezuela. They see Chavez wasting Venezuela's revenues at a rate greater than any previous government, as the people grow poorer. He spent over $300 million on his elections, wasting precious time needed to improve the economy, usurping the private television and ratio stations, traveling abroad more than any president, and doing so with huge entourages. With the billions that Chavez has wasted, he could have made a stab at restoring the devastation in Vargas, caused by the December 1999 floods. Instead he hosts OPEC heads of state and trots around Venezuela with Fidel Castro. And when the "spiritual son of Fidel Castro" (Le Monde mag.) travels abroad he makes statements like, "neoliberalism is the road to Hell," as he stated in Nicaragua. (11-00) But what is neoliberalism? Chavez never defines what this venomous term means. However his purpose is clear – to stir up hatred toward the United States.

"In the 21st Century, Caracas may produce as much havoc for Western civilization as Sarajevo did in the 20th Century," wrote Michael Rowan, on August 9, 1999 in Venezuela Online News. Chavez is just starting in Venezuela with his revolution, but his sights are on Latin America and the World!

Chavez has put his stamp on everything of importance in Venezuela. He calls his government the Fifth Republic. He now thinks of OPEC as his; he claims he raised the world price of oil in 1999; and in 2001, his Minister of Energy Ali Rodriguez, a former guerrilla, became the Secretary General of OPEC.

What Chavez has done with his efforts to become the leader of OPEC is to closely identify Venezuela with OPEC. Before this, Venezuela was one of the members of OPEC, and U.S. oil executives and government officials understood that PDVSA was not pro-OPEC. It was the Minister of Energy who dealt with OPEC and agreed to oil quotas. PDVSA dealt with its clients. This has now changed with Chavez running the country and PDVSA – the industry has merged with the government. As a result of this dramatic change, it should also be clear that U.S.

policy has a new direction. President George W. Bush has proposed a North American energy alliance with Canada and Mexico, and diplomatic initiatives to oil producing nations of the Persian Gulf.

President Bush plans to strengthen energy ties with Mexico, which is not a member of OPEC. "His administration would promote development of energy resources in areas outside of OPEC." (*Oil & Gas Journal*, 2/12/01, p.67) In plain words, Venezuela has lost its special status with the United States, which it has had since World War II.

And Chavez effectively changed Petroleos de Venezuela to Petroleos de Chavez! Please note: the petroleum industry that accounts for over half of all Venezuelan government revenues and four-fifths of all exports is now Chavez's.

CHAPTER III

A HISTORIC TRAGEDY: PDVSA

Abraham Lincoln, in January 1838, delivered a speech to the Young Men's Lyceum of Springfield, Illinois. The subject was **"The Perpetuation of our Political Institutions"** and it was filled with wisdom. Lincoln warned of danger, not from foreign invaders but from ourselves. *Government in infancy brings the best men forward and the best out of men when governing. "Their all was staked upon it." Later along comes a man seeking distinction who "would set boldly to the task of pulling down,"* what invading foemen could never do, **"the levelling of its walls."**

This is exactly what Luis Giusti did to Petroleos de Venezuela (PDVSA), he set boldly to the task of pulling down, and leveled its walls. Giusti gets credit for continuing the Apertura (Opening) of the oil fields in Venezuela to foreign oil companies. But what many forget, or did not understand, were the consequences of his restructuring of the Venezuelan oil industry in 1997. He effectively destroyed three totally integrated operating companies and the "mistica" in the industry, as well as, the merit system of promotions. By doing this, Giusti opened the doors of PDVSA for the total takeover of the Venezuelan oil industry by Hugo Chavez and Hector Ciavaldini in 1999. Once Giusti merged the three operating companies into PDVSA, it would be inevitable that Venezuela would need large foreign oil investments. The greatest irony is that in 1996, the last year before the merger, Lagoven, Maraven and Corpoven had their most productive years.

It was always understood that PDVSA as the holding company was the buffer between the Ministry of Energy (the government) and the four operating companies formed after nationalization in 1976. At a meeting I arranged for the four affiliate presidents: Frank Alcock (Corpoven), Carlos Castillo (Maraven), Jack Tarbes (Lagoven), and Renato Urdaneta ← (Meneven), in Washington, D.C. at the Capitol, in Rep. Billy Tauzin's office, in September 1985, this point was explained by Jack Tarbes to the Congressman from Louisiana.

51

Of course, this no longer mattered after 1997, when Giusti restructured the industry. President Giusti then became more powerful than the Minister, Erwin Arrieta, and could go over his head directly to President Caldera. As President of PDVSA, Giusti's salary was raised from $80,000 to $300,000 per year. And in January 1999, President Caldera allowed Giusti to retire before he was 55 years old; and then receive $2 million in prestaciones (severance pay) and a pension of $25,000/month (even though he had broken service to the industry).

Luis Giusti started working for Shell de Venezuela in 1966, after graduating from the University of Zulia as a petroleum engineer. Both he and Erwin Arrieta had scholarships from Shell to study in Venezuela, and fellowships for graduate school abroad. Giusti went to the University of Tulsa where he got his Masters in 1971. But after getting his degree and returning to Venezuela, he did not return to Shell that had paid for his education. Instead he started a data processing company, with his friend J. J. Martinez. The company went bankrupt after Carlos Andres Perez became President in 1974 (due to one of CAP's decrees against free enterprise), and Giusti then returned to work for Shell, which was nationalized in 1975, along with the other foreign oil companies. In the 1980s, Giusti was moving up in Maraven (Shell), and in 1990, he was appointed Coordinator of Strategic Planning at PDVSA.

In April 1992, Luis Giusti became an Alternate Board Member of PDVSA, and how this happened is worth retelling. The Foreign Minister in 1992 was Humberto Calderon Berti (past President of Intevep, Minister of Energy, and President of PDVSA), and Giusti got a friend to introduce him to Calderon Berti, as a "Copeyano," and plead for his appointment to the PDVSA Board. Calderon Berti, on his car phone on his way to the airport, phoned Carlos Andres Perez (who was President for a second term) to intercede for Giusti's appointment, and CAP granted Calderon's request. Calderon's request changed history, and Giusti repaid Calderon Berti as he did all those who helped advance his career. In November of that year, Gustavo Roosen, President of PDVSA, moved Giusti off the Board and over to Maraven, as Vice President, under Eduardo Lopez Quevedo. On March 17, 1994, Giusti supposedly told Lopez Quevedo that "tomorrow you begin reporting to me!" Giusti made many enemies, got even for every slight, and stabbed those who helped him in his strategic planning for the presidency, which started in a meeting in San Antonio de los Altos, in 1989.

President Giusti

When Giusti became president of PDVSA, on *March 18, 1994*, it was a shock to the industry. At 49 years, he was the youngest president of PDVSA and he had stepped over older more qualified men in line for the job. Actually, the position had been offered to Frank Alcock, the acting President of PDVSA, and Vice President of PDVSA since 1986, and before then, President of Corpoven. But Erwin Arrieta, the new Minister of Energy and Mines wanted his old colleague in Shell, as President of PDVSA. President Caldera turned Arrieta down twice when he proposed Giusti's name. Arrieta then brought in two of Caldera's oldest friends, Julio Sosa Rodriguez and Hugo Perez la Salvia, to change Caldera's mind, which he did. (Both Arrieta and Perez la Salvia would live to regret their efforts for Giusti.) When the appointment was announced at the press conference after the Asamblea Meeting, on March 18, there was a picture taken of Minister Arrieta making the announcement, flanked by Alcock and Giusti. The fact that Alcock was not told that Caldera had changed his mind was revealed on Frank Alcock's face. The clear use of such raw power was so *declasse*, some of us realized that PDVSA had peaked, and was heading downward.

In addition to the Giusti leapfrog, Arrieta also leapfrogged the two new Vice-Presidents. Claus Graf had been Vice-President of Corpoven, and Luis Urdaneta had been Vice-President of Lagoven. In other words, Arrieta preferred the three vice-presidents (Giusti, Graf and Urdaneta) of the three integrated affiliates over their presidents: Eduardo Lopez Quevedo, Roberto Mandini and Julius Trinkunas, who were inline for the top PDVSA positions, along with Frank Alcock, and others. Arrieta in effect ended the merit system of promotion in PDVSA, which enabled Luis Giusti to promote his friends and facilitators.

For twenty years PDVSA was a mercantile company, paying taxes and dividends to the Government of Venezuela; and its employees were not government employees, according to its by-laws. We often discussed how long the operating oil companies might remain independent, before the Government gained dominance as in Mexico (Pemex) and Brazil (Petrobras). Never was it imagined that the deed would be done by an oilman. With nationalization of the foreign major oil companies on January 1, 1976, four integrated operating companies were formed i.e., Lagoven (Exxon and Amoco), Maraven (Shell), Meneven (Gulf), and Corpoven (Corporacion Venezolana del Petroleo, Mobil, Chevron, and Texaco). Ten years later, in 1986, Meneven was merged into Corpoven, and the Venezuelan operating companies continued to be run by oilmen, who had been well trained by these foreign oil companies. As Jack Tarbes (now deceased) always used to say to me when I praised their accomplishments, "We had the best teachers." These four affiliate presidents, and the President of PDVSA at the time, Brigido Natera, were first class oil executives.

These Venezuelan oilmen took over a declining oil industry, melded their companies (14 nationalized, including three Venezuelan companies) into well organized modern producing companies, with loyal employees. This loyalty, which was called "la mistica," produced greater extraction of petroleum and larger reserves, with PDVSA reaching the position of the 2nd largest petroleum company in the world in 1995, according to *Petroleum Intelligence Weekly* (PIW). PIW based this on a combination of sales, reserves and refining activities. Venezuela was also the biggest supplier of imported oil to the United States. The three operating companies raised Venezuela's **oil reserves** of 18 billion barrels in 1976, to 72.6 billion barrels in 1996; and **production** was raised from 2.3 million barrels per day (b/d) in 1976, to 3.4 million b/d in 1996. Oil production figures were held back by Venezuela's production quota in the Organization of Petroleum Exporting Countries (OPEC). According to Orlando Ochoa, the monetary value of PDVSA in 1998 <u>was</u> between $100 to 150 billion! (PriceWaterhouse, that were accountants for PDVSA for 24 years, placed PDVSA's total assets as $49.99 billion, as of December 31. 1999.)

Luis Giusti wanted power and money, and in achieving both, he was Clintonian and prevaricate. At the top of his list of enemies were oilmen who had worked for Creole/Lagoven, and with few exceptions (Claus Graf) they would be vilified and removed to Siberia (Valle de los Caidos), a building across the street, in front of PDVSA headquarters. It was first Arrieta and then Giusti who destroyed the merit system in PDVSA, by moving his Shell/Maraven/Zulia people up into key positions. Unknown to most, even today, were the plans during the Gustavo Roosen presidency (before Giusti's), to divide up Maraven between Corpoven and Lagoven. Maraven lacked leadership, was giving very poor results, and was becoming corrupt.

After Carlos Andres Perez (CAP) named two non-oilmen (Andres Sosa Pietri and Gustavo Roosen) as president of PDVSA, Giusti must have concluded that in order to reach the top, he'd better find a political party. He chose COPEI, and the candidate he openly supported in 1993 was Oswaldo Alvarez Paz from Maracaibo, which is where Giusti is from. This was the first time that an oil executive openly supported a candidate, and the President of PDVSA, Gustavo Roosen sent out a memo reminding employees that PDVSA and its affiliates never engaged in politics nor should they support political parties. But the top for Giusti was not president of PDVSA, it was to be followed by President of the Republic of Venezuela, and in 1998, he would turn to the AD party, the largest of the political parties, in seeking the Presidency. After becoming President of PDVSA, Giusti started to court the political leaders of the parties, and in AD he discovered his political mentor, Luis Alfaro Ucero.

But Giusti did something else to further his potential political career. He spent millions of PDVSA's bolivars on some plans called the Armonicos de Oriente y Occidente, as a front to promote his campaign for the Presidency. In this way, he and his facilitators got PDVSA involved in politics, in order to promote Giusti's candidacy. One has to wonder how he ever thought he could win the Presidency? There seems to be an unwritten rule in Venezuela, Brazil and Mexico that no president of PDVSA, Petrobras, or Pemex can ever be elected President of their country. Calderon Berti has certainly proved this dictum to be true, having spent years running for President of Venezuela, after being President of PDVSA in 1983.

Giusti hoped to enter the 1998 Presidential campaign, but was probably deterred by the growing support Hugo Chavez was picking up from the poor and lower classes. Chavez had been campaigning since getting out of prison in 1994 (freed by the same President that appointed Giusti President of PDVSA), and in his last year of campaigning in 1998, Chavez relentlessly attacked both Giusti and PDVSA. Furthermore, the individual political parties never openly supported a candidate (as to who could defeat Chavez). On December 28, 1997, *El Nacional* (whose editor, Miguel Otero, had been charmed by Giusti), in its "Siete Dias" discussed Giusti's candidacy as one that might be by acclamation and careful planning. For many months, Giusti appeared to be seeking the support of the AD party. It was assumed that Giusti had been raising money to run, and had a sizeable slush fund, but he never announced his candidacy. Shortly before the election, Giusti in October invited Chavez to meet with the PDVSA Board. However, before the Board meeting, he sequestered Chavez alone and offered PDVSA's help in acquiring funds that Chavez might need after he was elected President!

A problem for Giusti was his age, becoming President of PDVSA when he was only 49. (The president of PDVSA is appointed for a 2-year term, and Giusti was reappointed president twice, by President Caldera.) What was he going to do next? President of Venezuela was the next logical step. Instead, today he lives in exile in the United States, and consults with foreign oil companies that he dwelt with as President of PDVSA. Already forgotten was the speech Giusti made in September 1994, in New York at the Society of the Americas, when he threatened the United States over reformulated gasoline. He said that Venezuela's U.N. Ambassador Tejera Paris would take the issue to the United Nations and that *the United States would have a supply problem, because Venezuela would sell its gasoline to other South American countries*!

Oil Industry as Provider (Cornucopia of Government)

The Wall Street Journal, on August 12, 1974, had a headline for an article on Venezuela: "Embarrassment of Riches Venezuelans Ponder How Best to Spend $10 Billion Windfall From Oil Resources," by Everett G. Martin. Mr. Martin wrote: "Venezuela is the fourth-largest petroleum producer in the Free World, and, because of rising oil prices, its national coffers will be enriched by $10 billion this year – about three times its oil income last year." And the old sage of the Ministry of Energy, Juan Pablo

Perez Alfonso, Minister in the Accion Democratica government of Romulo Betancourt, was quoted in this article as saying, "The 10 billion will crush us. After five years of this, we'll be in a worse state than ever. They've never appreciated the work ethic here. It's impossible to spend all that money wisely." He was right! Venezuela was producing 3 million b/d in 1974, and of this, half was produced by Creole Petroleum Corp. (Exxon). Soon after the Arab oil embargo ended in the spring of 1974, Venezuela announced cutbacks in oil production of 5%, or about 160,000 b/d to conserve natural gas being flared at oil wells.

The annual Venezuelan National Budget is largely determined on the income of PDVSA each year. The Minister of Energy and Mines was to set policy for PDVSA, and the Finance Minister was to gather its earnings through an onerous tax system. Even with this heavily taxed industry, it wasn't enough for the profligate government.

Under the 1975 Nationalization Law, Article 6, Section 5, 10% of the PDVSA operating companies' net profits from their exports were to be excluded from taxation. This was to enable the Venezuelan oil industry to generate its own capital requirements. It soon became clear, however, that with rapid expansion of the industry, more funds would be needed, and the Government thus agreed to establish an **Oil Investment Fund**, managed by the industry, to be utilized exclusively for oil industry projects and development. Venezuela was thus making sure PDVSA would not run into the experience of Pemex, which was chronically short of financing for its projects, and by 1982, its external debt stood around $25 billion. (Actually most of this debt was the Mexican Government's, which had used Pemex to do its borrowing in the international markets – something Venezuela was going to use PDVSA for, in the 1990s.) Through the industry's operation of the Investment Fund, and high interest payments on their foreign holdings, the Fund reached $8 billion by early 1982.

On **October 27, 1982**, Luis Herrera consolidated PDVSA's **$6 billion foreign exchange holdings** with the Central Bank holdings. And in December, the Government ordered PDVSA to utilize about $2 billion of the Fund to buy Government bonds of the public debt. PDVSA's loss of foreign exchange holdings, plus the subsidization of domestic gasoline prices, its onerous taxes and dividends to the Government, contributed to a growing cash flow problem.

PDVSA had to go to the foreign financial market and borrow billions of dollars, in order to satisfy government demands. In 1988, Venezuela asked the Bank of America and Salomon Brothers to arrange a $1 billion private placement of oil export receivables, i.e., sell future oil revenues to raise cash. In 1992, Venezuela's public sector deficit amounted to $2.75 billion, of which $2.2 billion corresponded to PDVSA's financing. In July 1993, PDVSA sold $1 billion of bonds to U.S. investors through their PDV America Inc. (Citgo), with Salomon Brothers arranging the offer. PDVSA was back again in the bond market in May 1998 for $1.8 billion, with J. P. Morgan, Credit Suisse First Boston, and ABN Amro underwriting the offering. PDVSA succeeded in convincing investors that the new bonds were safer investments than Venezuelan government debt, whose debt rating from Moody's Investors Service was Ba2. In PDVSA's 1999 Annual Report, they reported their long-term debt as $7.6 billion.

PDVSA first had to cut heavy oil development, therefore, it formed the strategic association joint ventures for the Oil Belt. Conventional oil recovery was cut next, which eventually led to the Apertura (Opening). Furthermore, PDVSA had to lend executive personnel to the government to fill key government positions, and continue to pay their salaries while PDVSA had to make do without their services. Carlos Andres Perez was one of the worst abusers of this arrangement (but he was later topped by Rafael Caldera), borrowing over 200 top men at a time, for periods of several years. This was the government's arrangement in the Ministry of Energy, Ministries of Finance, Health, Education, Environment, Corporacion Venezolana de Guayana (CVG), etc. Besides borrowing some of their best men, the government also borrowed their planes for trips, beginning with Jaime Lusinchi's presidency (1984-1989). The Minister of Energy, Arturo Hernandez Grisanti, took the PDVSA Falcon on his honeymoon and went all around the world: to the Middle East collecting wedding presents, staid at the best hotels and ate at expensive restaurants. Even the furniture in the Minister's office came from PDVSA. In 1985, I was making a presentation to the Minister in his office, along with a Vice President of PDVSA, and commented on the magnificent circular table we were sitting at. The Vice President quietly told me it used to be PDVSA's, but the Minister had asked that it be sent over. PDVSA even paid for the Government's consultants, e.g. when CAP wanted to hire Henry Kissinger, he had Citgo pay Kissinger's retainer of more than $250,000.

In spite of this total government control over PDVSA, the politicians were always suspicious of PDVSA – it was so unVenezuelan! It was run so efficiently, its employees were so loyal, worked such long hours, often through weekends, were well educated and widely traveled, many were fluent in English and French. The oil people even had a different system of time, i.e., the hour to meet was punctual. It was known as "la hora petrolera," as opposed to Venezuelan time, "whenever I get there." And to a large degree, oil people enjoyed each other's company and tended to socialize more within their own affiliate company, and kept friendships made in the oil camps, after they were transferred to Caracas or Maracaibo. This trust now exists only among those who have retired, or have left the industry.

Luis Giusti's rapid rise to power is associated with two words: *intrigue* and *betrayal*. The worst consequence of Giusti's ambition is the damage he did to the oil industry. He not only harmed those who had helped him, but those who were under his leadership. Giusti's principal "facilitator" for his intrigue and betrayal was Pedro Aponte, whom he appointed in 1994, as Corporate Manager of Loss Prevention and Control, which became known as "la policia de Giusti." (This is an office that first appeared in 1985, as Security and Loss Control, and the next year was changed to Loss Prevention and Control.) The Giusti Group purchased and used Westinghouse Audio Intelligence Devices, a sophisticated electronic bugging system, in the offices of the oil executives, in the Minister of Energy's offices, *and* in the offices of key politicians in Caldera's Cabinet. What fear Luis Giusti caused in PDVSA! "No passion so effectively robs the mind of all its powers of acting and reasoning as fear," said Edmund Burke in 1757.

To be a member of the Giusti Group (Gang) was not an honorable designation. The corruption in PDVSA under Luis Giusti became so bad that you began to suspect everyone as being on the take. It was this suspicion that drove Hugo Chavez, as a presidential candidate, to attack not only Luis Giusti, but the industry as a whole. Giusti proves Lord Acton's dictum that "power tends to corrupt and absolute power corrupts absolutely."(1887)

Now there is no one left – sufficiently experienced or respected – to take charge of PDVSA. Therefore, privatization is recommended. It is the only logical answer, for the Venezuelan economy. The first steps toward this route were taken under the Apertura, or Opening, and commenced with the Cristobal Colon LNG project. But it should be understood that this first step would have been <u>unnecessary</u> if the Government had not bled PDVSA dry. In the oil industry you must invest, invest, invest, in order to maintain your production and to increase your reserves. Furthermore, Venezuela has oil fields with a 25% annual reservoir depletion rate, in which PDVSA has to invest some **$4 billion/year**, just to offset this decline.

Before the Government began to pluck the Golden Goose, in addition to taking its Golden Eggs, PDVSA performed so well it rose to number two in the world, behind Saudi Aramco. PDVSA had some of the most capable men in the world oil industry. There is so much irony in PDVSA's present situation. The same politicians that bled PDVSA over the years were the ones who condemned PDVSA's efforts to bring back the foreign companies, in order to maintain Venezuela's oil production and exports.

Jose A. Mayobre, Minister of Mines and Hydrocarbons, in an address delivered in June 1967, to the North American Chamber Commerce of Venezuela (and published in the Caracas *Daily Journal*) said the following. "On seeking a maximum return, care should be taken not to kill the Goose that lays the Golden Eggs. Venezuela's oil returns have increased 50% in the last eight years. The share now received by the government from the industry is satisfactory." Further on, "Venezuela's chief petroleum problem at the moment is the relations with the United States. Venezuelan oil is of great strategic importance to the Hemisphere; the attitude should not be taken that it is merely to be had when needed. Venezuela is entitled to a new deal." (In March 1959, the Eisenhower Administration issued the Mandatory Oil Import Program, applying quotas aimed at Venezuela's oil exports, which

were produced by U.S. oil companies.)   Mayobre's message was
serious and logical – but quickly forgotten.

Apertura

Cristobal Colon

Lagoven spearheaded the Cristobal Colon LNG Project.
Venezuela at the end of 1990 had 233 trillion cubic feet (Tcf) of
proven, probable and possible reserves of natural gas. Of this
figure, 32 Tcf was nonassociated gas, and it was this gas that
Cristobal Colon was to develop offshore the Paria Peninsula, in the
northeast (Sucre State) of Venezuela, for export as liquid natural
gas (LNG), to the U.S. East Coast and to Europe. Lagoven
undertook an offshore exploratory program between 1979 and
1982, discovering 4 gas fields (Patao, Dragon, Mejillones, and Los
Testigos) and one gas-condensate field (Rio Caribe) in the
Caribbean, north of the Paria Peninsula. Feasibility studies by
Lagoven and Shell were concluded for the LNG Project in 1989,
and resulted in a proposal for an integrated project including
production and transmission of the gas, liquefaction, shipping and
marketing. A decision was made in June 1990 to invite Shell,
Exxon and Mitsubishi to join Lagoven as joint venture partners.
Each had a particular experience-expertise. Lagoven retaining a
33% share, already had spent $200 million in exploration, Shell
would take 30% share, Exxon 29%, and Mitsubishi 8 percent.

Before actually forming the joint venture company of Sucre
Gas, S.A., it was necessary to get Congressional approval, in a
joint session of the two chambers, under Article 5 of the
Venezuelan Hydrocarbons Nationalization Law of 1975. Renato
Urdaneta, former president of Lagoven had the difficult task of
getting this project through Congress. Finally, after three years,
the Venezuelan Congress approved the Cristobal Colon joint
venture on August 10, 1993. It was done with the support of AD
and COPEI parties, along with La Causa Radical party. The
smaller left-wing parties remained in opposition to the LNG
project. It was a very special victory, because it was going to be
the first direct foreign investment in Venezuela since the petroleum
industry was nationalized. The project was to be subject to
Venezuela's maximum corporate tax rate of 30%, instead of the
67.7% tax applied to oil and gas operations. Sucre Gas, S.A. was

formed on January 25, 1994, responsible for the $5.6 billion LNG project expected to produce 900 MMcf/day.

Unfortunately, in December 1996, after the partners had invested $50 million in the LNG project, they decided to postpone the project for five years, for lack of market. However, in January 2000, PDVSA revived talks with Shell, ExxonMobil, and Mitsubishi regarding the LNG export project. Using several new names, LNG of Venezuela, and Paria North LNG; and planning for less capacity and investment ($2 billion); new markets projected in the Caribbean, as well as the U.S. East Coast; and more than double natural gas prices; a new memorandum was signed in March. PDVSA assumed Lagoven's partnership and proposed that their share be reduced to 20%, from 33%, and operations begin in 2005. This new attempt surely had a lot to do with Trinidad's LNG production.

The question was often asked if Trinidad could launch an LNG complex ($1 billion, single train), which was commissioned in January 1999, why couldn't Venezuela? Furthermore, Trinidad's Atlantic LNG started exporting LNG to Puerto Rico in July 2000 – and before that to the Distrigas terminal in Everett, Massachusetts, in May 1999. Atlantic LNG had two more liquefaction trains coming on stream, one in 2002 and another in 2003, and a fourth proposed train under contract.

Whether Venezuela will build the Cristobal Colon (now North Paria) LNG complex, it has already served an important purpose by opening the way for other foreign investments in the Venezuelan petroleum industry. As an ex-Board member of PDVSA often said, "Cristobal Colon without any doubt was a pioneer in the real petroleum opening [apertura], and the essential reason for its deferment were gas prices at the time. The question is why did they build a plant in Trinidad, although of smaller size, if price was important, why there, and not in Venezuela?"

Strategic Associations

Three days after they approved Cristobal Colon, Congress on **August 13, 1993**, approved two strategic associations for the production of extra heavy oil in Maraven's Zuata section of the Orinoco Oil Belt. In the first strategic association, Maraven and Conoco were equal partners. In the second association, Maraven's partners included Total of France, Itochu and Marubeni, (the

Japanese companies later dropped out). These strategic associations are presently operating and producing 9 degree API crude, which is then upgraded at Jose, Anzoategui, on the Caribbean, into lighter 22 degree API crude (Conoco), and 32 degree API crude (Total/Fina), before being exported. Each strategic association was to produce over 100,000 b/d of upgraded fuel. The companies that were formed to produce this extra heavy crude from the Oil Belt are called Petrozuata (Conoco/PDVSA), and Sincor (Total with 47%, PDVSA 38%, Statoil 15%). Petrozuata began production in August 1998, and has now reached production of 120,000 barrels per day. Sincor commenced its initial production on December 20, 2000, and will have the lightest quality syncrude (Zuata Sweet), in 2002.

The Venezuelan Congress later approved two other strategic associations. In September 1996, Mobil Oil signed a memorandum of understanding with Lagoven (Julius Trinkunas, President) for the Cerro Negro strategic association. A month earlier, Arco had signed a deal with Corpoven for the Hamaca sector of the Oil Belt. Arco has since dropped out and the partners are now Phillips/Texaco/PDVSA, and the company is called Ameriven Hamaca. Cerro Negro (ExxonMobil, PDVSA, and Veba Oel) by January 2001, was producing 120,000 barrels per day, and will market a 16.5 degree API crude.

All four strategic associations have built or are completing delayed-coking upgraders at Jose. Petrozuata's investment in the project is to be about $2.8 billion, with Sincor and Ameriven each investing $4 billion in their projects, and Cerro Negro around $2 billion, for a total of close to **$13 billion**, to then produce between 500,000 and 600,000 b/d, mostly for export. Putting together the long term financing was no easy matter for these projects, particularly for Sincor. After Chavez became President, interest on long term financing for a project in Venezuela rose to 15% (i.e., 9% over U.S. Treasury bonds of around 6% interest). These extra heavy oil projects are subject to the 34% income tax rate, and their contracts are for 35 years.

The Oil Belt contains 1.2 trillion barrels of oil in-place, with ultimate recovery possibly reaching 270 billion barrels. The Belt is roughly 20,000 square miles and was divided into four sectors by PDVSA in 1978. The main producing areas are from east to west, with API gravity ranging from 13 degrees in Cerro Negro, to 3 degrees (bitumen) in Machete. This is the one area where foreign oil companies can and are greatly increasing Venezuela's production, and where PDVSA was forced to cut back because of lack of funds. PDVSA in December 1982 was forced to scale down the Oil Belt program, after five intensive years of evaluating the Belt and drilling 662 wells, processing 16,000 miles of seismic lines, etc., and spending $615 million, and with the mega DSMA project in the planning for Lagoven. PDVSA had just lost their $6 billion foreign exchange holdings in October, funds they had planned to use developing the Oil Belt. Their holdings were transferred to the Central Bank in an Executive Order. As one Venezuelan oilman said: "We have been the victims of a government coup (golpe de Estado). He was right on target. By 1998, the Venezuelan Government had managed to get **PDVSA indebted** by **$6.27 billion** in long term debt, and by 1999 indebted by **$7.6 billion.**

In 1993, PDVSA was banking heavily on Congressional approval for Cristobal Colon, and the two Maraven Oil Belt projects with Conoco and Total. The Executive branch had already agreed to the Apertura in April 1990, when it was approved by Carlos Andres Perez. His Minister of Energy, Celestino Armas, came up with the idea in September 1989. A particular irony: it was CAP, who nationalized the oil industry in 1976, and was now inviting the foreign oil companies back!

First Round – Mature Fields

The first small efforts were made in **June 1992**, when PDVSA signed contracts for rejuvenating old oil fields, which did not require Congressional approval because there was no equity oil involved. The fields offered had been produced and abandoned for 20 years, or marked off as marginal and uneconomic to develop by Lagoven, Maraven and Corpoven. The fields were called "squeezed oranges."

Winning bids were submitted by Shell for Production Unit 4 (Pedernales); Teikoku for Unit 9 (East Guarico); Benton Oil and Vinccler for Unit 3 (Uracoa, Bombal, Tucupita); and Lingoteras de Venezuela for Unit 6 (Cumarebo, La Vela on shore), and also for Unit 8 (West Guarico). PDVSA wanted to speed up foreign participation in Venezuela's upstream operations and increase production without tying up its resources in marginal projects. PDVSA's overall tax rate is onerous (89%), plus its enormous subsidies for domestic gasoline (for many years the subsidy amounted to $500 million/year), leaving insufficient funds for new production. PDVSA's budget for 1992 was $10.3 billion, the biggest until then, of which 52% was to go for capital outlays and 48% for operating expenses.

Operators for the winning bids would not own the crude they produced, but turn it over to Lagoven or Corpoven; they would assume all the risk for investments and were to be compensated on a per barrel fee basis for oil produced. The operators would only be taxed at 30% (34% after December 1994) on operating profits, instead of the 67.7% the government taxes PDVSA. The operating contracts were for 20 years.

Shell, the only major company to win in the first round (the Pedernales field, which in 1993 went to British Petroleum), refused to sign the contract, because of a dispute over a legal issue. Shell wanted any legal dispute to be resolved by arbitration outside of Venezuela. They had memories of their nationalization in Venezuela in 1975, when their compensation issue was settled in the Venezuelan Supreme Court. And Lingoteras, a Venezuelan group, planning to operate their winning bid in the Cumarebo and La Vela fields, was unable to raise the funds needed for production investment. That left two operators from the first round in 1992: Benton and Teikoku. Benton began the first production by a U.S. oil company since nationalization! It began producing 2,100 b/d from four wells in the reactivated Uracoa field in eastern Venezuela, in March 1993. Teikoku was the first Japanese company to undertake petroleum operations in Venezuela. Corpoven turned over East Guarico Unit to Teikoku on January 1, 1993, with production around 1,370 b/d, which Teikoku hoped to boost to around 18,000 b/d of light sweet crude (32 to 33 degrees API), but never exceeded 6,000 barrels per day.

Second Round – Mature Fields

In the second Round, 79 fields were consolidated into 13 operational units, in order to allow the contractor greater surface extensions to conduct their operations, and the possibility of significant amounts of crude oil production for an extended period of time. PDVSA, in February 1993, sent a team up to Houston and

Dallas, to make the marginal fields presentation. The team was led by Francisco Pradas, Coordinator of Exploration and Production, and we arranged with the Houston InterAmerican Chamber of Commerce, for him to speak before some 400 people, followed two days later at the Dallas Petroleum Club, at a breakfast briefing before 50 top oil executives. It proved both an opportunity to sell the Venezuelan program, and it also was an opportunity for feedback from many in the States, as to their questions and concerns.

In **September 1993**, the second Round of oil and gas marginal fields were offered for bid. Most of these fields were producing, with only Falcon offshore never produced. Again, contracts were for 20 years, operators must sell oil to one of the three PDVSA operating companies, for which they would be paid on volume basis, and the operators would be reimbursed for capital outlays. Under the second round, contractors would be allowed to drill beyond the original horizons delineated by earlier concessionaires.

The 11 new production contracts were awarded in **October 1993** to nine groups to revive marginal oil fields. Alirio Parra, then Minister of Energy and Mines, said that investments by the winning bidders called for outlays of $860 million through 1996. This would cover production infrastructure, new drilling, and some exploration, with targets for production of 140,000 b/d, by 1996, and 300,000 b/d by 2000. The winning **8** bidders and their blocks were: Mosbacker Energy Corp. for Guarico West; Teikoku Oil Co. for Sanvi-Guere; Norcen, Perez Companc for Oritupano-Leona; Tecpetrol, Astra for Quiamare; Total for Jusepin; Maxus (YPF) (and later British Petroleum) for Quiriquire; Shell for Urdaneta West; and Occidental for Desarrollo Zulia Occidental. Olympic got Falcon offshore, but later exited – leaving 8 groups of companies in the Second Round.

Maraven in December 1993, put out a call for bids for two oil field units: Falcon West, and Colon, offered earlier in September, but neither received a satisfactory bid. Falcon West along the coast, with 33 degree API light crude, was expanded to 1 million hectares, encompassing four different fields – completely inactive. Colon, also with 32 degree API light crude, was still active, and this area at the southwest tip of Zulia State is near the border with Colombia. In the second half of **1994**, Eduardo Lopez Quevedo, President of Maraven, announced the selection of a consortium of Corexland-Tecpetrol-Wascana-Nomeco to operate the Colon Unit (later CMS Energy took 43.7% and became operator); and the consortium of Samson-Vepica-Ingenieria 5020-Petrolago to operate Falcon West.

Boscan field was awarded to Chevron in 1996, by Maraven on a negotiated basis to raise Boscan's production of heavy crude in Lake Maracaibo, from 80,000 b/d to 115,000 barrels per day. The oil production was to be refined in Chevron's Pascagoula refinery in Mississippi, which has one of the U.S.'s largest cokers, able to process heavy oil into gasoline.

The sum of all this reactivation of mature (marginal) fields helped PDVSA maintain its oil production. The need for the Apertura in 1993 was a result of:

1) Reserves of light and medium crudes were down to 17.9 billion barrels in 1992, and Venezuela needed deep drilling projects (which are expensive) in order to increase these reserves. Venezuela's proved reserves of light and medium crudes were the lowest of major world oil producers, e.g. Saudi Arabia had 249 billion barrels, Iran 90 billion, Iraq 98 billion, Kuwait 91 billion, Mexico 56 billion, Russia 57 billion, and the USA 21.5 billion barrels, in 1992.

2) PDVSA did not have the needed cash flow – and the Government needed even more funds in 1994, to save the banking system, after the Banco Latino in January started a banking failure chain reaction.

3) Venezuela also needed the foreign oil companies' worldwide experience and development technology that it used to receive before nationalization.

Profit Sharing Exploration

First to clarify the number of so-called "Rounds." Some people do not count the first contracts for mature fields of June 1992, as I do, but instead start with the October 1993 Round. The second confusion is the types of contracts for different types of fields, from the first to the third Rounds. The first two Rounds were for "marginal fields." The next bidding should be called Profit Sharing Exploration contracts for reactivated oil fields with exploration rights, and they were tendered as Exploration

Association Contracts, and are called an Association Operating Agreement. British Petroleum was contracted by PDVSA in 1993, to make an overall geophysical study of Venezuela, and the selection of fields for the January 1996, and June 1997 bidding were made from this study. PDVSA sold geological packages of information on each respective area for $50,000 and companies were asked for $100,000 to bid. Furthermore, companies had to agree to a financial guarantee of $500,000 and a promised minimum exploration program of $40 million to $60 million.

It was no easy task to sell the idea in Venezuela that Venezuela should invite the foreign oil companies back, particularly when it involved new exploration areas. The Venezuelan Congress, on **July 4, 1995**, approved the offering of **10** exploration blocks, after many months of discussion. This opened Venezuela to exploration of light and medium crudes by private companies **in** association with a PDVSA affiliate (Corporacion Venezolana del Petroleo). Upon discovery, CVP had the right to buy-in to the project, at a percentage of between 1 and 35. This reactivated company, CVP, formed a Control Committee with the investor, and the Committee decided the program of the joint venture. The Control Committee is made up of an equal number of members designated by the investors and CVP, and presided by a CVP member (generally the President of CVP), who has ultimate power in decisions. The decisions of the Control Committee are not subject to arbitration, unless explicitly agreed to.

All investors in the contract are subject to the royalty of 16 2/3%, and income tax of 67.7 percent! And there was a so-called PEG (Participacion del Estado en las Ganancias). If the company should happen to make any money after exploration costs and onerous taxes, then the Venezuelan Government had this little profits tax that a company was forced to bid on (the PEG), up to 50% if the field was particularly sought after. Thus, when making its high bid (cash bonus) for an oil field, a company had to also bid on what percentage of its profits (the PEG) it would like to turn over to PDVSA/the government – in order to win the contract. The PEG is deducted from a company's gross profits during the first $1 billion of gross revenues from the sale of the production –

and varies after the first $1 billion in revenues. This was only the beginning of their Venezuelan taxes.

The following are more taxes and expenses that oil companies face: a 5% tax on the interest earned on loans given by a parent company to their subsidiaries in Venezuela; a VAT tax of 14.5%, a bank debit tax, municipal taxes, and licenses obtained in order to operate in a district or municipality. And, landowners can stop projects for months. Next, your workers: foreign oil companies must compete with PDVSA for personnel, so they pay higher salaries, and **90%** of all workers in a company must be Venezuelan citizens. Non-residents' income is taxed at the 34% flat tax rate. There is an INCE Educational Tax of 2% of the total amount of wages paid to the company's workers; and the housing policy contributions of 2% paid by employers. There is also Social Security company contributions, and unemployment benefit contributions. But the most onerous company payments after taxes were **prestaciones**. This severance payment, of one month for each year worked, drove labor costs so high that a company (or government) could not afford to *fire anyone*, and this payment was doubled in the petroleum industry and must be paid immediately when terminating an employee. Furthermore, the effect of pay raises was *retroactive* for the *computation* of *prestaciones*, so companies often gave bonuses instead of pay raises to their employees. In 1997, the Venezuelan Congress changed labor benefits and rescinded the retroactive amendment, eliminating one of the chief obstacles to new investments in Venezuela.

The Labor Law stipulates that 15% of a corporation's profits must be distributed in December among their employees as utilidades, which in the oil industry can amount up to 4 months pay. And an oil worker gets one month vacation and is paid for nearly 2 months. Finally, the oil companies had to comply with PDVSA's contracts with the unions. And they have to contend with high inflation and currency devaluation (at a specific rate).

With all of these unattractive conditions, the oil companies like lemmings rushed in to bid in Venezuela. Well not quite all— the high bidding was mainly by the independents and state oil companies (the Chinese were now **in** after the June 1997 bidding).

In spite of the most complex and onerous provisions in the new Association Agreement with PDVSA, the **January 22-26,**

1996 bidding went very well, on the first profit sharing contracts since nationalization. Even after winning a bid, each agreement was subject to approval by the Venezuelan Congress. There were 10 areas that were up for tender, and 14 foreign companies and one Venezuelan (Inelectra, as a partner with Enron) won in the bidding on **eight areas** and paid PDVSA a total **$250 million**.

On the first day, Mobil, Veba and Nippon joined in a consortium to get the La Ceiba area (which drew the highest number of bids) and paid a cash bonus of $104 million, and a PEG of 50%. They were followed by Conoco; Enron's group; British Petroleum with Amoco and Maxus (paid the highest bonus of $109 million, with a 50% PEG for Guarapiche); Amoco alone; Perez Companc; and Louisiana Land and Exploration with Norcen and Benton.

After this round of bidding there were 15 oil field operating agreements with the involvement of 22 foreign oil companies. But with these 8 association agreements, for the first time since nationalization, foreign oil companies could own **equity** in Venezuelan oil. Venezuela had raised its production capacity more than 200,000 b/d each year for 1994, 1995, and 1996, with a great deal of help from these foreign oil companies. PDVSA wanted to increase its total oil production to 6.3 million b/d by 2006 – double its production capacity of 3.4 million b/d in 1997. Of this increase, they expected 2 million b/d from foreign participation in the private sector.

In western Venezuela, in the Lake Maracaibo area, PDVSA was producing 1.6 million b/d in 1997, but much of the area is mature. It is in eastern Venezuela where most of Venezuela's future growth will come from, not only in light and medium crudes, and from the extra heavy oil of the Oil Belt, but also from natural gas development. In 1997, PDVSA's eastern production was 1.5 million b/d, but it was expected to grow to about 3.5 million b/d in the next 10 years.

The Lemmings Rush Off the Cliff

Known as the *Third Round* by Giusti, the bidding for reactivation fields by oil companies on **June 6, 1997**, was more than double what PDVSA expected. Luis Giusti and his group had traveled abroad and promoted this bidding. The total bonuses paid up front, to develop 18 of the 20 fields offered, reached **$2.19**

billion. All costs incurred under the 20-year <u>Operating Agreement</u> were to be paid by the contract holder, and the ownership of all hydrocarbons would remain with PDVSA, that will market production. PDVSA did not have to accept any production that exceeds the stipulated volume. This condition corresponds to Venezuela's quota with OPEC. The fields up for bid had already produced a total of 2.5 billion barrels, and the companies were expected to be able to recover another 2 to 3 billion barrels. The fields needed high technology to bring them up to full production capacity, and many of the fields had large sections that had never been explored. For this reason, the Exploration Operating Agreement offered a motive for some companies to go to Caracas and bid.

Five of the 20 areas had been reserved for bidding by Venezuelan firms. They could go in with foreign companies to bid, but they would act as operators of the field and have at least a 30% participation in the consortium. The five fields reserved for Venezuelans were: Kaki, Mata, Maulpa, Acema, and Casma-Anaco – all in eastern Venezuela. This was done to encourage the Venezuelan private sector to get into oil exploration and production activities in Venezuela. Venezuela already had good engineering and service companies. The highest bidder among the Venezuelan consortiums was Jantesa, together with Perez Companc (Argentine) for the Mata field for $111 million. This field was actually won by another Venezuelan group that could not come up with the funds.

Unfortunately, within a month after the bidding round in June, four of the nine Venezuelan companies that were successful in the bidding were in search of financial resources – to meet their commitments to PDVSA, by the first week of August. The <u>Factor de Valorizacion</u> (FDV) or **Bonus** offered for each area, proved more than these four companies could raise and they started to call on the "bigger fish" to sell their percentage in their winning bids.

Exxon had a large group of 60 geologists in Houston dedicated to studying Venezuelan oil fields and the Apertura, in 1997. Some of the majors like Exxon were interested in returning, or entering in pairs or alliances, and these companies opened offices in Caracas, in 1994-1995. But when the winning bids were announced on <u>June 6, 1997</u>, the major oil companies were

71

conspicuously absent. Exxon and Shell did not bid. **Chevron** was the exception, going in with Phillips, Arco and Statoil to bid **$251.3 million** for the LL-652 field in Lake Maracaibo. The wild bidders were Lasmos (U.K.) bidding **$453 million** for Dacion in eastern Venezuela, and Repsol (Spain) bidding **$330 million** for the old Mene Grande field, east of Lake Maracaibo. The next high bidders were the Chinese. The China National Petroleum Corp. won bids on Caracoles for $240.7 million, and Intercampo for $118 million.

Giusti and PDVSA executives were, of course, jubilant. They had just collected $2.19 billion for Venezuela, but one had to ask what were these high bidders thinking? How could they ever get a return on this investment? There were now **11** more foreign oil companies going into Venezuela – raising the number of foreign oil companies to **34**. When you add in petrochemical companies, the number of foreign companies with investments in the Venezuelan oil sector rises to **58** in early 2000. Since then, some have left Venezuela. PDVSA began talking about another Round for mid-1998, but it never came about. The Presidential campaign made it impossible, and thus *ended* the Apertura. Nevertheless, there were now more than **three times** the number of foreign oil companies in Venezuela, than there were in 1975, when the industry was nationalized (11 foreign).

In reviewing the Apertura in 2001, one can state that the Strategic Associations have been the most successful and the foreign oil companies continue to invest large sums in developing the extra heavy oil in the Oil Belt. Oil production in this area grows annually. The second most successful foreign investments have been the first two rounds of the mature fields (1992 and 1993). The least successful are the high risk exploration areas of the 1996 and 1997 bidding rounds, under Luis Giusti, particularly the operating agreements of 1997, where the foreign companies left $2.17 billion on the table. These agreements have turned sour, because conditions of the agreement were so bad, and the fields have not produced the expected oil. The taxes are onerous on these oil agreements, amounting to 90%, and political and economic conditions have greatly deteriorated.

The New Realities

Hugo Chavez made it clear that PDVSA would have to "rationalize" its ambitious 10-year expansion plan. Using one of his favorite terms, Chavez said he would look at PDVSA's investments "with a magnifying glass." Giusti responded that PDVSA's 1999 budget was at $3.8 billion, down from $4 billion in 1998, and way below the $6 billion/year it had been in recent years. The 1999 budget was the lowest in 10 years, and was going to be compensated by private sector investment through joint ventures, strategic associations, etc., amounting to an estimated $7.2 billion. This private sector investment would thus raise total investment in the Venezuelan petroleum industry in 1999, to a record $11 billion, according to Giusti.

This private sector investment of $7.2 billion for 1999, includes: $2.6 billion in operating contracts; $3.3 billion in strategic associations; $450 million in exploration and production risk contracts; and $500 million in petrochemical joint ventures.

Hugo Chavez campaigned as much against Giusti and PDVSA, as he did for the election. Referring to PSVSA as a "state within a state," Chavez vowed to subordinate PDVSA to the Venezuelan state. He did pledge to honor all agreements PDVSA had signed with oil companies operating in Venezuela. However, after his final elections and referendums were concluded in 2000, he started to move to get those agreements with foreign oil companies changed. In August 1999, Chavez's Government tried to get foreign oil companies to sign an acuerdo de principios (an accord of principles), whereby the companies would agree to a reduction of their return from 15% to 12 percent. For the first time, the companies got together and said "no". Their revenues had already been reduced under the OPEC quotas, and this government action was unjust, and a further disincentive for foreign investments in Venezuela.

The first action Chavez took after naming a new president of PDVSA, was to further cut oil production and comply with OPEC quotas. "We need to defend oil prices," he said. The price of Venezuela's oil was down to around $7/barrel at the end of 1998. Actually, there already was an agreement between Saudi Arabia, Mexico and Venezuela to cut oil production. This agreement came as a result of a March 28, 1998 meeting of their

73

three Energy Ministers in Erwin Arrieta's office in Caracas, and was signed a week later in Riyadh, Saudi Arabia. As a result, Venezuela agreed to cut 525,000 b/d, which had been nearly accomplished when Chavez became president and ordered still further cuts, for a total of 650,000 barrels per day.

It was because of these drastic cuts in production that some 6,000 oil workers lost their jobs, and some service companies went out of business. This is capacity that is now lost, because PDVSA was also forced to cutback on maintenance on the shut in wells. At the end of 1997, Venezuela was able to produce 3.5 million b/d, but in 2000, Venezuela could not produce 3 million b/d. Furthermore, the ranks of needed PDVSA exploration and production personnel had sharply declined. The one area where Venezuela can increase its oil production is in the Oil Belt, under the four big joint ventures with foreign oil companies.

In his book, El Gran Tabu Venezolano, (1997) Jose Luis Cordeiro writes about the *Estatizacion petrolera.* The petro state took over the nation's principal industry in 1976, assuming direct control. From that moment, the State usurped the Nation, and the Government stole from the people their patrimony – some **$240 billion** in fiscal revenue in the 20 years since nationalization in 1976. Mr. Cordeiro writes that the Government "in return gives us a country in crisis, oppressed, in misery, and with a good many of the population that would like to emigrate," and a foreign debt of $40 billion. The *$240 billion represents a massive transfer of wealth, mainly from the developed world to Venezuela*!

No Venezuelan was more effective in getting this massive transfer of wealth to Venezuela than Luis Giusti. With his many speeches and promises, foreign companies bid billions for exploration and production rights and entered Venezuela with even more billions in investments. Giusti helped make it possible for Hugo Chavez to spend the returns on these foreigners' investments. Where would Chavez get a billion dollars of oil to give Cuba? How could Chavez have afforded his many elections, his OPEC Summit meeting in Caracas, his new Caracas Energy Accord for the Caribbean, and his world travels? This would not have been possible without Luis Giusti's efforts to get foreign oil companies to invest enormous sums in Venezuela.

74

Restructuring: "the task of pulling down"

In addition to getting large foreign oil investments for Venezuela, Luis Giusti merged the Venezuelan oil industry into one giant PDVSA in 1997, and made it very easy for Hugo Chavez to take over Petroleos de Venezuela and make it Petroleos de Chavez. On July 15, Luis Giusti announced that PDVSA would undergo an organizational restructuring that would eliminate the three integrated operating oil companies of the holding, i.e., Lagoven, Maraven and Corpoven. In their place, PDVSA would adopt a functional organization, similar to that of major oil companies. Some people were aware that studies were being conducted on consolidating certain functions, however, the announcement came as a complete surprise to most of the employees.

On July 14, Giusti sent out to all the employees, a letter stating the need to change the organizational structure of PDVSA. He reported on the First Executive Congress of PDVSA and its affiliates that took place on the 10th, 11th, and 12th of July, in Barquisimento. Most of these 120 executives agreed with Giusti's proposed restructuring of PDVSA, to take place in January 1998. There would be three big new divisions under PDVSA: Exploration and Production; Manufacturing and Marketing; and Services.

Giusti concluded his 3-page letter to the employees with: "The results of the past do not guarantee the results of the future and to triumph we must change."

The rationale given for this restructuring was the expected saving of $10 billion over the next 10 years, and added value to the shareholder (the government). The oil workers unions were not pleased and claimed that 12,000 people would be negatively affected, but Giusti assured them there would be no layoffs. There was also criticism by men like ex-President of PDVSA Humberto Calderon Berti that there had been little consultation of the process when there was so much at stake. But outside of Venezuela, analysts and the press praised Giusti's action. A Bloomberg News article in the *Houston Chronicle* (7-16-97) led with this heading: "PDVSA to overhaul 3 redundant units."

PDVSA was supposedly following in the footsteps of the integrated majors and other state oil companies. What Giusti did not tell the public is that the big difference between PDVSA and the supermajors is that PDVSA has only one shareholder.

Today there are three categories of oil companies: 1) energy giants, now called supermajors, ExxonMobil, Royal Dutch Shell, BPAmocoArco (the new BP), Chevron Texaco, and TotalFinaElf; 2) the majors and independents; and 3) the national oil companies like Saudi Aramco, PDVSA, and Pemex.

The supermajors reflect the new competition in the energy business, i.e., energy convergence, from manufacturing oil-related products to becoming energy service companies, and selling units of energy. Enron Corp. has been the leader in energy convergence, going from gas to power, to the internet, etc. Enron's revenue shot up to $100.8 billion in 2000, from $40.1 billion in 1999, largely from buying and selling contracts in natural gas and electricity. Enron is the largest e-commerce company in the world. The digital age is very energy-intensive, therefore, the Internet is burning up a lot of fossil fuel in the process, as power consumption of our disk drives and screens is rising. Within the new decade of 2001, half of the electric grid will be powering the digital-Internet economy. In the United States, electricity is generated mostly with coal (56%), nuclear (20%), hydro (10%), and gas (10%) – and little from fuel oil. Thus, the oil companies are getting into power generation, which is a new growth area.

Then there is the recently developed gasoline-fuel processor for vehicles that run on fuel cells, a technology developed by General Motors and ExxonMobil. Fuel-cell powered vehicles are widely seen as the next generation of automobiles. Gasoline represents nearly half of U.S. consumption of oil, i.e., 8.8 million b/d of gasoline out of 19.8 million b/d total demand, in December 2000. With U.S. energy policy directed at cleaner fuels and away from conventional oil, and toward the fuel-propulsion mechanism, we may stop using crude from oil exporting countries long before they run out of reserves.

The restructuring of PDVSA created a new concentration of power in the presidency. With the removal of the three operating presidents, there were also some 160 resignations or retirements of top executives at the end of 1997. However, the most detrimental result of Giusti's restructuring of the Venezuelan oil industry was the removal of the three mercantile operating companies whose employees had pride in their work and loyalty to their company. But most important, the three former companies were no longer in the auditors' crosshairs. Auditors used to measure and compare one company against another for cost of their contracts, export sale prices, and every single bid these three companies made.

The familial loyalty was inherited from the original foreign company, established in their respective oil camps, an outgrowth from Exxon (Lagoven) and Shell (Maraven). But in the case of Corpoven, it was a particular accomplishment because it melded five different formerly foreign oil companies with Venezuela's national oil company (CVP), and in 1986, added Meneven (formed from Gulf Oil and three other companies), to comprise one of Venezuela's three great integrated operating oil companies.

This melding or merging of 10 oil companies to form Corpoven could never have been accomplished without the president who was able to turn this multiplicity of companies and cultural values into a cohesive first rate oil producing company. Frank Alcock and his executive team persisted in his quest to eradicate corruption from this assortment of companies and also cut costs, improve productivity, and made this all possible because he created a true mistica, i.e., an esprit de corps in Corpoven. Corpoven went on to become the lowest cost producer, and overtook Maraven as second in production capacity. In the 1984 Corpoven Annual Report, the President's letter states: "The achievements summarized here demonstrate most clearly the dedication, discipline, professionalism and involvement of our personnel, who every day work with a sense of loyalty and patriotic sentiment to obtain the results the nation demands from its petroleum workers." But this ended in January 1998, when the three operating companies were merged into Petroleos de Venezuela.

In this new era of globalization, it is difficult to have loyalty to a giant company, and one that is now so different, organized into large functional entities, with new executives and managers, many which have just risen upward because there was a rapid departure of the experienced executives. There was a great deal of chaos from then to the present. As Craig McCaw, telecom empire builder said in explaining why he likes to keep his companies separate: "merge, and the average IQ drops." (Forbes, June 12, 2000, p80) Unfortunately, the merged companies do not get better, and have a high failure rate, falling short of their corporate parents initial financial and strategic expectations, according to a study by Andersen Consulting (now Accenture) in New York. Cost savings from mergers are a one-time thing, and difficult to repeat. Oil companies are at the mercy of oil prices that they cannot control. In the end, it is the integration, down to the lowest levels in merging companies, that may be the most difficult to accomplish.

The good that Luis Giusti accomplished by raising Venezuela's oil production capacity and production through the Apertura bidding (June), he undid with such speed a month later (July) with his restructuring of PDVSA. The restructuring that Giusti started in 1997 was still going through changes, in 2000. The original Giusti organizational chart went through several changes of presidents and vice presidents for each of the three divisions of the new **PDVSA Oil and Gas, S.A.** These three divisions were divided into Business Units with their own presidents. One thing was obvious – there were a lot of new presidents – 17 – compared with the three of the former operating companies. It was never pointed out how 17 presidents could be cost effective compared to 3 presidents of the operating companies. Furthermore, with this corporate structure, there were no companies created for these presidents. Worst of all there was no longer a buffer between the oil industry and the government. The President of Venezuela not only appoints the President of PDVSA and the Board (as before), but now he appoints other top executives, as well.

And of course, under President Hugo Chavez there have been even more changes in the organizational chart of PDVSA. It is difficult to be loyal to a company in flux, and ever changing bosses. (There is an old adage my brother told me years ago: "if my boss phones, find out what his name is.") Actually, this was not new in PDVSA, but after January 1998, it was on a massive scale. Luis Giusti's legacy is the "pulling down" of PDVSA so that Hugo Chavez could make it his own, and transform it into Petroleos de Chavez. In the next chapter, I will discuss how Chavez went about doing this. Ironically, it was Roberto Mandini who did not support the restructuring, who first had to deal with the new PDVSA when he became President in February 1999.

The Mystery of the Price of Oil

Oil is <u>extracted</u>, it is not produced, although this is the verb we use when speaking of one of the seven operations of the petroleum industry. The cost of extraction does not determine the price of oil. Extraction costs are determined mainly by the location, rock formation and size of the field.

Oil is now the world's most watched commodity and one that influences the global economy, but very few people know what is happening in the market. Crude prices are set by the marginal barrel, i.e., the last barrel of oil needed, which is OPEC's oil. Thirty years ago the price of oil was determined by large oil companies, through long-term contracts of one to two years length, with about 4 to 6% of world crude sold on the spot market, mainly in Rotterdam, which was considered the most accurate of several spot markets. As the spot market reached record levels of $33/barrel in May 1979, when Saudi Light was only $14.54/barrel, OPEC began to withdraw crude from long-term contracts and sell it at spot prices. The spot market became the dominant factor in establishing the price of oil after OPEC quadrupled the price of oil in 1973-1974. And as the spot market exploded in the 1980s, so did the number of **oil traders** in Houston, New York, London, Rotterdam, Paris, Singapore, and Tokyo, buying and reselling the world's oil many times before it reached its final destination.

The oil traders and the spot market also were a result of the U.S. Federal Government's hopeless tangle of distorted equities caused by the 1975 Oil Entitlements Program of price controls on domestic oil (removed in January 1981, by Ronald Reagan). Refiners in order to avoid shortages of feedstock began relying on the spot market and oil traders. There was still another reason for the increase in oil traders, i.e., the shift in the international market from crude oil sales to oil product sales. Crude oil is of little use to anyone except to those who refine it into products. Thus, in the beginning of the oil industry in the United States, the purchaser/refinery would set the price by <u>posting</u> what they would pay for oil from a particular oil field.

Oil traders made it possible for refiners to buy either crude oil **or** products on the spot market. When it was more profitable to buy products than crude, domestic refiners could improve their profit margins by buying products on the spot market. Trading is now easier because refineries have been upgraded and designed to process a wide variety of crudes.

Thus, the oil market moved from posting, to long-term contracts, to the spot market, and oil traders, to futures trading. Oil traders started trading on the futures market at the New York Mercantile Exchange (the MERC, or NYMEX), and International Petroleum Exchange (IPE), in March 1983. The traders prevent the Chairman of the NYMEX or the OPEC Conference from setting the price of oil. The removal of price controls in the United States produced a free market and allowed the creation of a futures market! There is no futures market unless you have a free market.

The spot and commodity markets add liquidity to the oil market, particularly in the sale of products. Both OPEC and the U.S. Government created the need for what I call the 7th operation of the oil industry: the oil trader. This new operation changed the entire oil industry, causing the restructuring of oil companies and industry consolidation, upgrading of refineries, in order to produce more lighter products from heavier crudes, and the West had to face the upgrading and new refineries being built in some OPEC countries. This is a major shift in the international oil market – away from crude exports, and towards more oil products exports, which carry higher prices than crude. This new international market is more chaotic, and presented an increasing need for the oil trader.

The problem for the oil trader is the amount of oil en route, moving on the high seas. Counting the hundreds of millions of barrels in the supply chain is an inexact business because members of OPEC do not tell each other, much less others, what they are producing. But ascertaining the supply of oil in the market is crucial in setting the price per barrel, which in turn is dependent upon demand in the global economy. There should be some 4.5 billion barrels of oil in circulation at any time, and there can be large margins of error in estimating supply and demand. The main reason for this is the unreliability of the figures some oil producing countries give out. Speculators also play an important role in ensuring liquidity in a commodities market. Investment banks are now members of the oil trading system. They trade in paper barrels (cash), but do not take delivery of wet barrels. Therefore, no one can read the oil market that supports the volatile oil pricing in the futures market.

Besides the question of production (extraction) figures, oil producers are conservative about drilled reserves and are reluctant to add outlying estimations. Coiled tubing units can now drill out multiple radial holes in days, and install multi-zone producing strings that require little or no downhole intervention.

In addition to drilled reserves figures, oil en route, and production figures, no one knows exactly how much space exists in the world in which to store oil, or how much of that space contains oil at any one time. In determining the price of oil today, the oil in storage has become an important gauge of price. U.S. oil in storage is published every week under "API Crude and Product Stocks" (easily found in the Oil & Gas Journal) and ranges from 300 million to 285 million barrels for crude, and 538 million to 522 million barrels for products. The U.S. also has the Strategic Petroleum Reserve (SPR) with 568 million barrels of oil in caverns that have 680 million barrels of capacity. The next country with large storage capacity is Venezuela, storage mainly built by the foreign oil companies in the 1940s and 1950s. At the Amuay refinery on the Paraguana Peninsula, Creole Petroleum Company (Exxon) built storage facilities totaling 46 million barrels. This storage capacity includes the three largest open pits in the world. Open pit No 1 at Amuay holds 11 million barrels of resid, and was completed in 1955. And earlier, in eastern Venezuela, the first storage tanks with floating roofs were ordered built by my father, for Gulf's Mene Grande oil tank farm, at Guanta. Venezuela, in 1998, had approximately 80 million barrels of crude storage capacity, and 73.4 million barrels of refine products storage capacity. Venezuela also has 30 million barrels of storage capacity in the Caribbean (in the Curacao refinery oil terminal, and in Bonaire and the Bahamas). Stocks in storage are the markets buffer. Stock movements indicate whether there is a surplus or shortage of oil production. Unfortunately, no one knows exactly how much capacity there is or how much space is filled!

OPEC in 1999, by restraining oil production in member countries, jumped back into the catbird seat, thus causing world prices to rise again. However, technological changes are gradually eroding the organization's advantage, as a low-cost producer. This is creating possible substitutes for oil that could reduce long-term demand. Ironically, some OPEC members that started the nationalization trend of foreign oil companies in the 1970s, are now courting international investors to help develop their petroleum fields. However, after January 2001, and a more favorable investment climate in the United States with the new Bush Administration, U.S. oil companies may prefer to search and produce oil domestically.

Except for Saudi Arabia, OPEC producers, beginning with Venezuela, are largely tapped out for increases in oil supplies because of a lack of additional capital investments. With an economic recession, the petroleum industry would face further declines in investments in producing countries.

The capital cost of producing a barrel of heavy crude in Venezuela is about $28,000 (per barrel of daily production). In Saudi Arabia, the most expensive oil to produce is from Shaybah field, where it costs $5,000/barrel in capital investment to produce. Lifting costs of production, to operate and maintain wells and related equipment, is more often mentioned when speaking of average production cost per barrel. In Venezuela, in 1999, lifting costs were $2.72 per barrel. The simplest indicator of relative cost of a barrel of oil is the rate of flow of wells. Wells in Saudi Arabia flow at 9,000 b/d or better, while in Venezuela wells average less than 200 b/d. Location and well depth are also important in determining costs. With access to very low cost crude, a supermajor (like ExxonMobil in Saudi Arabia) can drive out of business some independents or state producers. Supermajor producer alliances can transform the petroleum industry in the near future.

For around 50 years, the world oil market was managed by private oil companies. Known as integrated oil companies, they explored, developed, produced, transported, refined and marketed crude oil and petroleum products. The major international petroleum companies were called the Seven Sisters: Exxon, Chevron, Gulf, Mobil, Texaco, Royal Dutch Shell, and British Petroleum, and they dominated the system until the mid-1950s. Newer companies weakened the Sisters control over the market, and after 1960, OPEC governments began to assert control over the petroleum industry in their respective countries. In October 1973, OPEC unilaterally seized control of international oil pricing, and began to nationalize the industry's crude production facilities within their respective country. The former concessionaire companies sought continued supply through long-term contracts – often paying a per barrel service fee. Thus, oil concessions gave way to long-term oil contracts, i.e., until the price of oil started to rapidly rise on the spot market.

Venezuelan Oil Industry Data

Venezuela has the largest petroleum reserves in the Western Hemisphere. Venezuela's reserves of crude oil and condensate at the end of 1999 were 76.8 billion barrels, and natural gas reserves were 146 trillion cubic feet. Of the crude reserves, only 35.7 billion barrels of the extra heavy oil of the vast Oil Belt were included. The Oil Belt contains 1.2 trillion barrels of which 22% can be recovered by conventional petroleum exploration methods. Venezuela's cumulative production since it started in 1914 through 1997 is approximately 50 billion barrels.

In 1997, PDVSA was ranked by *Petroleum Intelligence Weekly*, as the second largest vertically integrated oil and gas company, based on a composite of 1996 criteria of reserves, production, refining capacity and refined petroleum product sales. Venezuela has exported crude oil without interruption since 1914.

The Venezuelan oil industry commenced with a small oil field at La Alquitrana, my great grandmother's family coffee hacienda in Tachira, in the 1880s. Manuel Pulido and his associates formed a company called La Petrolia and built a small refinery. They never owned the mineral rights to their oil, because in Venezuela, as in most of the world except in the United States, the government owns the mineral rights. Pulido needed a concession to produce the oil on his hacienda. Thus, while Venezuelans started the oil industry in Venezuela, there were 60 years when foreigners dominated the industry (until 1976).

Since the return of the foreign oil companies in the 1990s, these companies have invested over $16 billion in Venezuela, including more than $2.4 billion in cash bonuses. Much of this investment has been in the construction phase of the heavy oil upgraders attached to the Faja (Oil Belt) projects.

Power and Petroleum

On July 14, 1936, in the newspaper *Ahora*, Arturo Uslar Pietri's landmark editorial, "Sowing Petroleum" appeared. "It is essential to extract the greatest possible income from oil, and to invest it all in assistance, facilities, and stimulus to national agriculture, livestock raising and industry. Instead of oil being a curse destined to turn us into a parasitic and useless people, the sudden infusion of wealth will become the good fortune that permits an acceleration and strengthening of the Venezuelan people's productive evolution under exceptional conditions." Uslar's expression is understood as the use of oil income to improve the living standard, education and health conditions of Venezuelans. Unfortunately, oil became the basis for a populist, protectionist paternalistic economy.

CHAPTER IV

COOKED and DEVOURED GOOSE

"On seeking a maximum return, care should be taken not to kill the Goose that lays the Golden Eggs." Jose Mayobre, Venezuela's Minister of Mines and Hydrocarbons, June 1967.

In the last 60 years of the twentieth century, Venezuelan oilmen and politicians often referred to their "Golden Goose that lays Golden Eggs." This was a reference to the petroleum industry that supplied such riches to Venezuela, and the need to protect this industry that Venezuela had become so dependent upon. The first significant grab for the Venezuelan Golden Goose was under the Herrera Campins' government, when the government appropriated PDVSA's $6 billion in foreign reserves, in 1982. Until then, PDVSA, since its creation on January 1, 1976, had been an autonomous oil holding company that controlled its own finances and paid taxes. In the 1990s we began to realize that the Goose was being plucked. In 1999, Hugo Chavez cooked the Goose, and in 2000 it was devoured.

In the 20 years after nationalization–1976-1997, the Venezuelan government received **$240 billion** in oil taxation, but succeeded in impoverishing 20 million Venezuelans, and creating a $40 billion foreign debt, one of the highest per capita in the developing world. Venezuela represents the most profligate waste of wealth in man's history.

How did Venezuela, a prosperous country in 1976, with European immigrants (after World War II), become a pauper nation 20 years after nationalization of the oil industry (and iron and steel industry), with its best citizens emigrating?

As Jose Luis Cordeiro shows in his book, El Gran Tabu Venezolano, between 1914 and 1975, Venezuela had an accelerated national growth period of 60 years. Why did growth stop after the Venezuelan oil industry was nationalized in 1976? The industry was well run by the Venezuelan oilmen. Unfortunately, the politicians got their hands on huge amounts of

85

oil revenues and benefited themselves and their friends, while depriving the people of needed schools, health services and needed government services, along with the rule of law. There is a quote by Venezuela's venerable author, Arturo Uslar Pietri: "Columbus discovered Venezuela, Bolivar freed it, and petroleum made it putrid (la pudrio)."

One can add that this happened because there are no private mineral rights in Venezuela, as there are in the United States. In the U.S., the government collects taxes from petroleum producers, and in Venezuela the government distributes revenues from the petroleum industry to the population. The Venezuelan Government impedes the generation of riches by the population, and without private mineral rights, Venezuelans have few places to invest. Therefore, there has always been a flight of capital. Venezuelans have some $100 billion invested overseas, in the United States and in Europe, etc.

An oil company survives on its production. A dictum in the petroleum industry is: invest, invest and invest. Otherwise you consume your production, and have little or none to replace what you produced. This is a depleting industry, because it is an extraction industry, for it does not make or produce crude. In Venezuela's case, it traditionally has had wells and fields that annually lose 25% of their production capacity. Thus, in order to maintain **or** increase production, oil companies in Venezuela have to maintain their oil wells and oil reservoirs by maintaining pressure flow (via natural gas, or water), as well as continue exploration and drilling for new reserves. It is a simple matter of investing in maintenance and technology – and for this you need funds and natural gas, and most of all capable oilmen.

Until 1998, PDVSA followed this efficient and productive policy. However, in 1999 and 2000, articles started appearing in Venezuela, e.g. by Alberto Quiros, and Jorge Olavarria, and abroad, e.g. in *Petroleum Intelligence Weekly*, and *The Oil Daily*, which called attention to the decline in Venezuela's oil production capacity, a decline from 3.6 million barrels per day (b/d) in 1998, to 2.9 million b/d in 2000. In fact, Venezuela would have a difficult time filling its assigned OPEC quota in 2000 (June), of 2.9 million b/d, because the country has an internal market of some 450,000 b/d. No wonder Venezuela has fallen from 1st place as the

U.S.'s leading supplier of oil imports, to 4th behind Saudi Arabia, Canada and Mexico. Not only has Chavez left "Venezuela lamed in the struggle for market share," (*PIW*, 6/00), it will be far worse, if Chavez does not allow needed investment in Venezuela's oil industry.

How truly ironic: Chavez was trying to revive OPEC's power in 2000, while trimming PDVSA's production capacity. In 1960, when OPEC was formed by five members, Venezuela, Kuwait, Saudi Arabia, Iran and Iraq, Venezuela's production nearly equaled the total production of these Middle East members. Venezuela in 1958, produced close to 3 million b/d and was the largest oil exporter in the world. In 1965, Venezuela was producing nearly 3.5 million b/d, as the third largest producer in the world after the United States and the Soviet Union. Venezuela peaked its oil production in 1970 at 3.7 million b/d, the same year U.S. production peaked at 9.6 million b/d. (In 1999, U.S. production dropped below 6 million b/d, while U.S. imports of crude and oil products went up to 11 million barrels per day.)

The decline in world oil prices in 1959, -- that brought about the U.S. Mandatory Oil Import Program (quotas on oil imports) in March 1959, a program that brought forth the founding of OPEC in 1960, -- was the direct result of new oil concessions granted in Venezuela in 1956 and 1957, which led to new oil production. Not until the 1990s and PDVSA's Apertura, did Venezuela have another effect (though slight) on declining world oil prices with its increased production (again, with foreign oil companies).

1998 Oil Price Collapse

West Texas Intermediate (WTI) crude dropped to $12/barrel in June 1998. The drastic decline in oil prices in the United States resulted in 41,000 jobs lost in the oil and gas industry, 136,000 oil wells and 57,000 gas wells shut in, and a decline in oil production of 360,000 barrels per day. This was followed by higher oil imports. The decline in oil prices in 1998, was a result of a decline in demand – particularly in Asia, which was going through a serious recession caused by the Asian financial collapse, -- as well as an increase in oil production within OPEC.

When Iraq oil exports began to flow again in December 1996, OPEC had no plan. According to Sheikh Ahmed Zaki Yamani, former Saudi oil minister, the economic collapse started in the Far East in the late summer of 1997, but OPEC chose to ignore the implications of this economic debacle. (*Oil & Gas Journal* 12/28/98) OPEC actually raised quotas in November 1997. By not cutting oil production, OPEC created a supply glut and massive oil inventories, and the United Nation's oil-for-food program in Iraq helped wreck the oil market in 1997-1998. In 1998, a decline in oil demand (by 300,000 b/d in Asia), and an increase in world supply by more than 1 million b/d in 1997, and a warmer winter caused a decline in oil prices.

Roberto Mandini (El Duque)

In the Venezuelan **Hydrocarbon Nationalization Law** of August 29, 1975, there was an important article. Under *Article 8*: "The directors, administrators, employees, workers of the companies ... once converted into a *mercantile society*, will not be considered public functionaries or employees." This is quite clear, they are not government employees. However, they are now!

The destruction of PDVSA and all it signifies is one of the most serious attacks by Hugo Chavez as President of Venezuela, according to Jorge Olavarria, former supporter of Chavez. But if Chavez destroys PDVSA, how does he maintain his Chavista economy? After all, PDVSA accounts for 78% of Venezuela's export revenues, 57% of fiscal revenues, and 26% of gross domestic product. And of those oil exports, about a half billion barrels per year go to the United States.

"El Duque" Mandini, who had been President of Corpoven from 1986 until 1994, when he went to Citgo Petroleum in Tulsa, returned to Venezuela as PDVSA President in February 1999, with the high hopes of its employees. Sadly, he lasted less than seven months. Every day was a battle of some sort: the oil production cuts that caused 6,000 workers to lose their jobs, along with budget cuts, and reduction of employee benefits; the new Decree for the Fondo de Estabilizacion Macroeconomica over which Mandini threatened to resign; and the Revolutionary Front led by Hector Ciavaldini. The PDV Penthouse could be described as a snake pit.

On Monday morning, August 30, 1999, Roberto Mandini resigned as President of PDVSA. When Mandini went to see

Chavez at Miraflores Palace on Sunday, he had told the President that he was under attack by a Marxist conspiracy led by Ciavaldini. He asked for Ciavaldini's removal. The President answered "Caramba no te puedo complacer." (Darn, I can't accommodate you.) The next day Mandini handed the President his resignation. Mandini had been president for less than seven months. He was pushed out of the Venezuelan oil industry after 38 years of distinguished service. The man who coveted his job was Hector Ciavaldini, who organized a Revolutionary Front (Frente Revolucionario) within PDVSA to push Mandini out. The day after Mandini's resignation, President Chavez announced he had appointed Ciavaldini, president of PDVSA, and was taking him along on his trip to Panama for the inauguration of the new president of Panama.

Mandini served an interim purpose, i.e., a respected oilman at the helm, and as cover while Chavez accomplished his political takeover of the Venezuelan petroleum industry. And Mandini served another important purpose. On Chavez's trip to the United States on June 8, 1999, to try and impress Wall Street and drum up interest in Venezuela's plans to sell $2 billion in international bonds, he took Mandini along to quiet U.S. worries about his threats against "savage neoliberalism," and his threats to review contracts with foreign oil companies. But even Mandini could not rectify or deflect the awkward, unpolished presentations of Chavez and his entourage of Ministers. Mandini was gone two and a half months later, having served Chavez's purpose.

It probably was Hugo Chavez's intent to appoint Ciavaldini president of PDVSA from the start. One only has to remember that following his presidential election on December 6, 1998, Chavez appointed Hector Ciavaldini to head a transition commission at PDVSA, something that had never done before. After his inauguration on February 2, 1999, Chavez appointed Ciavaldini to the PDVSA Board as Vice President of Planning. Ciavaldini at the time had a lawsuit against PDVSA before the Supreme Court. Ciavaldini was suing PDVSA for being terminated in 1995 from Bariven, a PDVSA affiliate, for various reasons, including extreme anxiety, intense depression and political intrigue. By August 1999, it was apparent that Ciavaldini was Chavez's *nemesis*, i.e., a source of harm or ruin of PDVSA.

When the new PDVSA vice presidents were appointed in February, Alberto Quiros Corradi wrote an article (14-2-99) in *El Nacional*, titled "PDVSA al Paredon." This was a reference to Fidel Castro's firing squads in Cuba in the 1960s, i.e., *to the wall*. Chavez had run much of his presidential campaign attacking the Venezuelan oil industry, calling PDVSA anti-national, with Saudi salaries, corrupt, and "a state within the state" (un Estado dentro del Estado). Quiros applauded the designation of Roberto Mandini as PDVSA President, and of Ali Rodriguez as Minister of Energy, but the constant attacks of calling Venezuelan oilmen *"corruptos"* that Chavez started, and the people now continued, was an unforgivable act. Then Quiros asked the obvious question for a reasonable observer. How do you expect to sell your foreign investments (Citgo), which you've announced you intend to sell, when you publicly attack it as a bad investment?

After "El Duque" Mandini resigned, he returned to his office, and in the afternoon, through a videoconference hook-up addressed the 40,000 employees of the Venezuelan oil industry. He spoke for several minutes telling his friends and employees of his resignation and with a breathtaking gesture of irony, he quoted Simon Bolivar (who Chavez quotes at ever opportunity). "If my death contributes to the end of parties and the union is consolidated, I will enter my grave calmly." After Mandini's thoughtful videoconference farewell to the Venezuelan oil men and women, the following comments were heard: "se fue Mandini, ahora tiene que irse Ciavaldini" (Mandini left, now Ciavaldini must go); and "PDVSA definitivamente se acabo" (PDVSA is definitely finished).

Roberto Mandini started his career in the Venezuelan oil industry in 1961, with Creole Petroleum (Exxon), as an engineer. Upon his return to Venezuela in 1999, he did not seem to grasp the new political animal. Mandini was a Roman at heart, often reminding us in conversation about the Fall of the Roman Empire. He was called back from semi-exile in the U.S. where he was Executive Vice President of Citgo Petroleum, in Tulsa. To Mandini, his appointment as President of PDVSA must have seemed like sweet revenge over Luis Giusti, who had been named president in 1994, when Mandini thought he should have gotten the position. When a President has enemies he names some of them as ambassadors and dispatches them abroad. Giusti did this to Mandini. Besides, Mandini was a former Exxon man and Giusti was from Shell, and he chose Shell people to fill his top positions.

There was a strange and cynical beginning to the brief appointment of the last professional oilman to head PDVSA. The new Board, consisting of Mandini and the five new vice-presidents were summoned to Miraflores Palace on February 9, to be sworn in by Chavez. What happened when they got there for their 2 P.M. meeting, which was to last 20 minutes, was most unusual. Chavez asked them to join his press conference, where there were 6 chairs for them. They sat and listened for over 3 hours – nearly falling asleep. They finally were able to leave at 5:45 P.M. The new PDVSA Board was never sworn in. After I was told this by one of the vice-presidents, I read the unusual title of "Executive President" given to Mandini in Decree 9 in the Gaceta Oficial. It was clear that the two oilmen (Mandini, and Vice-President Lopez Quevedo) would be in the Penthouse at PDVSA for a brief period. Three others on the Board consisted of two Armed Forces colonels and Hector Ciavaldini, and a fifth Vice-President, Eduardo Praselj was in charge of Pequiven. The new President of PDVSA was Hugo Chavez!

PDVSA Board by-laws call for 11 Board members not 6, and the Board had two vice-presidents not 5. The new Chavez Board was given line designation responsibilities for the first time. And when the PDVSA Annual Asamblea met on March 29, 1999, for the first time it was held at Miraflores Palace with President Chavez presiding. But of course, Chavez was the new President of PDVSA, and Mandini, merely the Executive President, and not the Chairman, as all previous presidents.

With the departure of Roberto Mandini, the industry that had played the dominant role in the development of Venezuela, started downward. PDVSA reached its lowest point under Hector Ciavaldini. Each new president of PDVSA, since Luis Giusti brought new purges of employees. Employees preferred their cajitas felices (retirement packages) than to stay, if they were close to retirement. By December 1999 (following Mandini's departure in August), some 1700 top level executives and managers had departed, some voluntarily, others fired, since Chavez became President. Their departure was called una caceria de brujas (a witch hunt). The merit system had turned into the "friendship system."

As for the foreign oil companies operating in Venezuela, they were not sure they were welcome. Conoco E & P President, Gary Merriman raised serious concerns regarding the climate for private investment in Venezuela: the escalation of costs, the uncertainty that surrounds the current political transition, and access to decision makers. In recent years, the later is one of the worst problems foreign oilmen face in Venezuela, for the Venezuelans seldom return phone calls and are often impossible to get an appointment with. A good reason for these complaints: Chavez makes the decisions, and no one is in place long enough or confident enough to risk a decision or an answer. Chavez keeps threatening the restructuring of PDVSA "with a magnifying glass," but no one knows his Bolivarian plans for PDVSA, and he has not a clue of how to run a world class corporation.

A word about the Fondo de Estabilizacion Macroeconomica (FEM), which Mandini objected to, after Chavez issued a decree changing the Fund (FEM). Chavez changed the Fund so that PDVSA during 5 years, after paying its income taxes, royalties and dividends, would put into the Fund 50% of the revenue acquired for oil sold over $9/barrel. It would simply mean PDVSA would have little cash flow for its expenses and oil investment programs. This occurred when the price of Venezuelan oil had started to climb in May 1999, to $12 and $14/barrel, and the FEM meant a straight jacket for PDVSA and a bonanza for the Government. A year later, the question was being asked, "where is the money?" Alberto Quiros Corradi, in one of his articles (March 14) asked where is the $2.5 billion that should be in the Fund? The price of Venezuela's oil had risen to $25/barrel, which would give the Fund the difference of $15/barrel on 2 million barrels per day. (PDVSA reported $589 million deposited in the Fund, in its 1999 Annual Report.)

In discussing and writing about the Chavez government, the word *surreal* keeps coming to mind. But surreal is soon followed by the words dangerous, and totalitarian. The Venezuelans are and will pay a heavy price for the government they have elected. As for the foreign oil companies who rushed into Venezuela during the "Apertura" of the 1990s, some have departed. With Roberto Mandini's departure from PDVSA, the magnificent industry that grew to be number two in the world under the dedication of some of the finest men and women I ever knew, will rapidly decline to just another state oil company in a poor country. It was Jack Tarbes, who used to often tell me, "we may last for 20 years as a commercial company, but eventually the government will politicize PDVSA and destroy it." He did not live to see, he had nailed it.

Hector Ciavaldini

Seldom has a man been placed in a position that was so far beyond his capabilities, as was Hector Ciavaldini. He is the best example of Chavez's new "friendship system" of running PDVSA. Ciavaldini visited Chavez when he was in prison at Yare, and began his "satanization" of PDVSA, a company that had fired him. Through his new friend, Hugo Chavez, he would get his revenge on PDVSA, and Chavez would use Ciavaldini to gain control of the industry. Finally, realizing Ciavaldini's many weaknesses, Chavez publicly fired him on his Sunday radio show, "Alo Presidente," on October 15, 2000. The excuse for his firing was his poor performance in handling the oil workers' October strike.

From the first, Hector Ciavaldini was Chavez's obvious choice for President of PDVSA. Right after his election in December 1998, Chavez appointed Ciavaldini to preside over his Transition Commission with PDVSA, with an office in the Penthouse. This man, who five years earlier had been fired with cause from Bariven, a PDVSA affiliate, and had a pending lawsuit for Bs 294 million for indemnification against the company, suddenly became Chavez's man at PDVSA. And after Chavez named him vice-president of planning of PDVSA, he took him on his overseas trips. Ciavaldini organized the Revolutionary Front in PDVSA to get rid of Roberto Mandini, and once Ciavaldini was in place as President, it was revenge time. Many executives left. Ciavaldini made public threats. "I'm not leaving without investigating administrative crimes of the past 10 years." (*El Nacional*, 16-7-00)

This was pretty ironic in view of what Ciavaldini is alleged to have done as President. In September, shortly after becoming President, Ciavaldini ended his Bs 294 million lawsuit in the

Supreme Court, and had his 5-year period out of the industry reinstated and added to his pension.

Ciavaldini will be remembered for his special form of corruption and intrigue, and for his questionable restructuring of PDVSA. Ciavaldini in June 2000, divided the company into two parts: Exploration, Production and Improvement (Mejoramiento); and Refining and Commerce. The 3rd division of Services was eliminated. Thus, PDVSA got a new organizational chart and a new Board of Directors composed entirely of chemical engineers. Not a single geologist or petroleum engineer was on the new Board. It should be pointed out that Ciavaldini was a chemical engineer. He declared in the PDVSA al dia (15-6-00), house organ, that one of the main changes in the restructuring was that of "culture," i.e., to make PDVSA more Chavista. The 14 months' reign of Ciavaldini was over October 15, 2000, replaced by Chavez's 3rd president of PDVSA in less than two years.

General Guaicaipuro Lameda

After Ciavaldini's scorched earth (tierra arrasada) politics at PDVSA, the appointment on October 15, 2000, of General Guaicaipuro Lameda Montero as President was welcomed by employees. They rejoiced upon Ciavaldini's departure: of how rapidly it occurred; and his not being able to see President Chavez at Miraflores (who refused to see him); and not being able to address the employees of PDVSA, as Mandini had done.

General Lameda, who wears his uniform with many medals to PDVSA, has good credentials as an army officer and military engineer, and went to PDVSA from the government's Budget Office (Oficina Central de Presupuestos). At 44 years of age, he is the 10th President of PDVSA, and the youngest. His specialization was in strategic planning and national security, with no background in the oil industry. He graduated at the top of his class at the Military Academy in 1974, and is a loyal friend of Hugo Chavez. Lameda's appointment completed the military appointments of Generals in-place, in Venezuela's state companies (even Citgo in the U.S. has a General).

When Hugo Chavez spoke in Houston at the Westin Galleria, to a large group of oilmen, on October 16, 2000, he said that he was reminded of a song, Te pareces tanto a mi (You seem so much like me), making constant references to the song in his comparisons. Then he made a reference to Alexis de Tocqueville and democracy. How unbelievably ironic, for it was Tocqueville who showed us how men can destroy democracy by voting for a despot. Chavez is the modern example of the elected dictator. He had gone to Houston to present his two new General presidents: General Guaicaipuro Lameda, appointed the day before as his latest President of PDVSA, and General Oswaldo Contreras, the first Venezuelan President of Citgo. What an interesting meeting for the U.S. oilmen, whose companies are invested in Venezuela, or who were interested.

General Lameda, announced in November shortly after becoming President that he was reviewing the pensions of retired PDVSA officers. He pointed out that one pensioner was receiving Bs 13 million/month, when 91% were receiving less than Bs 500,000/month. Much worse off were former presidents of the operating companies that receive Bs 250,000/month pensions. (At Bs 700 to the dollar that was $357/month.)

Of course there were further Board changes, with General Contreras going to Citgo and replaced, first by General Rafael Martinez, and then by General Arnoldo Rodriguez Ochoa. The Board was shortened to five members, with the two Generals and three from the industry: Domingo Mariscobetre, Aires Barreto, and Eduardo Praselj. Chavez continued to make changes, e.g. Domingo Mariscobetre and Aires Barreto were retired, and Jorge Kamkoff and Eduardo Praselj was appointed to his fluid Board of PDVSA.

Here one can make a dramatic contrast between Chavez and Vicente Fox, the new President of Mexico, who in February 2001 appointed his first Board of Petroleos Mexicanos (Pemex). President Fox appointed three prominent successful business leaders: Carlos Slim, Lorenzo Zambrano and Alfonso Roma. The new Director General of Pemex is a former Du Pont Company executive, Raul Munoz Leos. The contrast is stark. Fox's desire was to pick the best men to help turn Pemex from an antiquated monopoly into an efficient multinational corporation, and raise its oil export capacity from 2 million b/d to 4 million b/d, in five years. Chavez took an efficient multinational and did the reverse.

PDVSA Gas

    The Natural Gas Nationalization Law of 1971 prohibits foreign joint ventures or private investments in natural gas operations. Under this law, Corporacion Venezolana de Petroleo (CVP), established in 1960, could only produce associated gas. Thus, while natural gas produced with oil (associated gas) was used domestically, principally reinjected in oil wells to maintain production, Venezuela's potentially huge reserves of nonassociated natural gas remained undeveloped. Most of Venezuela's 146 trillion cubic feet (Tcf) of proven gas reserves is associated gas, and therefore, its production is dependent on crude oil production, which is subject to OPEC quotas. Of Venezuela's gas production of 6 billion cf/d, over 70% is used for gas injection, gas lift, as operations fuel, or other related purposes. The other 30% is consumed by the domestic market: in power generators (32%), petrochemical plants (21%), steel/aluminum producers (21%), and residential (5%). Some natural gas is still being flared in the production of crude oil.

    In late 1999, the Gas Hydrocarbons Organic law was decreed by President Chavez, after he obtained the Enabling Law from Congress that granted him power to legislate on defined areas via decree. Because the new law was "organic" it becomes Venezuela's "controlling authority" on the gas business and legally superior to all previous laws (like the Gas Law of 1971). The Chavez Government was promoting gas development: to add to the stability of the petroleum base, and to back out domestic consumption of crude oil, in order to boost oil exports.

    The so-called Project Gas calls for the development of Venezuela's 146 Tcf of mostly associated gas reserves, as well as exploration of potential nonassociated gas resources. Part of this Gas scheme calls for expansion of the country's gas transmission pipeline system, a natural gas distribution grid, and new gas processing and NGL projects, as well as LNG exports, and power and petrochemical projects fed by natural gas. The Project Gas proposes investments of as much as $10 billion during the next decade. The Anaco area is where future gas production is planned, but Project Gas is dependent on foreign investments.

    This Project is driven by politics. However, some of the scheme would be feasible if Chavez truly welcomed foreign investments and believed in the free market. On September 8, 2000, an ad appeared in the *Wall Street Journal* and other newspapers, as an announcement by the Ministry of Energy and Mines and PDVSA, of a Natural Gas Licensing Round 2000, for 9 exploration areas, and 2 proven reserve areas. Unfortunately, the news of the gas auction revived unpleasant memories among some energy companies that spent more than $2 billion for oil leases in Venezuela in 1997, and have yet to see a return on those investments. The new natural gas licenses call for a royalty of 20%, i.e., up from 16.7%, and a tax rate of 34%, down from 67.7% on crude oil production. This is seen as an attempt by the Chavez Government to increase its take from the oil sector, specifically from the foreign participants, because royalty is paid up front, while income tax accrues only if a profit is posted. PDVSA Gas is seeking joint venture partners, and other cooperative arrangements in an effort to move forward with exploration and production of nonassociated gas, etc. The potential is there, unfortunately so is the Chavez Government.

On June 29, 2001, the Ministry of Energy (not PDVSA) opened bids for the 11 natural gas areas offered. They only received bids on 6 of 11 areas, and these came from TotalFinaElf (French), Repsol (Spanish), Perez Companc and Pluspetrol (both Argentine). The highest bid over the 20% royalty was between 12.5% and 1.5%, with most at the low end. There was no up front bonus money, and no U.S. companies in the bidding. Curiously, the vice Minister, Bernardo Alvarez declared the bidding a great success.

Veba Oel – Ruhr Oel

PDVSA's first refining investment overseas was in West Germany, with Veba Oel AG. PDVSA paid approximately $233 million for a 50% share of Veba Oel's 220,000 b/d refinery in Gelsenkirchen, to form the joint venture called Ruhr Oel, on April 21, 1983. PDVSA was to supply its half of feedstock with 14 degree to 16 degree gravity heavy crude, and Veba its half with light crudes from the North Sea and Libya.

Venezuela's traditional oil market, the United States, has low transportation costs because of its proximity to Venezuela. However, the new commitments with Veba Oel carried higher freight costs. The Russians (Soviet Union) had very high freight costs supplying Cuba with its 200,000 b/d requirements (some of which they resold) and they approached Venezuela with a suggestion of a swap. Thus, Venezuela from 1985 to 1992 swapped 40,000 to 60,000 b/d of Ceuta and Lagomedio crude f.o.b. at Venezuelan ports, which the Soviets would take to Cuba, and then the Soviets would deliver a similar grade of crude (Ural crude) to Rotterdam for Venezuela's Ruhr Oel refineries. These swaps are common in the oil industry in order to reduce transportation costs. The Venezuelan Energy Ministry estimated that this arrangement saved Venezuela about $2/barrel on freight costs, i.e., millions of dollars annually. In 1992, Venezuela suspended its oil swap with Cuba and the Soviet Union (which broke up, in 1991), because Russia was not holding up its part of the bargain.

The Ruhr Oel joint venture was the beginning of PDVSA's new policy called "internationalization." i.e., diversifying sales, finding long-term markets for the country's increasingly heavier mix of crudes; as well as making downstream overseas investments. The Veba 50% participation was the biggest investment that the Venezuelan Government had ever made in any country, prior to the Citgo deal. It opened the door for PDVSA's purchase of overseas refineries, which in 1999 totaled 17 foreign refineries. PDVSA does not own all of these, but has an ownership share. However, before this was accomplished, PDVSA had to convince the Venezuelan politicians.

In 1984, there was an ongoing battle in Congress (particularly Celestino Armas and the AD Party) over whether PDVSA could engage in such foreign refinery deals, and whether Veba Oel had paid PDVSA $1 billion for the sale of Venezuelan crude. The deal had been made under the Herrera Campins Administration (COPEI Party) – therefore, the AD Party was vocally opposed and called it illegal because Congress had not approved the terms of the Veba agreement. However, the contract was "signed outside of Venezuelan territory," making it unnecessary to get Congressional approval. The Veba deal was done under Energy Minister Humberto Calderon Berti, who was a proponent of vertical integration, and who in January 1986, delivered a scathing attack on the Lusinchi (AD Party)

Government (1984-1989), for having stalled PDVSA's internationalization for two years.

It is incredible that PDVSA ever achieved the number two spot in the ranking of major oil companies, when their executives had to struggle and educate each new Congress with antagonistic political parties, in order to get Congress to allow PDVSA to proceed with carefully thought out development plans. Internationalization and the Apertura are prime examples of PDVSA's battles with Congress, in order to fulfill their mission.

Citgo Petroleum Corporation

Citgo Petroleum was PDVSA's vehicle to conquer the U.S. downstream market where Venezuela sells half of its oil production.

Citgo began as Cities Services Company, which was founded in 1910 by Henry L. Doherty, as a supplier of gas and electric power across the United States. In 1935, it got out of the regulated utility business and concentrated on its oil and gas activities. Then in 1946, it purchased the U.S. Government's refinery at Lake Charles, Louisiana. (Notice the irony, of who built this refinery and who owns it now.) Cities Service changed its gasoline marketing brand to Citgo in the mid-1960s, and in 1974, it moved its headquarters from New York City to Tulsa. Cities Service was a pioneer in resid conversion technology and ran the first H-Oil unit in the 1960s, at its Lake Charles refinery.

T. Boone Pickens of Mesa Petroleum put Gulf Oil into play and on the block in 1984, and also put Cities Service into play and broke it up in 1982. On August 13, 1982, Cities Service announced it was merging with Occidental Petroleum. Oxy (then run by Dr. Armand Hammer) paid $4 billion, and the deal was finalized in December. These were some of the most complex oil dealings, a result of T. Boone Pickens stalking oil companies. He first got Gulf Oil involved, then Marathon Oil, even Southland Corporation in his efforts to get Cities Service. Cities struck back and announced it was making an offer on Mesa, after Cities was given a briefing book by a banker on the Pickens group's tender offer plans. And after the deal was finally struck, Oxy's $4 billion purchase price forced it to start to unload Cities Service refining and marketing operations. Oxy began holding talks with domestic oil companies and oil-producing countries (Mexico and Arab oil producers) as potential venture partners.

In March 1983, Southland Corporation agreed to buy the Cities Service downstream operations, which included: the Lake Charles refinery, along with 65% interest in the Cit-Con lube oil refinery, about 350 convenience stores, 500 Citgo retail outlets, and certain transportation and wholesale businesses. Southland paid $250 million in Southland stock, plus construction costs on the refinery upgrading, which Cities Service had started in 1981. The Citgo refinery would supply Southland's 7,300 7-Eleven convenience stores with gasoline on more favorable terms. This purchase made Southland heavily leveraged, and Standard & Poors placed Southland on its Credit Watch list.

After a difficult start, the Citgo refinery in 1985 began to benefit from the new EPA strict lead regulations, because the Lake Charles refinery can produce 100% unleaded gasoline. The following year Citgo entered a joint venture with PDVSA, which gave it a steady source of crude oil, additional products, and $290 million for PDVSA's half of the refinery.

PDVSA President Brigido Natera signed the letter of intent to purchase 50% of Citgo with John P. Thompson, Southland's Chairman, at the PDVSA headquarters in Caracas, on September 15, 1986. And on September 30, the final agreement was signed in Tulsa. PDVSA agreed to provide 130,000 to 200,000 b/d of crude and other feedstock for Citgo's 300,000 b/d Lake Charles refinery for 20 years. The main feed for the refinery would be 24 degree gravity crude.

Then on November 7, 1989, PDVSA announced it would buy the other half of Citgo for $675 million. In the two years of PDVSA ownership, Citgo had expanded its retail branded outlets from 6,900 in 1986, to more than 8,300 outlets in 1989, and crude runs in the refinery were averaging 284,000 b/d, up from 238,000 b/d in 1986.

The price for the other half had doubled because Citgo was now a bigger company, but also because when PDVSA originally bought 50% in 1986, the refining industry had been through a major shake-out, caused by surplus capacity. Refiners were operating at 65% of capacity because demand had started to fall in the 1980s. The U.S. had mothballed a number of refineries after the decontrol of oil and the end of the Oil Entitlements Program, in January 1981. It became a buyers market for refineries. Furthermore, U.S. refiners had started planning upgrades for their refineries to comply with new environmental Federal standards (lead phase down), and to convert heavier crudes and resids, to lighter products. Most completion dates of upgrades were scheduled by or before 1984.

The irony here is that these costly upgrades (which for the refining industry amounted to billions of dollars) were carried out to process more heavy oil (with higher sulfur content) from the U.S., as well as Saudi Arabia, Venezuela, Mexico and Canada, and after completion, some of these refineries were snapped up by these foreign oil producers. Between 1982 and 1984, Citgo (Cities Service and then Southland) spent $500 million in upgrading the Lake Charles refinery, making it one of the most advanced in the industry. Then PDVSA bought 50% for $290 million, including percentages in two important pipelines, Colonial and Explorer; a lube plant; and over 30 terminals; and an established gasoline market, etc.

PDVSA would have preferred to keep its U.S. partner, and therefore, a lower profile, but Southland was forced to sell its remaining 50%, because it was in a serious financial bind. The three Thompson brothers, owners of Southland, had decided to buy the company back in 1987, and borrowed more than $5 billion at 16% interest, and were hit with the October 1987 stock market crash, as the buyout was underway. The Thompsons were forced to sell their half of Citgo, and the only other buyers would have been a foreign company (possibly Kuwait Petroleum), and thus PDVSA had little choice but to buy the other half of Citgo. It was a good decision.

Nevertheless, on occasion, a President such as Carlos Andres Perez, in 1992, might suggest selling off half of Citgo. It was reported in *Platt's Oilgram News,* June 11, 1992, that the Emir of Kuwait, Jaber al-Ahmad al- Sabah on a one-day trip to Caracas offered $3 billion for a 50% stake in Citgo. However, the Venezuelan argument was that "the other half should belong to U.S. investors, because in that way we'll have a company that can achieve the objectives that we're proposing, and we'll also obtain the *protection* that each company gives to other nationals." CAP said this to a group of journalists during a breakfast at Miraflores, and he added: "If we're going to have a company that is solely Venezuelan, one day the U.S. government or any other government could take reprisals for whatever motive, on Venezuela." (Caracas *Daily Journal*, August 29,1992) CAP does know something about nationalization – he did it in 1975, to 11 foreign oil companies. But there is something the Venezuelans do not realize. Very few US-Americans know that Citgo is Venezuelan owned, any more than that Shell is British-Dutch. Actually, the Citgo retail outlets, all 13,800 Citgo stations, are franchised, and are not owned by Citgo.

In 1986, Brigido Natera also signed a letter of intent in Caracas, with Union Pacific, the owner of Champlin Petroleum Company, to purchase 50% of the 160,000 b/d Corpus Christi, Texas refinery. The final agreement was signed in March 1987, with PDVSA paying $30 million in cash and contributing $63 million in crude oil and products. The joint company of Champlin Refining had assets estimated at $190 million, which included a petrochemicals facility, a distribution system of more than 50 outlets in 10 Southern states, in addition to the refinery, which PDVSA would supply 140,000 barrels per day.

Champlin began a $300 million upgrading project of its Corpus Christi refinery in 1981. The high-sulfur crude unit was completed in 1983 and sold to and leased back from General Electric Credit Co.

PDVSA acted on its option to buy the other 50% of Champlin Refining, effective January I, 1989, paying Union Pacific $50 million plus depreciation costs, and $25 million in retained Champlin earnings for 1987. PDVSA, thus, became the first foreign state oil company to become sole owner of a major U.S. refinery. And by the end of 1989, PDVSA would be the sole owner of a second U.S. refinery, Citgo – Louisiana's second largest refinery, and the 8th largest in the United States.

The following year, in September 1990, PDVSA said it was folding the Champlin Refining & Chemical Co. of Texas into Citgo Petroleum and making Citgo into a direct subsidiary of PDVSA, no longer answering to another affiliate (Interven). The previous month Citgo had announced it was acquiring Seaview Petroleum Co. for $42.5 million. Seaview, an asphalt refinery in

Paulsboro, New Jersey, producing 84,000 b/d, was a good fit for Venezuela's heavy crude oil. Venezuela's asphalt is among the best in the world, and it has been used in paving large parts of the U.S. highway system.

In February 1992, Citgo announced it would spend $1.7 billion over the next five years to comply with the new gasoline requirements under the Clean Air Act Amendments passed by Congress in 1991. These new requirements for reformulated gasoline were seen as costing U.S. refiners as much as $20 billion to upgrade their plants. Most of Citgo's upgrading was to process Venezuela's heavy crude into cleaner-burning gasoline. Chevron and Amoco said they would close some old refineries – as not economic for a costly upgrade. Ironically, a big part of this upgrading was for the construction of new MTBE (methyl tertiary butyl ether) units, used as an additive in gasoline to comply with the oxygen requirements, a product that in 2000 became a big problem in states like California. The problem was caused by the leakage from gasoline storage tanks in several regions and the contamination of groundwater.

Each decade, with new gasoline requirements issued by the Environmental Protection Administration (EPA), more refineries close, and the U.S. is forced to import more oil products. The U.S., thus, exports more of its capital, and our unfavorable balance of payments increases. And, the oil companies are blamed when there are shortages of gasoline or heating oil!

After PDVSA purchased Citgo Petroleum, the PDVSA Board found it prudent to continue to have a US-American as its president. A low profile was preferable, in view of considerable foreign bashing, which started in the United States against the Japanese, in the 1970s and 1980s. Thus, Ron Hall was president for 10 years, followed by Ralph Cunningham and David Tippeconnic.

Then on his "Alo Presidente," Sunday radio show, Hugo Chavez summarily fired Tippeconnic on October 8, 2000. He also announced he had appointed General Oswaldo Contreras Maza as the new president of Citgo, and would take him to Houston on October 15, to "swear him in." (In Venezuela, the President "swears people in" after he appoints them.) President Chavez had at least two reasons for taking this action. First, if he was going to keep Citgo, he wanted it run by Venezuelans. Second, Chavez wanted the "bad contracts" undone, i.e., petroleum supply contracts "unfavorable to Venezuela." Oswaldo, as he wants to be called at Citgo, was on Chavez's PDVSA Board for a year and a half, as Vice President of Human Resources, before going to the U.S. and Citgo.

As Alberto Quiros wrote in his *El Nacional* article, "Cuba, PDVSA, Citgo," (22-10-00), General Contreras as a person is not the issue. The point is that Citgo is a U.S. company with U.S. clients, and to change its image, to "Venezolanize" it is not a good commercial strategy. First, the head of Citgo should be a professional oilman, expert in the market, storage, distribution and finance, in order to run an operation of 16,000 [sic] outlets that are not the property of Citgo but franchised stations, various refineries, pipelines, docking terminals, transportation fleets, contracts with third parties, and small revenue margins on a gallon of product sold. Quiros then continues: "It is necessary to know this type of business, and you need to know the country." Furthermore, Citgo's activities have little to do with PDVSA's primary activities, and "I would not name a president of Citgo as President of PDVSA." And to make matters worse, Chavez's declarations that General Contreras was to go to Tulsa and straighten Citgo out, and undo the contracts signed under the previous administration was "stupid and imprudent."

One reason Chavez may keep Citgo is the new subsidiary he created in 2000: Citgo International Latin America (CILA). CILA was created for PDVSA to expand fuels and lubricants wholesale and retail marketing operations in the Caribbean, Central and South American regions. PDV brand has already been launched in Costa Rica, next Ecuador and Puerto Rico. Cuba, undoubtedly.

Venezuela's overall refining capacity in 2000 was 2.6 million b/d, and of this 820,798 b/d was in the United States. Of Venezuela's U.S. refining capacity, 729,548 b/d was from Citgo's four refineries (Lake Charles, La; Corpus Christi, TX; Paulsboro, NJ; and Savannah, GA). PDVSA owns 50% of the Hess refinery in St. Croix, U.S. Virgin Islands, which is the 6th largest refinery in the world. PDVSA paid $625 million for their share of the 525,000 b/d refinery, in 1998. The Paraguana Refining Center (the

Amuay and Cardon refineries) in Venezuela is the largest refining complex in the world with 940,000 barrels per day capacity.

In 1999, PDVSA's overseas assets were around $9 billion, with $7.5 billion of this amount invested in the United States. PDVSA, through its U.S. subsidiaries is one of the largest refiners of crude oil in the United States. PDVSA's U.S. subsidiaries are: Citgo, Midwest Refining, 50% of Chalmette Refining, Sweeny Joint Venture, and Hess Joint Venture – all under PDV America. Citgo has 4,200 employees.

Citgo Petroleum, ranked 5th in U.S. market share, had 8% of the U.S. gasoline market in 1999. ExxonMobil ranked 1st, and BPAmoco was 2nd in market share. Citgo is PDVSA's largest subsidiary abroad, and in 1999, sold over 1.5 million b/d of products. Overall marketing of Venezuelan crudes and products averaged 3.1 million barrels per day. Thus, Citgo accounted for nearly half of all of PDVSA's market. Until 2001, PDVSA sold its oil to Citgo at an arms length price, but for tax reasons did not receive dividends. Instead, Citgo reinvested almost all of its profits in U.S.-based operations. In October 1999, a Treaty to Avoid Double Taxation between the United States and Venezuela was signed, and became effective in January 2001. Consequently, PDVSA received $213.75 million in dividends from Citgo from its 2000 earnings. Under the treaty, Citgo's U.S. tax burden dropped from 30% to 5 percent.

With overseas refineries, Venezuela was able to increase its crude exports over its product exports, which were limited by Venezuela's own refining capacity of only a little over 1 million barrels per day. The purchase of foreign refineries was also necessary because more and more there were fewer refineries that could refine Venezuela's heavy crudes, which need deep conversion upgraded refineries. However, with each OPEC quota cutback of Venezuelan crude production, PDVSA has to continually purchase crude and oil products (at higher prices) in the international market, in order to meet its overseas refining and marketing commitments.

Finally, when PDVSA has to go to the U.S. financial market for loans, it has excellent collateral: Citgo.

Saudi Arabia, Kuwait and Foreign Integration

In 1988, Saudi Arabia followed Venezuela in entering the downstream operations of the U.S. oil industry, when Saudi Aramco bought 50% of three Texaco refineries and Texaco's distribution and marketing system in the East and Gulf Coast area. This amounted to a $1.25 billion investment by Saudi Aramco in Texaco, a company that helped to develop the Saudi oil industry before nationalization of Aramco (Chevron, Texaco, Exxon and Mobil) in the 1970s. The new U.S. joint venture between Texaco and Saudi Aramco was named Star Enterprise.

Kuwait's foreign downstream investments preceded Venezuela's and Saudi Arabia's. Kuwait, however, eschewed joint ventures. On October 1, 1981, Kuwait's Kuwait Petroleum Corporation (KPC) purchased Santa Fe International Corp., a large diversified energy services-engineering-construction firm based in California, for $2.5 billion. Santa Fe had a business association with Kuwait since 1964, through joint operation of Kuwait Drilling Company. The Santa Fe deal brought with it about 40,000 b/d in U.S. production, and involvement in exploration and production in areas ranging from the North Sea to China – all outside of OPEC quotas.

Gulf Oil and British Petroleum's Kuwait Oil Company was nationalized in March 1975. Their market for Kuwait's oil had been Europe. Gulf had built its European downstream infrastructure to run on Kuwaiti crude, which it no longer had. Thus, on October 1, 1981, my old friend Edward B. Walker III, the last president of Gulf Oil Corp., offered Gulf's European assets for $1, to Ali Khalifa al-Sabah, Kuwait's oil minister and chairman of Kuwait Petroleum Corp. This occurred in Geneva during an OPEC meeting recess. Kuwait would have to buy the oil inventories. It would cost KPC hundreds of millions of dollars to upgrade the facilities, which included 2 refineries and about 1,500 service stations, pipelines and storage tanks. In February 1983, Kuwait made its first purchases from Gulf – the Benelux assets – and one month later took the Swedish and Danish assets.

Kuwait's three modern upgraded refineries, along with its three European refineries (Denmark, Rotterdam, and the last one in Naples, purchased from Mobil in 1990) enable Kuwait to sell mainly oil products, and far less crude. Kuwait Petroleum

International replaced the Gulf logo with "Q8" (wordplay for Kuwait) on its network of European service stations, which rose to 6,500 after it purchased Mobil's downstream network in Italy, in early 1990.

Most OPEC members lack Kuwait's financial reserves, small population and ability to move fast. Before the 1990 Gulf War, Kuwait had financial reserves of nearly $100 billion, and oil reserves second to Saudi Arabia. Kuwait Petroleum Corp., as a large holding company had subsidiaries including: a tanker company to control the global movement of Kuwaiti oil; and a finance company (KPI). In July 1989, Kuwait sold C.F. Braun Engineering to Halliburton for $100 million. Braun was an affiliate of Santa Fe International.

Through foreign integration, these large OPEC producers were seeking new ways to market their oil and become competitive. If you have a refining and marketing operation you have a great deal more control over your production. Integration also makes it difficult for OPEC to control official prices because prices paid become invisible when oil is transferred to their own refineries. Reintegration can only benefit the world economy. Refineries running mainly on one country's crude means not having to change temperatures and pressures to accommodate different crudes, thus cutting refining costs. In the United States, nearly 25% of the nation's distillation capacity is now owned by non-U.S. entities. This contributes toward an economically stronger U.S. refining industry and more interdependence with producers and producing countries.

The U.S. and European major oil companies had control of upstream (production) and downstream (refining and marketing) operations before they were nationalized in many OPEC countries, in the mid-1970s. They, thus, lost their foreign crude operations, while the OPEC members needed the marketing outlets that the majors controlled. A good example of this change was Gulf Oil and Kuwait. Gulf had built up its marketing operations in Europe in order to process its Kuwaiti production. After Kuwait nationalized Gulf and they lost their Kuwaiti production, it was short of feedstock for its European operations, while Kuwait needed Gulf's refining and marketing assets. To be concise, this process was a worldwide trend of *reintegration* of oil industry operations.

Saudi Arabia, Kuwait and Venezuela were founding members of OPEC in 1960. As members of this organization, they differ widely. Venezuela is the only non-Muslin member of OPEC, and Venezuela has never embargoed oil to the United States, as the Arab producers did in 1973. Hugo Chavez may be very friendly with the other members of OPEC, but the Venezuelan people never looked with favor upon the Arabs or OPEC.

Petroleos de Chavez

The system that Luis Giusti set up when he restructured PDVSA was superb for Chavez to gain complete control of the Venezuelan oil industry. Giusti removed the buffer between the industry and the President of Venezuela. Chavez, by naming the Directors of the Board of PDVSA as Vice-Presidents of operations, controls not only their appointments but the appointments for the operations of the industry. The Board of Directors now function as the operators. The Venezuelan state is now really in the "state of PDVSA" – and the by-laws of PDVSA have been discarded. Furthermore, there is no cohesive Board, for the Directors as operators can go directly to the President. "This is a state enterprise and I plan to run it for the benefit of the national treasury," said Chavez.

What Chavez does not understand is that petroleum only has value if someone has a use for it. With the development of consumers, oil acquires value. Chavez says "do not touch petroleum, which belongs to the state as a direct right." He thinks he is the state and has sovereignty, and not the Venezuelans, over petroleum. Venezuela's oil is Chavez's.

The basis for Chavez's future control over Venezuela will be his personal control of PDVSA's oil revenues. To become President of Venezuela, Chavez needed the votes of the poor, who were the majority. But to remain in power, Chavez needs his big oil company, which can now be properly called Petroleos de Chavez. During his first year as President, in 1999, PDVSA's revenues increased by $4.5 billion, due to the doubling and tripling of the world price of oil. But where was this money spent? There was no longer any transparency, and no accounting to the public.

Thus, as the new President of Venezuela and as the President of his own oil company, he can do as he pleases, accountable to no one: a dictator with black gold, another Qadhafi, or Saddam Hussein. And he is a dictator who is in a position to help Castro and Cuba.

Chavez has surrounded himself with both the Old Guard and Young Communists. His revolution to change Venezuela and reunite Simon Bolivar's Gran Colombia by taking over Colombia and Panama (and gain control of the Panama Canal) will be carried out with Venezuela's oil. But maybe not!

Orlando Ochoa has pointed out that in 1971, Venezuela had an oil production of 3.6 million b/d with a population of 11 million. Thus, Venezuela's oil production has been dropping as its population increases. Production costs have also been rising due to the increased production of heavy and extra heavy crude. Venezuela's own consumption of oil products, now 450,000 b/d, has been rising as PDVSA is forced by the government to subsidize oil products, particularly gasoline, which sells for about 24 cents a gallon. (Some of Venezuela's 370,000 b/d of gasoline leaves the country as contraband across the border to Colombia or Brazil.) It, therefore, becomes ever more difficult for PDVSA to sustain the Government.

The Goose was cooked and being devoured. The vast reserves of oil, extra heavy oil, and natural gas are still in Venezuela, as is most of the modern infrastructure, but the capable, experienced oilmen are gone.

CHAPTER V

CUBA and FIDEL CASTRO

"Communism is the creed of spiteful and avarice men who, in order to have shoulders upon which to raise themselves, pretend to be impassioned defenders of the disenfranchised." Jose Marti

Fidel Castro and Cuban Marxists claim Jose Marti as the "intellectual architect" of the Cuban Revolution. Marti's life refutes everything Castro and Communism stand for; Marti is the antithesis of Castro.

There is an incredible coincidence and irony between Marti and Venezuela. In March 1881, Jose Marti arrived in Caracas, during the presidency of Guzman Blanco. While living in Caracas, he started the *Revista Venezolana*, and in its first issue honored the Venezuelan teacher, Cecilio Acosta, who was alienated from President Guzman. Marti, a Cuban, was teaching a course in freedom in Venezuela. However, Guzman Blanco told Marti to leave Venezuela, and so he returned to New York. In his departing letter to friends he wrote: "Let Venezuela give me a way to serve her, and she will find in me a son."

Unfortunately, Venezuela gets rid of its great sons. Andres Bello went off to Chile, and established their remarkable education system. Humberto Fernandez-Moran went to the United States and Sweden, with his scientific discoveries, Baruj Benacerraf went to France and the United States and received the Nobel Prize in Medicine and Physiology in 1980. They proved Jose Marti's doctrine: "Only the genuine is fruitful." Marti dreamed of true liberty.

Now that Hugo Chavez has become Fidel Castro's best buddy, Castro is the daily subject of Venezuelan political discussions. Many in Venezuela remember Castro's attempt to take over Venezuela in the 1960s, the Cuban guerrilleros that blew up Venezuela's oil pipelines, and their attacks on the population. These attacks were particularly severe during the government of

Romulo Betancourt. It was at this time that I left Venezuela with my family and returned to the United States. Our lives seemed to be in constant danger, in merely taking and picking my sons up at school, grocery shopping, or in whatever normal activities one engaged in day or night.

It is strange, indeed, that in the United States when journalists write about Castro's terrorism and guerrilla wars in Latin America, they never mention Venezuela. Their list only includes Guatemala, El Salvador, Nicaragua, Colombia and Bolivia. Perhaps the U.S. ignorance of Castro's terrorism in Venezuela stems from President Romulo Betancourt's success in combating Castro's guerrillas. Betancourt had been a Communist and understood their tactics, and he never lost the support of the rural population that knew where the guerrillas hid.

Kennedy Abandons the Cubans

How is it possible that Fidel Castro is still in Cuba, controlling the Cubans, but also still a threat to other countries, even after the fall of the Soviet Union that subsidized Castro's dictatorship for over 30 years? The answer: The 1962 Kennedy – Khrushchev **secret accords** supposedly made the United States the bodyguard of Fidel Castro. President John F. Kennedy's October 27, 1962 message to Nikita Khrushchev stated that "there would be no attack, no invasion of Cuba, not only on the part of the United States, but also of other nations of the Western Hemisphere." Thus, after Soviet SA-2 missiles were discovered in Cuba, in October 1962, Cuban exiles were to be deprived of the right to fight for their freedom, and the U.S. Government would jail those Cubans in exile who tried to invade and liberate their own country.

These secret accords, however, came into question in 1997, when newly declassified documents revealed that President Kennedy later retreated from the pledge. Both countries took steps to implement the agreement, including Soviet removal of offensive nuclear missiles in Cuba, and the U.S. removed all IRBMs in Italy and Turkey confronting the Soviets; but a formal agreement ended in failure. Ironically, Kennedy was worried about how a no-invasion pledge would affect the U.S. ability to respond if Cuba undertook a major arms buildup, shot down U.S. planes, or attacked a pro-American country. George Ball, State Department official, pointed out to Kennedy that a no-invasion pledge could not supersede U.S. rights under the Rio Pact. Nevertheless, each U.S. Administration has honored the pledge. Regardless of whether or not, President Kennedy did change his mind about the no-invasion pledge to Khrushchev, he had already abandoned the Cubans when they tried to take back their country at the Bay of Pigs (Playa Giron), in April 1961.

The **Missile Crisis** in 1962 was triggered by the U.S. discovery that the Soviets had sent offensive missiles to Cuba. Placing missiles outside of the Soviet Union was a break with Soviet policy. The Kennedy Administration at first ignored (and even publicly denied) information, as early as January 1962, that the Soviets had installed missile pads and submarine pens in Cuba. (Braden, pp.401-402)

The island of Cuba is underlain with huge caverns, which the Russians took advantage of to put in two-lane underground highways in many places. In this way they were able to transport missiles, which were installed from underneath and could be camouflaged from high flying planes. Some of these caverns were converted into submarine pens so that submarines can enter underwater from the ocean without being seen. The Russians built a submarine base on the southern Cuban shore in Cienfuegos. A big electric power plant was also built for use by the submarine base. (Braden, p442) Bill Gertz reported in a December 2000 article in the *Washington Times* that Castro's military forces are underground. The Cubans have built an extensive network of underground bunkers and tunnels for key military forces, air-defense sites and command facilities, according to a classified Defense Intelligence Agency report. The bunker construction was carried out throughout the 1990s despite the withdrawal of Soviet aid. One can assume these bunkers are in those huge caverns.

A less known event concerning the Missile Crisis was the appalling intervention of the U.N. Secretary General U Thant, who went to Cuba in late October to tell Fidel Castro that he should not permit U.S. inspection on the ground of missile sites or on ships of missiles, since it would infringe on Cuban *sovereignty*. (Braden, p425)

When John F. Kennedy was campaigning for the Presidency in 1960, he charged U.S. failure to aid Cuba had turned Cubans against us. On October 20, 1960, Kennedy advocated direct intervention. Richard Nixon, the Republican candidate running against JFK could not speak out because of the planned invasion. Kennedy knew what the Eisenhower Administration was doing because as the Democratic candidate, he was given daily briefings by the CIA. This gave Kennedy a lucky political break. Then as President in 1961, Kennedy set about changing the plan, vacillating at every turn, finally straddling two horses by imposing ruinous conditions and reserving the right to cancel at the last minute.

It had been President Eisenhower who had approved the CIA plan in 1960, to help Cuban exiles return and fight a guerrilla war in Cuba. But, this one attempt was botched by the Kennedy Administration at the Bay of Pigs. Kennedy wavered; and finally dismembered the original Zapata invasion plan, changing the daylight invasion to night when it was more dangerous over the coral reefs. The key to success was the destruction of Castro's small air force on the ground, before the invaders hit the beaches (which Kennedy scratched from the town of Trinidad in Las Villas Province, to Playa Giron, far less preferable), on **April 17**. This was to be done by three air strikes of 16 planes each coming in from Nicaragua to the south coast of Cuba, 48 sorties was the minimum. The first air strike was cut in half by orders from the White House, and the 2nd and 3rd strikes were cancelled.

The Cuban brigade on the beach was betrayed. They had been told they would have continuing supplies arriving on the beach. They never got any supplies. Castro's jets sank two of the five ships sent to supply them.

President Kennedy further compromised the invasion when in an April 12th press conference, he stated that "there will not under any conditions be an intervention in Cuba by U.S. armed forces." This propaganda for world consumption had a devastating effect on Cubans in Cuba. If they rose against Castro it would be at their own risk. Kennedy thus eliminated the vital premise for success of the invasion. And Kennedy protested so much that Castro was sure an invasion was coming, and mobilized to smash it. Castro's police and militia rounded up a quarter of a million people suspected of being disloyal.

President Kennedy's statement tied the hands of the United States in advance. The Kennedy Administration had been in office for three months, and Arthur Schlesinger and Adlai Stevenson were crucial in the defeat of the invasion plan: Schlesinger in dismantling it; and Ambassador Stevenson at the United Nations for calling off the third strike by the Cuban Brigade's Air Squadron. Kennedy's decision to cancel the third strike to appease Stevenson doomed the invasion. There were 1,500 Cubans already on their way to the Bay of Pigs. They had been mobilized, trained, and sent on their mission by the United States. Then, they were abandoned, for purely political reasons.

And then, Kennedy paid *tribute* to Castro with $55.9 million in goods, after 20 month's of *negotiations* over what goods Castro wanted; before he would finally free 1,199 Bay of Pigs prisoners. Mario Lazo in his book, Dagger in the Heart (Chapter 18, Lives for Sale), describes how the American people were misled and deceived. It all started with a speech by Castro on May 17, 1961, where he demanded tribute in the form of 500 Caterpillar bulldozers, "not with rubber tires, no." These were worth about $28 million. However with the delays Castro upped his demands and finally got $55.9 million of goods in exchange for the survivors of Brigade 2506.

Through a committee of private citizens headed by Eleanor Roosevelt and Milton Eisenhower, President Kennedy tried to maintain the fiction that all aspects of the negotiations and critical decisions, from raising funds to actually freeing the prisoners, were private. This committee soon came to naught. On March 29, 1962, after being in captivity almost a year, the prisoners were tried as war criminals in a mass trial, and received 30-year prison terms. The Cuban exile community in Miami then organized a "Cuban Families Committee," and with their enormous efforts [complicated by the intervention of the October 1962 Missile Crisis with the Soviets], and with the participation of at least *14 branches of the U.S. Government*; drug and food companies; and with everything coordinated out of Robert Kennedy's Justice Department; the last of the prisoners arrived in Florida, on Christmas Eve, 1962. Every Castro demand had been met and he received twice what he originally demanded!

The United States botched the Bay of Pigs so badly that words do not exist to record the shamefulness of this action by a U.S. Administration. The Bay of Pigs saved Fidel Castro. There

114

was never again to be a significant resistance movement inside Cuba.

Cuban History

The following is a brief historical perspective on Cuba.

Cuba was a coveted prize in the international wars of past centuries between England, France and Spain. The buccaneers and pirates of England, France and The Netherlands fought over Cuba as a strategic point of operations. In 1762-1763 a British force occupied Havana. French refugees fleeing Negro revolts in Haiti after 1790 settled in Cuba. Thus, it has a mixed population and a pattern of violence since the days of the Spanish Conquest. Bartolome de las Casas, in the sixteenth century, began his crusade for Indian rights in Cuba, after witnessing Spanish atrocities. Cuba's location is uniquely central in the Caribbean, and the Spaniards could organize their conquest of the mainland from the fine natural harbour at Havana. Havana was the headquarters of Spanish power in America. And, as the Indians were killed, slaves were imported from Africa. Cuba, as a military base for the Spaniards, remained important after Spain lost its colonies in Latin America, in the early nineteenth century. As trade in sugar and other Cuban crops increasingly developed with the United States, Spain tried to restrict this trade, and in doing so, provoked the independence movement in Cuba.

Such ironies: after Mexico and most of South America were freed of Spanish domination between 1810 and 1824, only Cuba and Puerto Rico remained under Spanish control in the Western Hemisphere. Royalists from Mexico and Gran Colombia fled to Cuba, where they helped to block intervention by Simon Bolivar's forces. United States' interest in Cuba continued to grow, particularly after the acquisition of Florida from Spain, in 1819. John Quincy Adams in 1823, spoke of the physical gravitation of Cuba "toward the North American Union, which by the same law of nature, cannot cast her off from its bosom." (Adam's letter to Nelson, April 28) President Franklin Pierce in 1853, offered to buy Cuba from Spain for $130 million.

Columbus brought sugar cane to Cuba. The Spaniards, in the 1520s, started the Cuban sugar plantations, and to work on the plantations they imported Negro slaves. Cuba made money from sugar, but also suffered years of slavery, and unrest because of this

115

crop. In each of the island's political upheavals, 1868, 1895, 1930-33 and the 1950s, revolutionaries burned cane fields and promised to improve the lot of the cane pickers. Fidel Castro promised the same when he reached power in 1959.

Nature endowed the island with the right conditions of sunshine, rain and soil to grow the lowest cost sugar in the world. By 1894, Cuba's sugar production was over 1 million short tons, and in 1952, it was 8 million tons. Before Castro, Cuba was the chief vendor of cane sugar in the world market. Under Castro, the crop of cane dropped to 3.8 million tons in 1964, and to 3.2 tons in 1998.

The island's economy depended on marketing its sugar and tobacco in the United States. However, in 1894, Spain canceled the trade agreement between the Cubans and the Americans. The consequences were disastrous, and their losses persuaded Cuban businessmen the time had come for Cuba libre.

The Ten Years' War (1868-1878) cost the Cubans 200,000 lives and some $700 million in property loss. In the settlement with Spain, slaves were to be emancipated, which was fulfilled in 1886. This brutal war hardened the determination of Cubans to be free.

The Cuban independence war that started in 1895 was actually a continuation of the Ten Years' War. **Tomas Estrada Palma** headed a government-in-exile in New York, which included **Jose Marti**, who more than any other Cuban, helped to create the conditions that later prompted American intervention. Marti spent the greater part of his short life in exile, the last 15 years, in the United States. From the U.S., he launched the Modernist Movement in Spanish poetry; and he wrote a bi-weekly column, carried in nearly every newspaper in Latin America. Marti saw the connection between economic freedom and individual liberty. He wanted to introduce this system in Latin America.

In 1895, Marti, Antonio Maceo and Maximo Gomez and their recruits landed in eastern Cuba. Marti was one of the first to be killed in battle. But volunteer expeditions continued to reach the island. Then Spain appointed Valeriano Weyler commander-in-chief, who quickly gained the name of el Carnicero (the butcher). He herded several hundred thousand men, women and children into concentration camps (<u>reconcentrados</u>), where some 50,000 in Havana province alone, died! Crops and cattle were systematically destroyed, in order to starve out the patriots, who in turn retaliated by burning Spanish-owned sugar plantations. The patriots were driven back to the eastern end of the island by 1896, and the battle for liberty seemed lost. However, the United States had been provoked; and had a strategic motive. (It was also at this time that the U.S. became involved in Venezuela's boundary dispute with British Guiana.)

Washington wanted a canal across the Isthmus of Panama and having Spain in control of the largest island in the Caribbean seemed unwise. Furthermore, there were humanitarian reasons to help the Cubans. The U.S. public was appalled at the savagery with which the Cuban patriots were treated. Joseph Pulitzer's *World*, and William Randolph Hearst's *American* sold piles of newspapers on the stories of Spanish atrocities in Cuba. On February 15, 1898, the <u>U.S. Maine</u>, anchored in Havana harbour to protect U.S. citizens in case of emergency, mysteriously blew up, with the loss of 266 U.S. seamen. "Remember the Maine," reverberated across the United States, and on April 11, President William McKinley laid the case before Congress, and called for armed intervention. U.S. forces on land and sea expelled Spain from Cuba, Puerto Rico and the Philippines, and gained control of what was left of Spain's empire. Cuba was now free, mostly.

Thus commenced, between 1898 and 1902, the U.S. Army's pacifying and organizing of Cuba. Tens of thousands were homeless and starving, and fields lay in weeds. Departing Spaniards stripped island offices, and bandits ruled country roads. Under Dr. Leonard Wood's command, the Army set about distributing food and clothing to the population; the patriot army was disbanded and its members received a $3 million bonus from the U.S. Treasury. Courts and customs services were reorganized. Cattle were imported. Landholders received help in cultivation of fields. Harbours were dredged, highways and railroads were begun, public schools increased in number, even the University of Havana was reopened. And, the eradication of yellow fever, a scourge for four centuries, was accomplished by Dr. Walter Reed and other physicians.

But the Cuban people would be content with nothing less than national independence. When Dr. Wood was seeking a transfer of his authority to an elected assembly drafting a constitution, Washington laid down some demands. The infamous Platt Amendment, largely drafted by Elihu Root, was to set limits upon the island's activities, so as to make it a safe neighbor. The Cuban Government was limited in its powers to make treaties and in its freedom to contract public debts, and it promised "coaling or naval stations" (Guantanamo Bay) to the United States. Most galling to Cubans, was "Cubans consent that the U.S. may exercise the right to intervene for the preservation of Cuban independence." The U.S. Government demanded the Platt Amendment be inserted in the new Cuban Constitution of 1901.

Tomas Estrada Palma was chosen the first President of Cuba, and in May 1902, Governor Wood turned over the government to President Estrada and sailed for New York. Cuba lived under the Platt Amendment until 1934. Estrada won a reciprocal trade treaty from the U.S., reducing sugar duties, and in force until 1960. This favorable advantage stimulated an increase in sugar production.

In reviewing the list of Cuban presidents after Estrada, one is struck by the lack of admirable executives that followed the honest efforts of their first president. Plunder is a verb that can be used for most of these presidents. Various forms of tyranny in Cuba became the rule, rather than the exception. Cubans continued to flee to the United States. With the fall of the Gerardo Machado (1925-1933) government, and the successful efforts of U.S. Ambassador to Cuba, Sumner Welles, to abrogate the Platt Amendment in 1934, an era ended in Cuba.

Cuban graft was inherited from the early days of the Spanish conquest. *Grafters* took as high as 50 to 60%. Even though the economy bore an appalling burden, the Cuban standard of living was one of the three highest in Latin America. This corruption, of course, provided fodder, for Communist blamed the corruption on the "American imperialists." If US Americans wanted to do business in Cuba it meant paying bribes and making contributions to political parties. It was a case of extortion. The corruption was a many centuries old Spanish tradition, which is why it is so prevalent in Latin American countries. But in Cuba, big business was US business and it provided graft and extortion running into millions annually. In Cuba, the lottery was the center of corruption in the early days, with people in power winning the big prizes. Huge amounts were stolen through the distribution of jobs, *botellas*, by government officials. Many of these botellas required no work.

U.S. Pushes Batista Out of Cuba

After 1934, **Fulgencio Batista** emerged as the arbiter of Cuba's destiny, first ruling through puppets, and in 1940 assuming the presidency. Batista as the strong man behind a succession of presidents, piled up a huge fortune. He was the first president in Latin America to appoint Communists to his Cabinet. In 1944, he allowed the election of Dr. Ramon Grau San Martin, and in 1948 Carlos Prio Socarras became president. Batista again seized the presidency in 1952, and departed in January 1, 1959, after the U.S. State Department informed him that he no longer had U.S. support. The Assistant Secretary of State for Latin American Affairs, Roy (Dick) Rubottom and William Wieland were particularly helpful in pushing Batista out, and in doing so, assisting the Castro brothers in gaining power in Cuba. But there was someone else who played a very important role in delivering Cuba to Castro, and that was Dr. Milton Eisenhower, the President's brother. Dr. Eisenhower never went to Cuba and did not speak Spanish, but he was his brother's adviser on Latin American affairs, and through him Wieland and Rubottom were able to influence President Dwight D. Eisenhower's Cuban policy. And they influenced Cuban policy directly through the Secretary of State, John Foster Dulles, who stated at a press conference on November 8, 1957, "There is no Communism in Latin America."

The U.S. Government has a long history of claiming it cannot intervene – but doing exactly that, by refusing help! And over the past 100 years, Cuba is the best example of U.S. meddling, with incredible arrogant ignorance!

According to Earl E.T. Smith, U.S. Ambassador to Cuba in 1958, "we were consistently intervening in our day-to-day actions to bring about the downfall of the Batista dictatorship, and to turn the government of Cuba over to Fidel Castro." (The Fourth Floor, p. 134) In his testimony, on August 30, 1960, before the U.S. Senate Sub-Committee to Investigate the Communist Threat

Through the Caribbean, former Ambassador Smith stated: **"Without the United States, Castro would not be in power** today. I will put it as straight as that to you, sir." (In response to Sen. James O. Eastland) "Senator, we are responsible for bringing Castro in power." In the spring of 1958, some of the U.S. press (particularly Herbert Matthews of the *New York Times*) carried exaggerated and false stories depicting chaotic conditions and violence in Havana. Tourists stopped arriving and the hotels were empty.

Ambassador Smith in his book, The Fourth Floor, relates an incident of U.S. day-to-day intervening in Cuba. President Batista purchased 15 training planes from the U.S. to be used by the Cuban Air Force for training of pilots. The delivery of the paid for planes was stopped by the State Department's Fourth Floor. The refusal of delivery had a demoralizing effect on the Cuban armed forces and government officials. The U.S. Government's refusal to sell Batista any arms, while at the same time permitting clandestine shipment of arms to reach Castro in the hills, was construed by the Cubans as the U.S. backing Castro and working for Batista's defeat. An additional irony: the State Department sent a bill to the Cuban government for storage and servicing of the planes in Fort Lauderdale. The U.S. failure to deliver the 15 training planes and 20 armored cars was done because "the State Department did not want to take any action which might help the Batista government and receive the protests of the revolutionaries [Castro]." In the meantime, Raul Castro, Fidel's younger brother, began kidnapping U.S. citizens (47) in the area under his control. Next, the Castros demanded a "loan" of $500,000 from the Texaco Corporation, which the company refused to make. Cuban rebels hijacked a couple of airliners in 1958. And, the Cuban economy began to deteriorate.

General elections under Batista, postponed from June 1, were to be held November 3, 1958. And Castro, from his rebel quarters in the Sierra Maestra Mountains (where he spent a year and a half), issued on October 10, 1958, his Revolutionary Law No. Two, which called for *capital punishment for all candidates to public office*. One candidate, Anibal Vega was executed in this way. Castro ordered to shoot and machine gun the citizens that lined up at the polling places. Castro made the same threat to the

Venezuelan people in their presidential elections in 1963, when Romulo Betancourt was President, and again in 1968 when Raul Leoni was ending his presidency.

Castro Gets Cuba

Fidel Castro never won a military victory in Cuba! In 1958, terrorist activities were stepped up: in an attempt to cut the island in two, disrupt the main transportation arteries, and prevent the sugar harvest from getting to the mills. Batista left Cuba because the U.S. withdrew its support. The fact that the U.S. was no longer supporting Batista had a devastating effect upon the moral of the armed forces and the labor leaders. Roy Rubottom delivered the U.S. coup de grace on December 14, to oust Batista and bring in Castro, in instructions to U.S. Ambassador Earl E. T. Smith. The Ambassador was to advise President Batista that he no longer had the support of the United States and that he should leave Cuba. (Actually, Ambassador Smith was told in 1957, before going to Cuba, that he was assigned to Cuba to preside over the downfall of Batista – to be replaced by Castro.)

Batista was told that he should leave his own country! As Mario Lazo said in his 1968 book, Dagger in the Heart: "This interview brought about the fall of the Batista government, which Castro could never have accomplished militarily without State Department support." The publication in 2000, of The Venona Secrets: Exposing Soviet Espionage and America's Traitors (Regnery), documents the astounding Soviet penetration of the United States during the Franklin Roosevelt Administration, and Truman's disinterest in Soviet spying in the United States. The U.S. foreign service and the State Department, and amazingly even Bill Donovan's Office of Strategic Services (OSS) were penetrated by the Soviets. Thus, it is no surprise that the State Department supported Castro.

After Batista departed Cuba on January 1, 1959, it appeared that fighting might break out in Havana. Non-Fidelista students occupied the Presidential Palace. On **January 6,** Ambassador Smith was asked by the Eisenhower State Department to deliver a note of recognition to the Castro government. Castro had not even arrived in Havana to take over the government (he arrived on January 8). The United States usually withholds recognition until there is a formally established and operating government, and waits until assurances are given that the new government will honor its international obligations, has the support of the people, and will maintain law and order – and is not Communist. As a result of the State Department's undue haste, and not following normal procedures to receive assurances from Castro **before** granting recognition, the U.S. was in a weak position to protect the millions of dollars of property of U.S. citizens in Cuba.

Dictator Castro proceeded to unlawfully expropriate close to $2 billion of U.S. investments. But that hardly compares to the more than $25 billion of private property owned by Cubans that Castro confiscated by the end of 1960. In one of his violent speeches, Castro declared he would take all the property away from Americans "down to the last nails in their shoes." Cuban gasoline consumption had been dependent on the Esso and Shell refineries in Havana, and the Texaco refinery in Santiago de Cuba. These refineries had been obtaining their crude from the Venezuelan oil fields. In June 1960, Che Guevara notified the three refineries that they now would be processing Russian crude. When the oil companies contested the arbitrary order, Castro seized the refineries, valued at $140 million, and canceled the Cuban Government's $60 million debt to the companies.

Five edicts were promulgated between August 5 and October 14, 1960, confiscating all of the remaining important privately owned property, both Cuban and American. Cuba's free enterprise system was destroyed during those nine weeks: ranging from public utility services, banks, sugar mills, industrial plants of all kinds, railroads, and down to small businesses. The amount of U.S. private property and assets expropriated by the Cuban Government is the largest **uncompensated** taking of American property by any foreign government in U.S. history. The value of these properties as adjudicated and certified by the U.S. Foreign Claims Settlement Commission was $1,851,057,358. At a rate of 6% interest per annum, the present value is well over $6 billion, including interest. This property was taken under force of arms with no compensation ever paid to the 5,911 property owners. Over many years, Americans had been encouraged to, and did, invest heavily in Cuba's economy, including large industrial and financial grants.

Castro's Executions

Once Castro gained power in Cuba, in January 1959, he set about eliminating the heroes of his revolution in the Sierra Maestra Mountains, e.g. Major Pedro Diaz Lanz, and Major Huber Matos. After they entered Havana, both Majors objected to Castro's communist indoctrination and both resigned. Camilio Cienfuego, early colleague of Castro, simply disappeared, reportedly died in a plane crash.

Castro had Matos tried as an *anti-communist* and sentenced to 20 years in prison, in October 1959. The principal witness against Matos and 34 of his officers was Castro. Castro gave a 7-hour speech, which he had broadcast over radio and television, where he harangued the prisoners, calling Matos a conspirator and a coward. Huber Matos, the longest serving political prisoner in the world was finally set free in December 1979, after serving his 20-year sentence. In 1968, the President of Bolivia offered to exchange Regis Debray for Matos; and in 1976, Chile (President Pinochet) offered to trade two of their Communist prisoners for the release of Vladimir Bukovsky in Russia and Matos in Cuba. Bukovsky was traded by the Russians, but Castro would not release Matos.

Major Diaz Lanz, who was Chief of the Air Force, and had been Castro's personal pilot, resigned, defected; and reached Miami in a small boat with his wife. On July 14, 1959, Major Diaz testified, before the Senate Internal Security Subcommittee, that Castro was a willing tool of international Communism.

(Castro at age 21 had been a leader in the *Bogotazo*, the Communist uprising in April 1948, in Bogota, Colombia, on the occasion of the 9th International Conference of American States. After Colombian Liberal Party leader, Jorge Gaitan was assassinated, Castro and his comrades burned, looted, and over 1,000 people were killed in a two-day frenzy. This uprising led to the 20-year period in Colombia, known as "la Violencia," with more than 300,000 deaths; to be followed by the narco traffic violence and the guerrilleros, which only escalates each year as the drug cartel and the rebels acquire more territory in Colombia.) (See Chapter VII for more on Colombia.)

During the first two weeks of Castro's regime in 1959, more than 500 persons were condemned to death and executed [*al paredon*] under penal laws drawn up in the Sierra Maestra, in 1958. This was just the beginning of thousands of Cubans and some Americans, including Howard Anderson, commander of the American Legion Post in Cuba, who were to lose their lives; and thousands of others who were arrested and sentenced to long prison terms. It was a reign of terror in Cuba, which was to spill over to Latin America, and later to some African countries. More than twice as many people were killed in a single year in Cuba, than during the 17 years that Batista had held power.

Three months after Fidel entered Havana in January 1959, he went to the U.S. in a widely publicized visit, a trip arranged by Assistant Secretary of State for Latin America, Roy Rubottom. As he arrived in Washington, his firing squads were executing large numbers of Cubans, judged by revolutionary tribunals to be enemies of the state. Castro spoke at Harvard and Princeton, and met with the Senate Foreign Relations Committee, though few knew what he was saying. At every stop he was an immense success with celebrities. He was the figure of machismo and charisma, even pitching a few baseball innings.

Out with Religion

In Castro's first year in power, he seized all 250 Catholic schools, expelled 500 of the 700 Catholic priests and drove out all but 200 of the 3,000 Catholic nuns. It was important to get rid of religion in Cuba, a Catholic country, in Castro's effort to form the "new man." The nuns and priests had to go. Others he imprisoned and sent far from home, because it is difficult for resource-starved families to make visits. In 2000, there were still thousands of political prisoners in filthy Cuban dungeons. The world forgot about human rights violations in Cuba. The last real effort to counter human rights violations in Cuba was made by the Reagan Administration in April 1987, when the United States lost a United Nations vote to investigate Cuba. Voting against the U.S. resolution, which failed by one vote, was Venezuela.

Communism Arrives

Under the May 1959 Agrarian Reform Law, a super state was created called INRA. "The land must belong to the state – not the people," said Castro. He also made a dire prediction at an INRA meeting in the spring of 1959: "Let us see who dares to oppose us when we are confronted with a hungry population! This is something that Karl Marx never dreamed of. *Hunger will be the midwife attending the birth of a socialist state in Cuba.*" (Castro visited Chile in November 1971, when Salvador Allende was President and gave him the same advice during his 27 day "good will visit." One has to wonder if he gave the same advice to Hugo Chavez. Will the Venezuelans follow the Chilenos with the March and Banging of the Empty Pots?

During Fulgencio Batista's presidency, there were no Embassies of Communist countries in Cuba. A year after Castro took power, he signed a five-year commercial contract with the **Soviet Union**, during Anastas Mikoyan's visit to Havana. It opened up the Soviet era in the Western Hemisphere. But many in the U.S. still thought that Castro was a misguided nationalist, while the liberals were still condoning his excesses. And, the U.S. press chose to ignore, or were ignorant of, what Castro did in Venezuela shortly after taking power in January 1959.

Eisenhower Administration, on January 3, 1961, finally severed diplomatic relations with Cuba, following Castro's demands that the U.S. reduce its Embassy staff in Havana to 11. And, after the Bay of Pigs tragedy, Fidel Castro on May Day 1961, declared Cuba a "Socialist state," in which no elections would be held. In a TV speech on December 2, 1961, Castro proclaimed himself a "Marxist-Leninist," and would be so until the day of his death." According to Salvador Diaz-Verson, Cuba's Chief of Military Intelligence (1948-1952), during Dr. Carlos Prio Socarras' government, Fidel Castro became an agent of the Soviet Union in 1943, at age 17.

In February 1962, the United States imposed a total trade embargo on Cuba.

Castro's First Invasion: Venezuela

The following are facts little known in the United States about Fidel Castro in Venezuela.

Less than two weeks after Fidel Castro entered Havana, he flew to Venezuela, uninvited we thought, on the eve of Venezuela's one year anniversary of Perez Jimenez's departure (January 23, 1958). We now know Castro was invited by the radical left, the FCU, to come to Venezuela to stir up the people to revolt. (Garrido, p80) He arrived on a Friday evening and left the following Monday. His visit almost caused a revolt in Caracas. At

El Silencio, he worked up a huge cheering frenzied throng. This was the first speech I ever heard in Venezuela, where the United States was torn up into little bits and thrown to the winds. He talked on and on – for hours, and we listened via radio. The next day we listened to more of the same, as he spoke before the Venezuelan Congress, protected by his gun toting guerrillas, all, including Fidel Castro, dressed in olive khakis – speaking in a voice that was very hoarse from all of the ranting of the previous night. From Congress, he was rushed to University City (to the Aula Magna) where he continued to speak – barely audible by now, but unrelenting in his attacks on the United States and Puerto Rico, and the injustices inflicted upon the Cuban people by foreign monopolies and imperialists. He called for the uniting of all Latin America, and accused the Organization of American States of do nothingness.

Junta President, Edgar Sanabria did not stay to welcome Castro, but left Saturday morning for Quito, Ecuador, with a planeload of officials on a state visit.

Romulo Betancourt, the President-elect, was off visiting military installations, and wasn't informed that Castro was going to speak – nor would he have been there if he'd been invited. The following is taken from a taped interview, which Mr. Betancourt granted me, September 23, 1970:

"I wasn't even informed that Castro was going to speak. He left the plane and entered Caracas accompanied by the man I had defeated – Larrazabal. I was touring the country, visiting military installations. When I heard the speech from El Silencio, I was so angry, I called Caracas and cancelled an interview I was supposed to have with him on Saturday. Instead I went to spend a week-end, because I was very tired. And when I returned [to Caracas], my friends convinced me, that courtesy never is at a loss, and I had the interview. Life magazine took a picture through a window of this interview, where you see Castro gesturing and I am looking at him.

Castro tells me that between the two of us he wants to *"stir up a lot of trouble for the United States"* (hacerle una gran jugada a los gringos) and he wants Venezuela to lend him $300,000,000 to do this. Then I calmly tell him, 'Look Dr.

Castro (for I never called him Fidel) here we cannot lend you $300 million because what the dictatorship did not waste, it robbed.' So then he asked, 'Well then why don't you lend it to us in petroleum?' I said, 'To lend it to you in petroleum is the same as lending you money.' He said no more, but the truth is that he was irritated."

This was the beginning of the great hatred Fidel Castro had for Romulo Betancourt. It took root even before Betancourt assumed power (February 13, 1959) - and just after Castro took over Cuba. It is ironic that the Venezuelan people, who were to suffer greatly, as a result of Castro's terrorism unleashed upon Venezuela, had given substantial support in arms and ammunition to the Castro movement in the Sierra Maestra Mountains. (When Castro was in Venezuela, he said the Andes reminded him of the next Sierra Maestra.) Castro's sister, Emma Castro, had come to Venezuela to raise money, and had been warmly received. During 1958, Betancourt arranged for all the Cuban groups fighting Batista, to meet and sign the **Pact of Caracas**, thereby pledging close cooperation in the struggle to overthrow the Cuban dictator, Batista. The Pact also promised the establishment of a democratic government.

In other words, Venezuela had extended the hand of friendship and was repaid by violent attempts to overthrow its new democratic form of government. Venezuelans may have thought that they were helping Cubans free themselves from a dictator, in order to follow Venezuela's path to a constitutional democratic government, but after Castro's visit to thank them, they knew he was a Communist. Besides his bitter speeches, his long private conversation in his hotel bathroom with Gustavo Machado, head of Venezuela's Communist Party, removed any hopes for Cuba's future.

Shortly after his visit to Venezuela, Castro invited Jose (Pepe) Figueres of Costa Rica, to speak at a mass meeting in Havana. Figueres was not sure of the reception, for he had helped other Cuban exiles, not Castro's 26th of July Movement, and he was well aware of what Castro had said in Caracas. He was told not to speak about Puerto Rico (or Governor Luis Munoz Marin, a close friend of Figueres, and Betancourt). The Figueres speech, besides congratulating Cubans, dealt with the importance of not changing one dictatorship for another, and reminding them that Latin America must stand with the West. Castro jumped up and in a long tirade attacked the United States, the West, Figueres, Betancourt, and the other democratic leaders in Latin America, as agents of imperialism. Castro shouted that Latin America could not stay with the West.

However, the United States **still** seemed to have deaf ears. If more U.S. government officials had understood Spanish, perhaps some higher up might have gotten the message. It certainly was clear – deafeningly clear.

In the early summer of 1960, the first Soviet arms arrived in Cuba, and by the end of October, Castro boasted that he had a militia of *250,000 equipped with weapons supplied by the Communist bloc.* After OAS Foreign Ministers met in Costa Rica in August 1960, and signed a resolution condemning all subversive activities in any country in the Americas, whether by China or the Soviet Union, *Castro went after the countries that voted for this resolution, starting with Venezuela.* Castro mounted an insurrection against Betancourt's government that progressively escalated into murders of women and children on the El Encanto train in tunnel No. 10, in September 1963; murder of policemen and national guards; assaults on commercial planes; and the pirating of the Anzoategui; a campaign of exploding bombs; bank robberies; burned U.S. owned factories and warehouses; and blowing up oil pipelines and power plants.

Venezuela broke diplomatic relations with Cuba, on **November 11, 1961**. And in Punta del Este, in January 1962, the Betancourt Government presented documentary evidence to the Organization of American States, of Castro's violent attacks all over Venezuela; after which Cuba was *expelled* from the OAS. As Romulo Betancourt wrote in an article in The Reporter, in 1964: "Venezuela was a coveted prize that Castro wanted to offer his master, Nikita Khrushchev." It should not be forgotten that Venezuela was the first Latin American nation to mobilize its armed forces in October 1962, during the U.S. Missile Crisis, and sent war ships, planes, and its only submarine to take part in the U.S. blockade of Cuba.

In November 1963, the Betancourt Government brought charges, again, to the OAS against Cuba, after the discovery of four tons of foreign arms on the Venezuelan northwest coast. After an OAS investigation, which found clear evidence that the arms did come from Castro's Cuba, the OAS in July 1964, declared Cuba *guilty of aggression and intervention in Venezuelan affairs*. Severance of all diplomatic ties and suspension of trade and sea transportation were recommended. All the Inter-American States, except Mexico, took these steps by the end of 1964.

As late as May 1967, Castro was still transporting guerrillas to the coast of Venezuela. The Venezuelan government of Raul Leoni requested the OAS to convoke still another meeting of Foreign Ministers to consider Cuba's "policy of persistent intervention in their internal affairs in violation of their sovereignty, by fostering and organizing subversive and terrorist activities in the territory of various states, with the deliberate aim of destroying the principles of the Inter American System." The Foreign Ministers submitted a 92-page report "confirming all Venezuelan claims."

Castro's regime was the center for Communist activities in Latin America. From Castro, Latin American communists obtained everything, money, arms, and training in terrorist activities. "Bullets and hate" propaganda from Castro, which Cuba's officials explained as *people without hate cannot win*. In 1967, Castro claimed that he had guerrilla movements in nine Latin American countries [four of consequence: in Venezuela, Colombia, Bolivia and Guatemala]. However, with the death of Ernesto "Che" Guevara in Bolivia, in October 1967, Castro's revolutionary efforts in Latin America to create "two, three ... many Vietnams" suffered a severe blow.

Castro's support of guerrilla activities in Venezuela continued for *ten years,* until **Rafael Caldera** became president in 1969 and offered amnesty to the guerrillas. Some of these former guerrillas were in Hugo Chavez's Government and Congress, e.g. Luis Miquilena, Jose Vicente Rangel, and Ali Rodriguez, with powerful positions, and as Chavez's chief advisers. Curiously, some of these former Castro guerrillas like Teodoro Petkoff are among Chavez's most severe critics of his dictatorial power. It was also Rafael Caldera (at age 78), who, after being inaugurated for a second term as President, February 4, 1994, ordered Hugo Chavez released from prison for his February 4, 1992 rebellion. It was also Caldera, who as a Senator in February 1992, made a passionate speech examining the causes for the discontent that fueled the revolt. By thus supporting the 1992 Chavez military officers' rebellion, Caldera was on his way to win the next presidential election in December 1993, and Hugo Chavez was now set to win the following election in December 1998. Rafael Caldera is very much to blame for his own miserable government **and** the disastrous one that followed.

There are two important points to remember: Fidel Castro terrorized Venezuela because of his hatred for Romulo Betancourt and his new democratic administration, and because Betancourt was his chief rival in Latin America; and, Venezuela solved its problem with Castro **without** the help or interference of the U.S. Government. The Kennedy Administration, in reaction to Castro's revolution began the Alliance for Progress aid program for Latin America. About 120 military advisers in counter-insurgency training were sent to Venezuela, and trained Venezuelan forces to play guerrilla with five hunter battalions of about 175 men each. They lived and moved like guerrillas, never letting the rebel forces rest, and covering the entire insurgent area. The hunter battalions were aided by the campesinos, who told them where the guerrillas were hiding. This was not a U.S. bang, bang media war, as later occurred in El Salvador.

In addition to the above, hardly anyone in Venezuela did not improve their standard of living in he 1960s and 1970s. Venezuela did not develop a strong class structure in its early history because it was less important to the Spanish than Mexico, Peru or Cuba, therefore Venezuela had traditionally been a relatively mobile society. The Betancourt and Leoni governments adhered to the Constitution of 1961, and did not abuse civil rights. Finally, the guerrillas were foreign backed and could not win popular support, and the U.S. was no menace.

Dictator Fidel Castro did not only bring misery to his country, his guerrillas operated first in Venezuela, and then spread out in Latin America, winding up in Nicaragua and El Salvador. Fidel never forgot that Nicaragua was the staging area for the 1961 Bay of Pigs invasion. The Cubans united, trained and equipped the rebel Sandinistas in the field. Anastasio Somoza was overthrown in July 1979, and Fidel Castro after 20 years achieved his first triumph in Latin America. Castro now also had a strategic base to conduct operations throughout the region. Salvador was next on the list, then Guatemala and Honduras.

The Cuban revolution was made for export. Cuba became the strategic Soviet beachhead to communize Latin America and ultimately the Western Hemisphere. Castro saw himself as the one who would bring the United States down, even bringing the world to the brink of nuclear war to do this.

Exodus from Castro's Hell

The exodus from Cuba began January 1, 1959, by the Batistianos, in *planes*. They were followed by businessmen, landowners, and professional men and women: university professors, school teachers, lawyers, doctors and engineers. Toward the end of 1961, the number had reached 175,000. Later waves brought the less educated. The Cuban Refugee Emergency Center in Miami began keeping records in 1961, of Cuban refugees who managed to reach the U.S. on the sea-going flotilla. To flee Cuba, over 90 miles of sea to the United States, has been to scale Castro's "Machine Gun Alley." We do not know how many were riddled by machine gun bullets from Castro's wolf pack patrol boats or his planes, and never made it alive to Florida. Coast Guard radar often showed gunfire in the distance, and when searchers reached the spot they would find only murder – all dead, riddled with bullets. Besides Castro's bullets, the escapees battled shark attacks in the Straits of Florida. Sometimes there was only one survivor left, for they also faced a blazing sun, hunger and thirst, as they drifted in the Florida Straits. It is estimated that for every one who won freedom, three died.

The reason most of them gave for leaving Cuba: **"To save the children."** Operation Peter Pan, started under President Eisenhower, airlifted 14,048 children from Cuba to live in freedom in the United States.

Castro's control of the children was in full throttle. Through study groups and youth organizations the children were taught to spy on teachers and parents. Castro closed the schools during 1961, so they could submit large groups of youngsters to brain washing, could screen and reorient teachers, *and* write new texts.

This indoctrinated generation first took to the *boats* in the Marielito exodus of 125,000 Cubans in 1980; and in the last 20 years the people have left Cuba in *rafts*. Another irony, in 1962 it was Mariel where the Soviet armada started unloading MiG fighters and missiles, using only Russians – Cuban residents were evacuated. Furthermore, Castro <u>allowed</u> this mass exodus in 1980, in order to distract U.S. attention from military activities going on in Cuba and throughout the Caribbean. Some of the Russian combat brigade of 20,000 men in Cuba were building nuclear weapons facilities on the southern coast of Cuba, along with construction at the submarine base at Cienfuegos. And, Castro, in the 1980 Marielito exodus, emptied some of his jails and mental asylums.

By 1965, Castro had deep problems from internal dissatisfaction. Air travel between Cuba and the U.S. was cut off after the Missile Crisis in 1962, and only a handful could get out each week. Castro was holding between 60,000 and 90,000 prisoners; and 3,000 U.S. citizens and their families were being held in Cuba in violation of all standards of international conduct. Castro, on September 28, 1965, in an angry speech said "all of those who wish may leave." President Lyndon Johnson then went to New York and to the Statue of Liberty and signed into law an Amendment to the Immigration Act, whereby the U.S. could accept Castro's offer to let Cubans come to this country. Castro immediately reneged on his offer, and over 30,000 Cubans who applied to leave wound up in concentration camps and Castro had his slave labor on state farms. However, President Johnson's airlift, between Cuba and Miami, which cost the U.S. taxpayer $52 million in 1965, brought out 243,664 Cuban refugees to the United States by 1971. The *Economist* magazine, in 1971, wrote that the Cuban revolution "has been shedding admirers like autumn leaves." You could say the same about Hugo Chavez in 2000 and 2001.

Cuba under Castro in the 1970s had proportionally the largest number of *political prisoners in the world*! It also has one of the highest proportions of exiles—some **2 million!**

Cuban Adjustment Act of 1966

The Cuban Adjustment Act of 1966 provided Cubans who fled Castro's regime an opportunity to apply for permanent

States. The 1966 Act only provided a procedure for seeking permanent residency, not an entitlement to it. The 1976 Amendment to the 1966 Act, had to do with "not requiring the Secretary of State to reduce the number of visas authorized to be issued in any class in the case of any alien who is physically present in the United States on or before [January 1, 1977]." This was important because beginning in 1968, an <u>overall annual quota</u> on Western Hemisphere immigration of 120,000 became effective. The Cuban refugees were not to disadvantage immigration from other Western Hemisphere countries.

The Refugee Act of 1980 amended the 1966 Act to reduce the presence requirements for adjustment from two years to one year.

Unfortunately, the Clinton Administration in 1994 changed the long standing immigration policy of admitting Cubans who reached our shore, and Clinton adopted the shameful *"wet foot-dry foot policy,"* the **Clinton- Castro Agreement**. On **September 9, 1994**, the U.S. Government <u>and</u> Cuba after concluding talks in New York, announced that "migrants rescued at *sea* attempting to enter the United States will not be permitted to enter the United States, but instead will be taken to safe haven facilities outside the United States." Furthermore, "Cuba will take effective measures in every way it possibly can to prevent unsafe departures using mainly *persuasive methods.*" And, "The United States ensures that total legal migration to the United States from Cuba will be a minimum of 20,000 Cubans each year." The use of the word "minimum" is exceedingly strange. What is clear is that the quota was a <u>maximum,</u> not a minimum.

The Clinton White House on May 2, 1995, released a press statement to "build upon the September 9, 1994 *agreement.*" They tried to address the 26,000 Cuban refugees at the U.S. Naval facility at Guantanamo Bay, Cuba, which Attorney General Janet Reno said would have to return to Cuba in order to be processed for entry into the United States.

More than 32,000 fled the island in 1994, most of them in August. Without the Soviet Union's huge annual subsidies, the Cuban economy was even worse off. With the flight of Cubans, Fidel Castro gets rid of some of the discontents, and he also has less mouths to feed, as Cuba's food shortage escalates. Ironically, the **Clinton-Castro Agreement**, creates an *Iron Curtain* in the Caribbean so Castro can punish his <u>gusanos</u> in peace, and is a partner and agent of the United States. This Agreement clearly violates international law, because it asks Castro to repress the right to freely leave Cuba.

The previous Cuban Adjustment Act of 1966 and the 1976 Amendment, and the Refugee Act of 1980, were laws passed by Congress; however, the Clinton-Castro Agreement was an Executive Order. But Congress has not reversed Clinton's "wet foot-dry foot" test, and thousands of Cubans that were picked up by the Coast Guard before they stepped on U.S. soil were returned to Cuba. It was thus that little Elian Gonzalez after being saved by the dolphins in his inner tube, and found on Thanksgiving Day 1999, off the coast of Florida by two men fishing, who then turned him over to the Coast Guard, was sent back to Cuba, in June 2000. Easter Holy Week, U.S. Attorney General, Janet Reno made the decision to take the law as well as the child into her own hands, when she ordered the Immigration and Naturalization Service (INS) to kidnap Elian from his home in Little Havana, Miami. "Her decision strikes at the heart of constitutional government and shakes the safeguards of liberty," wrote Prof. Lawrence H. Tribe of Harvard (op-ed in *New York Times*, April 25, 2000).

Under the Clinton-Castro Agreement, Cubans fleeing Cuba have to be on guard against Castro's patrol boats <u>and</u> the U.S. Coast Guard! One of the most curious statements made by Janet Reno in her May 2, 1995 White House press briefing on Cuban refugee status, was:

"Cuban migrants intercepted at sea, attempting to enter the United States or who enter Guantanamo illegally will be taken to Cuba where U.S. consular officers will assist those who apply to come to the United States through already-established mechanisms. *Cubans must know that the only way to come to the United States is by applying in Cuba.*"

This statement raises serious moral questions. Did the Attorney General of the Clinton Administration not know that no one can leave Cuba without Castro's permission? Why did hundreds of thousands flee Cuba in the dead of the night on small boats and rafts, risking shark infested waters to reach freedom?

Why have two million Cubans fled this island utopia? Why does Castro bar his people from leaving his paradise?

Of course, the Clinton-Castro Agreement did not work. In August 2000, the Clinton Administration, i.e., Secretary of State Madeleine Albright (8/28/00) accused the government of Cuba of "increasingly obstructing the safe legal and orderly migration of individuals from Cuba." Thus, Cubans denied the exit permits continue to take to unseaworthy boats, resulting in an unknown number of deaths. The U.S. Interests Section in Havana issues visas for family reunification, and for applicants who can demonstrate a well founded fear of persecution. And, a lottery is used for the remaining 20,000 who can legally leave for the United States, each year. However, they still need an exit permit from the Castro regime to leave Cuba, and for this Castro charges around $600, when the average salary in Cuba is about $10 a month. Fidel's interest in family reunification ended with his campaign to get Elian Gonzalez back.

The Cuban exodus to the United States, since 1959, has been an astounding economic and democratic success for both the Cubans and their adopted country. Their arrival in Miami has turned the city into a thriving international center. Cuban Americans have greater economic security than any other Latin American group. There were 1.37 million Cuban Americans in the U.S. in 1999, according to the U.S. Census Bureau. They live primarily in Florida, as well as New Jersey, New York, California, and Texas, and in every state in the Union.

In 1898, at the time of Cuban Independence, 30% of Florida's population were Cubans, mostly employed in the cigar industry. In the nineteenth century, Cubans in an effort to get away from the Spaniards went to Tampa. In 1886, the Cubans established the cigar industry in Tampa. At Ibor City (part of Tampa), Ignacio Haya built factory No.1; the railroad arrived, and with it the Cuban cigars got access to New York and Europe. There were more Cuban cigars rolled in Tampa than in Cuba once machines transformed the cigar industry, and the "5 cent cigar" was born. In the 1950s, Cuba's second export was tobacco, the best in the world for cigars, and furnished about 7% of Cuba's export revenue.

The Floridas – Captaincy-General of Cuba

Lest we forget, Florida was once Spanish domain just as Cuba was. The peace Treaty of Madrid in <u>1670,</u> between Spain and England, established the boundary in the Floridas (West and East) to the Mississippi River, and north to Savannah. It recognized England's right to retain full sovereignty over as much land as it occupied at that time. Florida's boundaries from that time on became a serious problem. The Spanish, by the beginning of the eighteenth century, had established missions and small forts and were exerting a fair degree of administrative control over the provinces of Santa Elena, now in South Carolina.

President James Madison plotted to wrest the territory of Florida from Spain, in 1811. Madison attempted to instigate a popular uprising against the Spanish. When President Thomas Jefferson had authorized negotiation for the purchase of New Orleans from France, and Napoleon indicated he would sell all of Louisiana in 1803, Jefferson's secretary of state, James Madison made sure the eastern boundaries of the eastern territory were left unclear. Their purpose was to create a claim to Florida. *The Floridas were governed by the Captaincy-General of Cuba.* Both West Florida and East Florida were outposts of the Spanish Empire, an empire that was breaking up in the New World. The first stirrings of patriotic rebellion against Spanish authority would break out in 1810.

Spain did not have troops to defend West and East Florida. Furthermore, there was a great war in Europe, which the United States got involved in, declaring war on Britain, in June 1812. Britain was Spain's ally against France. Seizing Florida was a necessary defense measure once war with Britain was underway. However, it was John Quincy Adams who arranged to get Florida in the Treaty with Spain, in <u>1819</u>. (Article VI of the Treaty: "The inhabitants of the territories which His Catholic Majesty cedes to the United States, by this treaty, shall be incorporated in the Union of the United States, as soon as may be consistent with the principles of the Federal Constitution, and admitted to the enjoyment of all the privileges, rights, and immunities of the citizens of the United States.") The Spanish subjects of Florida became U.S. citizens when the U.S. Army legitimately occupied the territory in 1821, and by 1845, Florida was a state.

In other words, Florida and Cuba were once both governed by Spain, under the Captaincy-General of Cuba. Two hundred years ago it was a Cuban regiment that was sent to Florida to protect His Catholic Majesty's lands.

The Trade Embargo

The ban on U.S. trade with Cuba was imposed in several stages, beginning with an arms and ammunition embargo in 1958, when Batista was president. In October 1960, the embargo was extended to all goods except non-subsidized foodstuffs, medicines and medical supplies. Later, these goods required export licenses. In 1960, sugar imports, Cuba's main export, were banned. This was followed by a ban on all imports from Cuba in early 1962.

In order to steady the Cuban economy, dependent on sugar exports, the U.S. in 1934, had established quota arrangements under the Jones Costigan Act, whereby one-third of U.S. sugar imports came from Cuba. Until June 1960, when Cuba lost its U.S. market, the U.S. had paid $150 million a year more for Cuban sugar than Cuba could get elsewhere, i.e., in the world market.

In 1959, Cuba's quota far exceeded present total U.S. quota imports by 3-to-1; Cuba's sugar quota was 3 million out of U.S. total of 4 million metric tons. In 2000, total U.S. sugar quota allocation was only 1.1 million metric tons. The source of the United States' largest sugar imports is now the Dominican Republic. However, that is changing over time to Mexico, which under NAFTA will have unlimited sugar exports to the United States by 2007-08. Mexico has replaced Cuba in sugar production with 5.4 million tons in 1998, to Cuba's 2 million tons. (Brazil is one of the largest exporters of sugar.) Curiously, Mexico has also replaced Venezuela in terms of petroleum production and their export to the United States.

The U.S. embargo saved millions for the U.S. taxpayer. Castro's Western creditors (Canadian, French and Spanish) in 2001, were attempting to recover loans amounting to over $10 billion. There are no U.S. banks in the Paris Club, a consortium of Cuba creditors, which means U.S. banks and Congress will not be hitting U.S. taxpayers to cover their losses in Castro's Cuba.

Spain and Canada have been the two primary free world countries trading with Cuba. Neither were members of the OAS. Under the regulations of the U.S. embargo, U.S. citizens were not permitted to travel to Cuba for pleasure. Family visits and licensed travel for academics, some business and journalism purposes were allowed.

The Foreign Ministers of the Organization of American States applied a trade embargo on Cuba on July 26, 1964, after Venezuela brought charges against Cuba. And, the U.S. Maritime Administration had placed a blacklist of all ships that visited Cuban ports. The Cuban Democracy Act of 1992 bars foreign ships trading with Cuba, or vacation cruise lines that stop in Cuba, from docking at U.S. ports for a period of six months. The law expanded the total U.S. embargo on trade with Cuba to foreign subsidiaries of U.S. companies.

Cuba's trade with the U.S. was replaced by trade and enormous subsidies from the Soviet Union, and trade with China. For 33 years, the Soviets propped up Castro's brutal dictatorship. Boris Yeltsin's new Russian government announced that the Soviet Union's $6 billion a year package would end, in January 1992. However, in 1997, Moscow reported an increase in Russia's oil-for-sugar swap, to 9.75 million metric tons of oil for 3.25 million metric tons of raw sugar – a ratio of 3 to 1/oil-for-sugar. This amounted to nearly $500 million of a subsidy for Cuba per year. The deal did not cover Cuba's crude oil needs. Enter Venezuela and Hugo Chavez.

Cuba merely exchanged dependence on the U.S. for dependence on the Soviet Union. This dependence on countries several thousand miles away created a monstrosity, economically. The Soviets produced more sugar than Cuba did, and did not need its chief export. Then there was the breakdown of U.S. equipment, which put Cuba in a perennial crisis in spare parts. Serious shortages began to appear in early 1961. Cuba used to export meat, now it was unobtainable for Cubans. Even sugar production had dropped, due to general mismanagement, allocation of funds to industrialization, and the resistance of the campesinos to state control.

In 2000, the U.S. Congress continued to be concerned about the Russian intelligence complex near Havana, i.e., the *Lourdes* operation (SIGINT), calling for its abandonment. Congress' opposition to Russia's operating an intelligence facility in Lourdes, Cuba, spying on U.S. citizens and companies was put in a House bill prohibiting President Clinton from rescheduling Russia's Soviet era debt. "If we are to have a new relationship with Russia, and if the Russian Government seeks the support of our nation such as debt relief, then it's time they heard from our government . . . This is about espionage," said House International Committee Chairman Ben Gilman (R-NY).

1996 Helms-Burton Act—LIBERTAD

The Helms Burton Act, which is the Cuban Liberty and Democratic Solidarity (LIBERTAD) Act of 1996, passed Congress by overwhelming vote, after Cuban MiGs shot down two unarmed Cessnas, killing 4 Cuban Americans, on February 24, 1996. The Act of 1996 had two key objectives. First, to expedite the demise of the Castro regime by drying up his new source of hard currency. The second objective was to determine who was trafficking in Cuban confiscated property, and stop them by providing claimants a civil remedy whereby traffickers are liable for damages, if they continue to traffic in confiscated property. President Clinton, however, ordered one 6-month suspension after another (10 in all, the last one just before leaving office) of this provision, of protection of property rights under Title III, of the Helms-Burton Act. These 6-month suspensions have resulted from European objections to the law's infringement on their rights to profit from the use of stolen property.

The *Wall Street Journal* in an editorial, on January 8, 1997, put a question to the Europeans, "Do its leaders believe that its OK for little dictators to steal property? Or is it OK only if the property belongs to Americans?" And, Paul Greenberg in his syndicated column on January 11, 1997, seemed to answer the question: "*Because there's money to be made by trading with regimes that oppress their own people.*" "Never mind that none of our allies has joined the American embargo against Cuba, and that all seem determined to trade with the tyrant, even in stolen property." Ironically, Castro claimed in 1993 that he had settled claims made by Spanish, Canadian, Swiss, English and French firms. Castro said he would settle with the U.S. **if** the U.S. would pay him economic costs of the U.S. embargo against Cuba, which he estimated at $40 billion.

This ruse by Castro indicates that the U.S. embargo has been effective, certainly in the post-Soviet ($18 million/day subsidy) era. The principal motivation for the Helms-Burton Act was U.S. concern over Castro's new financial reliance, on *foreign joint ventures with Cuban state companies*, many of which operate on stolen U.S. properties. Known as <u>empresas mixtas</u> (joint enterprises) they are not subject to minimum wage, environmental, anti-discrimination, antitrust or capital repatriation laws. Castro wants partners to support his communism, not to replace it!

The confiscation of private property in Cuba became a burning issue, again in 1993, with Castro's desperate attempts to attract foreign investment. The first to be heard from was the Bacardi Corp., the rum giant whose first distillery was confiscated by Castro in 1960, as well as three breweries. Castro was searching for joint venture partners for the rum business. Bacardi sent out letters to major brewers, distillers and trade associations around the world, as well as embassies from foreign countries, alerting investors that Bacardi considered its properties were stolen, and would take legal action if necessary.

Castro started the process of trying to peddle his stolen property with a list of 131 properties, that Cuban officials circulated at a "Conference of Foreign Investment in Cuba," held in Cancun, Mexico; and in Havana, in July 1993. The Cuban list of confiscated properties included:

Boise Cascade,	Certified Claim for:		$279.3 million
ITT	"	"	$130.7 million
Borden	"	"	$97.4 million
United Brands	"	"	$85.1 million
Amstar	"	"	$81.0 million
Exxon	"	"	71.6 million
Texaco	"	"	$50.1 million
Freeport Minerals	"	"	$33.0 million
Coca Cola	"	"	$27.5 million
Lone Star Industries	"	"	$24.9 million
Colgate-Palmolive	"	"	$14.5 million
Atlantic Richfield	"	"	$10.2 million

(Source: U.S. Foreign Claims Settlement Commission)

Castro and His Destruction of a Pearl

And why did Fidel Castro show up in Venezuela two weeks after entering Havana? I learned from Romulo Betancourt that

Castro wanted $300 million to combat the Gringos, but he also went to Venezuela to elevate his stature from a national to an international figure. Cuba was too small for Castro. He saw himself as the leader of the Latin American nations, against the United States! And where did this hatred of the U.S. come from?

Jean-Francois Revel, well known French author, once explained that the leftist revolutionary *myth* in Latin America always came with a corollary, i.e., the United States is the enemy, responsible for the poverty and backwardness of the republics south of the Rio Grande. The United States as a scapegoat for all their frustrations has been a cover for their feelings of inferiority.

Cuba gained her independence from Spain, finally, after the U.S. sent in troops. Cuba reaped rich rewards through its association with the United States. Cuba ranked among the most advanced countries in the Spanish speaking world. The Cuban sugar industry was a highly-mechanized operation, utilizing one of the three best developed railway networks in Latin America and up-to-date highways and ports. Cuba was second in gold reserves and foreign trade per capita. Over two-thirds of the population could read and write, and Cuba ranked 3rd in the number of physicians. The island had the largest number of television stations and receiving sets in Latin America, which were of enormous help to Castro in his non-stop speeches to the people. U.S. citizens, capital, and know how were at least partly responsible for this high standard of living. It would seem that Cuba had a revolution **because** there was a measure of economic development.

It certainly was not the poor country it is today, after over 40 years of Fidel Castro's totalitarian government. In Cuba, while most are now very poor, in 1958, Cuba had a wealthy class, and a middle class that probably were the most frustrated, because Cubans compared themselves with the U.S., and not with the rest of Latin America. This created intense nationalism, and the Wall Street dragon was blamed invariably for the island's difficulties. Cuba's almost total dependence on the United States had beneficial as well as negative repercussions. Cuban society was weak and dependent, children of American tutelage, as much as of past Spanish rule. Castro succeeded in removing Cuba from the U.S. sphere of influence in the Western Hemisphere.

In 1958, Cuba was emerging from a one-or two crop economy, to become an industrial state, ranked fifth in Latin America, after Brazil, Argentina, Mexico, and Chile. Under Batista, Cuba had everything except liberty. Cuba ranked third in per capita income, at $353 (or 353 pesos) per person among Latin American nations, behind Argentina and Venezuela. Today, after receiving over $75 billion in Soviet economic and military aid, between 1959 and 1991, Cuba ranks only above North Korea, as the most repressed , centralized, and government planned economy in the world. The annual Index of Economic Freedom, published by the Heritage Foundation and the *Wall Street Journal* each year, gives Cuba this ranking, as "rife with corruption and graft." Cuba outlaws foreign ownership of private property, and there is no recourse to enforce property rights, contractual obligations, or the rule of law. Castro's ruinous economic policies and his destruction of the free market, along with the emigration of Cuba's educated, entrepreneurial class to the United States, account for the dramatic change in Cuba, since 1958.

Fall of the Soviet Union

With the fall of the Soviet Union in 1991, the scaling down of Soviet and Eastern bloc economic assistance shrank Cuba's GNP a further 20% by 1992. Cuba's sugar for oil trade agreement with the Soviets was scaled back. The end of aid and the energy shortage caused enormous problems for Castro, e.g. rationing of gasoline and diesel fuel, and LPG for cooking, reduced electrical power generation with frequent blackouts, factories closed, etc. etc.. Castro was now increasingly shunned by his Latin American neighbors, i.e., until Hugo Chavez came to power in Venezuela, in 1999, and came to his aid.

After the fall of the Soviet Union, Cuba began to suffer its worst economic crisis in 30 years. In the first half of 1991, Russian trade with Cuba fell about 25%. In October 1991, the three presidents of Colombia, Mexico (Salinas) and Venezuela (Perez) met with Castro at Cozumel, Mexico, and told him they could do little to help him, nor could they provide oil at a subsidized price to replace Russian oil. In May 1992, Cuba was in desperate straits, trying to survive on one/third of the energy supplies it had three years before. Entire neighborhoods were dark at night, theaters closed, and workers transferred closer to their jobs. Bicycles replaced cars for transportation. Castro lost not only Russian oil supplies, but replacement parts for weapons and military equipment. There was not enough fuel for aircraft military or civilian needs.

In July 1992, Fidel Castro had a disastrous trip to Spain for the Ibero-American Summit, where he was mocked in the Spanish press and made fun of from his concern for his security to his human-rights record. His host, Spanish Prime Minister Felipe Gonzales, underscored his alienation from Castro by meeting for two hours with Cuban exiles, the day after Castro returned to Cuba.

The Cuban crisis, after the end of Soviet aid in the early 1990s, brought back into focus the U.S. trade embargo. The embargo not only forced Castro to cut government spending, but also to curtail his support for Third World Communist revolutionaries and terrorist groups. For the rest of the Hemisphere, and Africa this was great news – no more Cuban guerrillas. Thousands of Cuban soldiers died in Castro's African and Latin American adventures, while draining Cuba's coffers, and increased popular dissent. Castro's involvement in the drug smuggling business to earn hard currency, had a second purpose, i.e., to impose more social and law enforcement costs on the United States.

Vladimir Putin, President of Russia, made his first trip to Cuba, December 13-17, 2000. President Putin and Castro toured Lourdes, the primary source of Russia's strategic intelligence gathering aimed at the United States. The leaders signed a number of agreements, a $50 million line of credit, a draft protocol agreement for 2001-2005, and cooperation agreements. Russia will deliver to Cuba between 1.5 to 2 million metric tons of crude oil, between 100,000 to 150,000 metric tons of agricultural chemicals, as well as equipment and parts for the sugar industry. Cuba in 2000 had fewer than 100 mills reported grinding sugar cane, thus raw sugar production declined even further. This would make it difficult for Cuba to deliver to Russia between 2.2 to 2.8 million metric tons of raw sugar, as part of the new trade protocol, without the new equipment for the sugar industry.

The Deceit of Castro

It should not be forgotten that when Fidel Castro gained power in January 1959, 90% of the Cubans were "Fidelistas," or were for Fidel. The motto of the new government was "<u>Pronto,</u>" hurry up. Why the hurry? Castro expected U.S. intervention. At the Havana Rotary Club on January 22, 1959, Castro in a speech stated:

"If the marines should land in Cuba, we would kill 200,000 before they could take the Island, and they would find dust and ashes, because we would burn everything."

But the Cuban revolution was against Batista, not the United States. Ah, then what was Castro thinking about when he made this speech to a shocked group of Cuban Rotarians? It must have been about Guatemala in 1954, when the U.S. helped the patriots overthrow the Communist infiltrated government of Arbenz Guzman.

Why didn't the United States and the OAS intervene, as they had the right to, under the Rio Treaty and the Declaration of Caracas? Thousands of lives would have been saved by an early intervention, not only in Cuba, but in the rest of Latin America and Africa. Even as late as April 1961, if the Kennedy Administration had supported the Cubans at the Bay of Pigs, history would have been so different. It was a **watershed** event in U.S. history, not to mention Cuba's. As a result of a U.S. President's ignorance (Eisenhower), and another President's weakness (Kennedy), Cuba became a huge arsenal, as Russia incorporated Cuba into the Soviet bloc, and Castro got a tremendous boast in Latin America for his plans to spread his revolution. Furthermore, if we couldn't help the Cubans who are on our doorstep, how was the United States going to save the Vietnamese who are across the Pacific Ocean? Or any other people? President Johnson and President Reagan did hold up U.S. honour, and President Bush did unite our allies to save Kuwait, but did not finish the job in Iraq. Then there is the Clinton Administration's foreign policy, about which there is nothing honorable or admirable.

The tragedy of Cuba was the deceit of Castro, who came to power in the name of a democratic revolution and used his new power to impose a totalitarian government. The Cubans wanted the kind of revolution that Castro had been talking about since his

July 26, 1953 Movement. They objected to the kind he introduced and as a result Castro had to rely on force to stay in power. Castro began to speak over the radio and television daily for four, five, six hours. The legislature was dissolved and the courts were purged of judges who had supported Batista. A new Fundamental Law of the Revolutionary Government was promulgated on February 7, 1959 (a month after Castro marched into Havana) to take the place of the 1940 Constitution. The death penalty, banned in the 1940 Constitution, was reintroduced. The show trials commenced, and the condemned were imprisoned or shot – *al paredon*! The Cuban Communists took over offices in all parts of the country, and they yelled *"Viva Fidel"* at every opportunity.

Does any of this sound familiar to Venezuelans now living in Chavezuela, or Chavezlandia?

Instead of "the sea of happiness" as Chavez calls Cuba, it is "a prison surrounded by water," as Juana Castro, Fidel's sister, called it in 1964.

Why have so many fled Cuba, not only to the United States, but to Mexico, Argentina, and Venezuela? The Clinton Administration's September 9, 1994 Agreement with Castro, i.e., "Cuban migrants intercepted at sea ... attempting to enter the United States will be taken to Cuba," forced some freedom seeking Cubans to seek asylum elsewhere. In June 1997, the Venezuelan Foreign Ministry reported that over 100,000 Cubans had arrived in Venezuela, mainly illegally, in the previous three years. Cubans for decades immigrated to Venezuela. The most famous are the Gustavo Cisnero family, which have a media conglomerate, and according to *Forbes* magazine's "The World's Working Rich" 1999 issue, the Cisneros are worth $2 billion. Since the father, Diego Cisnero, arrived in Venezuela in the 1930s, the Cisnero Group has become one of Latin America's largest conglomerates. In March 2000, the Cisnero Group indicated it would relocate its business headquarters to Miami. Insecurity in Venezuela was to blame for the move.

First the Cubans, Now the Venezuelans

It would now seem the turn of the Venezuelans to start flooding Florida. In 1997, the number of people leaving Venezuela began to climb. Again, like Cuba, it was the educated and well-to-do, who were the first to leave. The first wave was the young educated, who could not find jobs in a declining economy under the Rafael Caldera Government. But it was also rising crime, soaring inflation and inefficient public services, and the anticipated election of Hugo Chavez that drove many, particularly the middle class (what was left of it) to leave Venezuela. Sammy Eppel in an article in *El Universal* (7 September 2000), suggested that like the Cuban exiles who are the main source of funds for Cuba, Venezuelans in exile may be doing the same thing for Venezuela in 20 years. "There are already more than 500,000 men and women from the land of Bolivar that have left, and around 250,000 of these are in the land of Uncle Sam . . . " In 2000, one of the few businesses making money in Venezuela were moving companies – packing up over 500 families a month, whose destinations were Florida, Canada and Europe. There was an added urgency now for the children – the new military classes in all the high schools, started in the Fall 2000; and Chavez's Decree 1011 on education.

Cuba has known 450 years of dictatorship and only eight years of constitutional government (Grau San Martin, and Carlos Prio Socarras, both of the <u>Autentico</u> party). The Cubans have had only <u>8 years of democratic government</u> in their long history. Venezuela has been somewhat more fortunate than Cuba. It achieved its own independence through its native son, Simon Bolivar, but not until the twentieth century did it gain more benign presidential rule, and several good presidents like General Lopez Contreras, General Medina Angarita; and Romulo Betancourt, the first constitutionally elected president in 1958. Today, Venezuela has a constitutionally elected dictator, Hugo Chavez.

Cuba has had two main export products, sugar and tobacco, which the world can get along without, as neither is considered good for human health. Venezuela, on the other hand, has an export product, petroleum, and in vast reserves, that the world currently needs. One cannot say whether this will be the case in the distant future, because energy needs have changed over history, e.g. from whale oil, to coal, to petroleum and nuclear. What will it be in the future? Thus, a country should sell a product while there is a demand for it, because if a substitute is found, your product loses its value.

Reading between the lines, Venezuelans will read so many comparisons of Hugo Chavez to Fidel Castro, in the preceding pages. A great irony in comparing Hugo Chavez to Fidel Castro is found in a quote from Theodore Draper:

"Fidel Castro – as much demagogue as idealist, as much adventurer as revolutionary, as much anarchist as Communist, or anything else – was suddenly catapulted into power without a real party, a real army, or a real program."

But in Hugo Chavez's case, he had Castro to guide him **and** Castro's road map. Their first focus was anti-Americanism. Indignities and insults heaped upon the United States. Next, the arrests and executions: in Cuba in the first week alone, Raul Castro had 250 people executed in Santiago de Cuba. (At this time of writing, there are no apparent executions in Venezuela, however, there are many deaths from violence.) And of course, **lie!** The truth will be buried. Curiously, this is not so easy in Venezuela where many have computers in their homes and readily use the Internet. Some 500,000 people are connected to the Internet in Venezuela. (Of course, Chavez will take care of this in his *Ley sobre Mensajes, Datos y Firmas Electronicas.)* The Cubans descended into poverty before the computer age and have little money to buy computers. Internet connections are prohibited without government permission, and in 2000, only about 40,000 officials, businesses and foreigners were authorized to link up, according to a *Washington Post* article (12/26/00).

CHAPTER VI

CHAVEZ: CUBA and CHINA

"Among a *people generally corrupt, liberty cannot long exist."* Edmund Burke, 1777.

"It is necessary only for the good man to do nothing, for evil to triumph," attributed to Burke.

Venezuela in one year, 1999, moved from a country in crisis to a country in chaos. As a director at the Central University of Venezuela put it, "all the Venezuelans are damaged" (damnificados). There seemed no way to stop the Chavez takeover train because the opposition was incompetent and could not prevent Venezuela's new totalitarian gaining complete control. Chavez wrote the new Constitution; Chavez fired the Congress; Chavez removed the Judges of the Supreme Court, and appointed a new Comptroller General and Public Prosecutor.

It is logical to remember the past, how Fidel Castro took over Cuba, as we study and contemplate Chavez' new Venezuela.

How very opportune for Cuba, the election of Hugo Chavez in Venezuela, not only on December 6, 1998, but again on July 30, 2000. With the election of Vicente Fox of the PAN party as President of Mexico on July 2, 2000, Cuba probably lost its strongest ally in Latin America. Castro had always counted on Mexican support when the PRI party was in power (for 71 years). Venezuela now becomes Cuba's strongest ally in the Western Hemisphere, and its biggest hope in the future.

"Chavez can help us a lot, particularly with petroleum." (Chavez nos puede ayudar mucho, sobre todo en el tema de petroleo.) "He's a great friend of Cuba." This said in Cuba by people in the street, after the July 30, 2000 election of Chavez to a 6-year presidential term.

However, how much help can Chavez be to Castro, if Venezuela is isolated? Chavez takes every possible opportunity to attack the United States, which is Venezuela's principal market for its oil exports, and the main source of its imports; and Venezuela

148

has a $50 billion external debt, mainly to the United States. If Venezuela lost its U.S. market, and decided not to repay it huge debt, it would soon have an economy that mirrored Cuba's. In an article, in *El Universal*, "Cuba, China y otras…" (29-7-00), Linares Benzo wrote, "we cannot relegate our luck to become a petroleum Haiti." But how can Venezuela avoid this fate, when Chavez reiterates over and over, that "Venezuela is sailing in the same sea of happiness that Cuba navigates." A few Venezuelans thought that Chavez was just blah, blah, blah, and, therefore, not as dangerous as many believe. Perhaps the sum of the man is found in his following statement: *"The revolution is like a building. It requires a lot of material, but the one element that is essential is blood. Lamentably, that is true."* It was Fidel Castro who gave Chavez the advise that worked so well: Get dressed as a democrat before the real revolution. Chavez was fond of saying that he was not a Communist. But he talked like a Communist, and acted like a Communist!

Chavez has already saved Fidel with the greatest gift – petroleum! Venezuelans consider this one of the most corrupt acts by the "megabanda Chavista 5th Republic": the gift of $10 billion of oil to Cuba under the Caracas Energy Accord. There is a new book on this subject, by Leonardo Montiel Ortega, called <u>Analisis de una Estafa Petrolera Anunciada</u>. An obvious reason that Chavez has not nationalized Venezuela's resources the way that Castro did in Cuba is that Chavez already has possession. Petroleum represents 70% of GNP.

Betancourt and Chavez

For someone who spent her childhood in Venezuela, and adult life studying Venezuela, its history, government and oil industry, I cannot help but compare Romulo Betancourt to Hugo Chavez. (I wrote my Ph.D. dissertation on Betancourt's two governments.) First, Betancourt's rhetoric was remarkably erudite, Chavez's is in the gutter. Betancourt's young revolutionary passion evolved into a dedicated democrat, bent upon helping his people and the rest of Latin America, as well. Chavez is still a revolutionary, without a clue of how to govern. Betancourt, as a student organized the university students in Caracas against the dictatorship of Juan Vicente Gomez. Chavez led a group of military forces against the government of a duly elected president, Carlos Andres Perez, in 1992. Betancourt joined the Communist party in exile, in Costa Rica, but left it before returning to Venezuela in 1936, after Gomez's death. Chavez is a declared friend of Fidel Castro, and a declared Maoist – both Communists.

Betancourt became active organizing labor, the students, and the <u>campesinos</u>, into what became the <u>Accion Democratica</u> (AD) party, in 1941. Chavez is his own party, and his most hated opponent is Betancourt's AD party, which he rails against as "corrupt cliques," or "vipers." There was no doubt that this party and the Christian Democrats (COPEI) party, the two main political parties, had become corrupt and all-powerful in Venezuela. However, Chavez's attacks were strongest against the "adecos" (AD), perhaps because Rafael Caldera, founder of COPEI, had ordered his release from jail when he became President in 1994.

Betancourt was Junta President after the overthrow of the Medina government in 1945, however, he turned over the presidency in 1948, to his former teacher, Romulo Gallegos, following Venezuela's first general election. In November 1948, after the overthrow of the Gallegos Government, Betancourt went into exile a second time, for ten years. Chavez has never been forced into exile, which can be a humiliating and learning experience. After Betancourt's popular election, and inauguration in 1959, he started a new era in Venezuela's history. In order to better utilize Venezuela's oil royalties, he promoted economic diversification through industrialization, and the Agrarian Reform. A singular achievement during the Betancourt regime was the inauguration of the Lake Maracaibo Bridge, on August 24, 1962. This bridge was not only significant for the development of the State of Zulia, but for Venezuela. His greatest contribution was in fostering a middle class, which would stabilize democracy in Venezuela. And, his greatest moment in history came on March 11, 1964, when he turned over the Venezuelan government to freely elected Raul Leoni, thereby actualizing Simon Bolivar's dream of a strong democratic Venezuela.

As for Chavez, for the first time in memory, the Venezuelan economy **shrank over 7%** in 1999, his first year in power, and $8 billion left the country in capital flight. By August 1999, six months after taking office, 500,000 had lost their jobs.

Over 20% of the workforce were unemployed, and 50% were in the underground – off the books economy. And the middle class, what was left of it, left for Miami, were planning to leave for Miami, **or** are now in the poor class.

The number of small and medium businesses, 3,000, that went bankrupt in 1999, tells the story of what happened to the middle class. In 1999, some 600 medium and small petroleum-related businesses shut down, according to Hugo Hernandez, president of the Venezuelan Petroleum Chamber. With so many businesses closed (a quarter of the small businesses, in year ending June 30, 2000, according to Fedeindustrias) and so many out of work, the number of street vendors (buhoneros) has grown to thousands. In Caracas, the smog-choked streets are clogged with armies of peddlers. The Venezuelan middle class population is decreasing in two ways: by those who are leaving, and by those who are killed daily (21) in the streets or in their own homes as they are being robbed.

Chavez has impoverished Venezuela with his poor management and threatening policies. Public expenses rose 47%, and government debt rose $15 billion, according to economist Orlando Ochoa, (38 year-old with Oxford Ph.D., and consultant to former presidential candidate, Irene Saez, in 1998). The 1999 payment on the foreign bond debt was $3.4 billion. Chavez's 5 electoral campaigns in two years left the country exhausted and impoverished, while he gained total power!

And finally, the comparison of Betancourt and Chavez hangs on Fidel Castro. Betancourt became a strong opponent of the Cuban regime of Fidel Castro, because it was totalitarian communist, and for its exportation of revolutionary terrorism, particularly in regard to Venezuela. These two men, Betancourt and Castro, came to power at the same time, Betancourt to lead a freely elected constitutional government, and Castro to turn a prosperous Cuba into a poverty stricken, suppressed Communist island. Betancourt fought every attempt Castro made to take over Venezuela; and 40 years later, Hugo Chavez gives Castro the Bienvenida (Welcome), and invites him into Venezuela – to help him gain complete control over Venezuela, as he, Castro, had over Cuba. Remember, Fidel Castro ordered the invasion of Venezuela in the 1960s – the only foreign invasion of Venezuela.

Betancourt turned into a statesman, and Chavez turned into a demagogue dictator. The first man had a fine mind, the later thought he knew everything (sabelotodo) and saw himself as *predestined* for the heights of Bolivar, if not higher! This was evident when Chavez addressed the world leaders at the United Nations' Millennium Summit in New York, on September 7, 2000. He said: *"The hour has arrived, let's save the world,"* in urging the heads of state to end the misery in the developing nations. (Before he spoke in his allotted 5-minute speech, he made the Sign of the Cross. He who has blasphemed the priests, the bishops and the Catholic Church in Venezuela, and states that he is not a Catholic.)

The deeds of a former Venezuelan president (now deceased) remained to haunt the current president. Romulo Betancourt was successful in organizing the union movement, as well as the Accion Democratica (AD) party. Chavez had an Achilles heel: the labor unions, which have turned into his opposition, first the oil worker's unions that won 60% raises, and then other unions that marched and called for strikes. But Chavez held a referendum on December 3, 2000, and with 1.5% of the vote closed down all of Venezuela's unions, thus taking care of that opposition. Or did he? On February 20, 2001, more than 100,000 teachers stayed home, closing 20,000 schools in Venezuela. The teachers were demanding that the Chavez Government resume talks on increasing their pay – from $360/month to $430 per month.

The AD party had had its problems with the unions, particularly those that were not willing to place themselves under its guardianship, going so far as repression of some unions.

In April 1960, the AD party split over the signing of a new contract between the foreign oil companies and Fedepetrol (Federacion de Trabajadores Petroleros). Domingo Alberto Rangel (an adviser to Chavez when he was in prison in Yare) was an adviser to Fedepetrol and had agreed to the terms, but once the contract was signed he violently attacked it, arguing that it was disadvantageous to the workers. The AD party leaders were furious at Rangel's action, but the youth organization of AD supported Rangel, who was expelled from AD. This group, expelled, or quit, formed MIR (Movimiento Izquierda

Revolucionaria) in July 1960, and became violent opponents of the Betancourt Government.

Actually, the only connection between these two Venezuelans is Fidel Castro, who was Betancourt's mortal enemy, and is now Chavez's buddy! Castro, 74 years old in 2000, in power for 41 years, and Chavez 45, in power for two years, make a strange team. The first is the teacher, the second the adoring pupil, 30 years younger. The younger is the savior of the older man.

Having lived through those early days of the 1960s when Fidel Castro tried through terrorism to take over Venezuela with his guerrilleros, his presence in Venezuela now, is beyond imagining. The terrorism increased in Betancourt's last year in office. Caracas was subjected to nocturnal bombings, banks were held up, warehouses burned, and the police and the military were singled out for assassination. United States businesses were prime targets for sabotage. So many oil pipelines and power stations in the oil fields were blown up, that President Betancourt placed the oil fields under military control.

The guerrilla campaign was aimed at triggering a military golpe in order to prevent the December 1 elections, forcing foreign enterprise out of Venezuela. The restraint of the Betancourt government, along with the support of all Venezuelan leaders and organized labor, contributed to maintaining public support. Thus, Fidel Castro's "Operation Caracas" failed to disrupt the elections of December 1963, when three million Venezuelans voted, i.e., 96% of the registered voters. The victory was for democracy.

Betancourt, in an article he wrote for *The Reporter* in 1964, describes what happened.

"At first, nobody in Venezuela could believe – and let this be a warning to other countries – that time bombs, exploded in crowded places without regard for how many would be killed or wounded, would be used as a political instrument."

"Far from concealing their role, the Cubans publicly and boastfully proclaimed their support for the pyromaniacs and dynamiters who were doing their bidding. Venezuela was a coveted prize that Castro wanted to offer his master, Nikita Khrushchev."

Chavez and Castro

Fidel Castro

In 1994, after Chavez was released from prison, Fidel Castro invited him to come to a conference on Simon Bolivar at the University of Havana. He received Chavez as a head of state, the man who had tried to overthrow Carlos Andres Perez, whom Castro had phoned after the coup attempt to offer his solidarity. When President Caldera received Cuban exile leader, Jorge Mas Canosa at Miraflores in 1994, Castro was furious, and he then invited Chavez to Cuba. And thus, began the Castro-Chavez alliance. Chavez's first trip overseas, a month after being elected President, was to Cuba, on January 16, 1999.

As Chavez's advisor, it is easy to surmise that Castro advised: give them lots of elections so that international opposition cannot mobilize against you; and "do not give your opposition clemency," as Brian Latell of *The Washington Post*, suggested in his article, a "Disguised Dictatorship." And, the two dictators must have a well developed reciprocal secret intelligence operation. Chavez in his threats against the leading Venezuelan newspapers has openly threatened the owner of the *El Universal*, Andres Mata Osorio, *"Se donde te mueves en los Estados Unidos," "porque tengo amigos en todas partes."* (I know where you move in the United States, because I have friends everywhere.) This particular threat was done on his Sunday morning show "Alo President," November 5, 2000.

Just as with Castro's request for money or oil from Betancourt in 1959, 40 years later in 1999 when Chavez came to power, Castro was back with the same request to a Venezuelan president. In the beginning it was a request to be included in the San Jose Pact, which Cuba was excluded from when it was signed in 1980, between Venezuela and Mexico. These two oil producing countries agreed to sell 160,000 b/d (80,000 b/d each) of oil, to 11 participating countries in Central America and the Caribbean, at favorable subsidy terms. Mexico denied the Cuban request, in 1999, therefore, the Cuban supply of oil became a bilateral accord with the Chavez Government, in October 2000.

The question asked in Venezuela is why does Cuba have to be Chavez's model for government? Communism is bankrupt in the world. Equality is only accomplished downward, and in Venezuela under Chavez that means a return to "el rancho," i.e., the hut. The most despised person by a Chavista is a cultured person, or someone educated from the middle or upper classes. Elitism now is bad. To stay in power Chavez must keep Venezuelans poor, just as Castro has in Cuba for 40 years. This is certainly not Simon Bolivar's revolution. He was fighting for his people's freedom from Spain, and Bolivar came from the best and wealthiest of Venezuelan families, as did many of his officers. Just how does Chavez equate these two men, Bolivar and Castro, in his own personal "social revolution"?

Fidel Castro is the illegitimate son of a bigamous father, Angel Castro, and a servant in his household, Lina Ruz, with whom Angel had seven children: Angela, Ramon, Fidel, Raul, Juana, Emma and Agustina. Castro's mother, Lina, was of mixed ancestry that included Chinese blood. He was raised by his barefoot, illiterate Galician father, who worked in the sugar cane industry in the Oriente province. Fidel Castro's father was born in one of Spain's poorest provinces, Galicia, in December 1875, and he arrived in Cuba as a Spanish soldier to fight the Americanos in the Spanish American War of 1898. In Cuba, Angel Castro built a small fortune, partly by tipping his cane scales, and "his boundary fences would frequently be moved out over a neighbor's land, and cattle and other property belonging to a neighbor would often end up on Angel's side of the fences," writes Mario Lazo, in Dagger in the Heart (p111). Mario Lazo points out that the main part of Angel's fortune came from growing sugar cane during a period when sugar prices were high.

Unlike other Cubans, the Castros seldom bathed, chickens had the run of the house, and there was no running water or toilets in the house in Fidel's youth. Fidel's mother carried a pistol in a holster when she went about her chores in the house and outdoors. Because of his personal hygiene, Fidel acquired the nickname of bola de churre ("greaseball") in the Jesuit-run Colegio de Belen in Havana. Even then, his tendency for conversations became monologues. Castro graduated from the University of Havana in 1950 (age 24) with a law degree.

Without Herbert Mathews and his articles in the *New York Times*, Fidel and Raul Castro might never have been heard of again after their unsuccessful landing in Cuba, on December 2, 1956. The Castros and their 10-member rebel group made it into the Sierra Maestra Mountains and were forgotten. Without a press, Castro's little band was going nowhere, for Fidel was believed to be dead. In January 1957, Castro sent an emissary to Havana looking for a foreign journalist. Castro needed an audience in the United States, and he found The New York Times liberal Herbert Matthews, who in mid-February went to the mountains to see Castro. As Lazo and many others point out, Mathews' three articles "represent the most reprehensible act of journalism attributed to a reputable newspaper." (p.124) Matthews later said he altered the course of Cuba's history, for his articles on Castro had an explosive impact in the United States and throughout the Western Hemisphere. The *New York Times* open promotion of Castro was the beginning of an unprecedented barrage of publicity and support for Castro.

Hugo Chavez

"Hurricane Hugo," breaks protocol with vigor and takes every opportunity to expound his ideas. He always talks, "blah, blah, blah," and seldom listens. Hugo Chavez Frias is a mix of black and Indian ancestry, but he favors the Indian side and says he is the Yaruro Indian. He was born in Sabaneta, Barinas, July 28, 1954, the second son of six sons of Hugo de los Reyes Chavez and Elena Frias. His parents were school teachers, in the Llanos cattle ranching State of Barinas. He was born in the village of Sabaneta, but went to school in Barinas.

He entered the Military Academy in 1971, when he was 17; and was a member of the 1975 graduating class, receiving his sword of command from President Carlos Andres Perez, on July 5. Such irony, for this was the President he would try to topple, in February 1992. The next two years after graduating, Chavez was stationed in Barinas, where he joined a counter-insurgency battalion. The battalion was sent to Cumana to crush a new guerrilla outbreak. Chavez now began to feel sympathy for the guerrillas he was supposed to fight, and formed his own rebel army group, the Ejercito de Liberacion del Pueblo de Venezuela

(ELPV). His group was to be an underground movement *within* the armed forces.

Chavez was an instructor at the Military Academy, first as a sports instructor, and then as a tutor in history and politics. In 1982, he began to organize a political conspiracy with Jesus Urdaneta Hernandez and Felipe Acosta Carles (who was later killed in El Saqueo rebellion in 1989), called the Movimiento Bolivariano Revolucionario–200 (MBR-200). The "200" was the anniversary of the birth of Simon Bolivar, who was born in 1783. These officers swore an oath under the tree at Saman de Guere near Maracay. The oath was Bolivar's made at Monte Sacro, Italy, in 1805, when he swore to liberate Venezuela from Spain. Major Francisco Arias Cardenas joined the group in March 1985. They became known as the COMACATE organization (for Commanders, Majors, Captains and Lieutenants).

Hugo Chavez joined the elite paratrooper battalion in Maracay in August 1991, and rose to Lt. Colonel. He was one of the leaders of the February 4, 1992 coup attempt, that left 15 soldiers dead, 51 wounded and 133 officers out of 1,000 soldiers arrested. Chavez was sentenced to 4 years in jail, but after 26 months was pardoned by President Caldera. After his release from prison in May 1994, Chavez made a tour of Venezuela's 22 states. "We appeal to the 70% of the population who don't vote," he said. In 1997, Chavez, with leftist civilians, organized the Movimiento V Republica (MVR), and with two other leftwing parties (MAS and PPT) formed a coalition called Polo Patriotico, and won the December 1998 presidential elections.

Chavez never visited the United States until after he was elected President. He tried to visit the U.S. after he got out of prison, but was denied a visa by the Clinton Administration. As President-elect, Chavez met with Clinton at the White House in January, a week before his inauguration. This visit required the U.S. to rescind his visa denial. In June 1999, Chavez arrived in New York with his entourage to drum up interest in Venezuela's plans to sell $2 billion in international bonds. He then went to Houston to meet with U.S. oilmen. This was the trip he took Roberto Mandini along on to reassure Wall Street and U.S. oil companies. Chavez fired Mandini two months later.

Chavez remarried in 1997, to former television presenter, Marisabel Rodriguez, with whom he has a 4-year old daughter. He has three children by his first marriage. His father, Hugo de los Reyes, was elected Governor of Barinas in November 1998, a month before Chavez was elected President. And, Chavez's elder brother, Adan, is a professor at the University in Merida and was a member of the Constitutional Assembly. According to Douglas Bravo, it was Adan who was a member of the Partido de la Revolucion Venezolana (PRV), and who put the revolutionaries in touch with Hugo Chavez, and others within the Armed Forces.

Chavez attempted to earn a degree in political science, but did not, because he had studied in prison, and the highly regarded Simon Bolivar University in Caracas did not accept his thesis. Was it because he writes as he speaks with bombastic words, is careless with the facts, or just because he was a poor student, that he was denied a college degree. In an article in *El Universal* (23-7-00), "The Cadet Didn't Study," Manuel Caballero writes about simple direct questions he and other professionals asked President Chavez on Carlos Fernandes' television program. Chavez did not answer any of the questions, merely called the men names: "sacred cow (vaca sagrada), "ignorant," and "puntofijista." Mr. Caballero wrote in his article that he now understood why Chavez did so poorly in school, and why Hugo de los Reyes took Chavez out of high school in Barinas after he failed, and put him in the Military Academy.

Chavez claims to admire three Venezuelan heroes. The first is Simon Bolivar, next is Simon Rodriguez, who was one of Bolivar's teachers, and the third is Ezequiel Zamora, a general in the Federal War in the 1850s, who was ardent, impetuous and a leader of the campesinos against the hacendados (landowners, ranchers), in the Llanos. Zamora is no one to admire. When Zamora would enter a town he would burn all the property titles and turn over the land to the campesinos. His slogans were "death to the whites," and "everything for the poor and nothing for the rich," and "death to those who know how to read and write." He acquired wealth before he was shot in an assault on a small town. This is the man that Hugo Chavez invokes as a Venezuelan hero to be emulated. And in June 2001, a new guerrilla group appeared in

Venezuela calling itself the <u>Ejercito Revolucionario Bolivariano Zamorano</u> (ERBZ) ready to fight and defend Hugo Chavez.

Venezuelan Indian Tribes

Since Chavez calls himself a *Yaruro Indian*, a short history of Venezuela's Indian population can be helpful. From the last Venezuelan census there are 145,230 Venezuelan Indians (a difficult feat of counting, since they are mainly scattered in the unpopulated southern regions).

At the time of the Spanish conquest, Venezuela had everything from cannibals to fruit farmers. The most advanced culture in Venezuela was that of the *Timote Indians* who lived in the Andes near Merida. They worshipped a supreme being who lived on the mountains and in the lakes. They lived in stone-walled houses grouped in orderly rows around a temple. The Timotes were farmers, planting their crops on terraced slopes, with irrigation ditches.

The *Quiriquire* tribe inhabited the area east of Lake Maracaibo, and fiercely resisted the Spanish. They were superior boatmen and dominated Lake Maracaibo and nearby coastal waters until the Spanish galleons wiped them out. These Quiriquires were lake-dwellers, building their houses on piles, for protection from their enemies. It was this custom that reminded the Spaniards of one of Europe's most civilized cities, Venice. And they called the land "Little Venice," Venezuela.

The *Caracas* tribes, the most westerly of the Carib cultures, combined fishing and agriculture, growing cotton, tobacco and maize to supplement their diet. They had a political organization with a graded military class, and had <u>caciques </u>(chiefs). In time of war they often formed a confederation under a single leader. The Caracas gave the Spaniards their most formidable opposition in the conquest of Venezuela, and produced Venezuela's first national hero – <u>Guaicaipuro</u>, chief of the *Teques*. Guaicaipuro produced a fighting force of 10,000 braves and massacred the first expeditions sent to conquer his land. He attacked the first two Spanish settlements in the Caracas area: Nuestra Senora de Caraballeda on the Caribbean, and San Francisco further inland. Both were abandoned soon after their founding in 1562. But the Spaniards eventually destroyed Guaicaipuro, attacking his camp at night. He became the symbol of Venezuelan liberty. There are other tribes further to the east of the Caracas tribes whose social customs were even higher, and chiefs who were generally hereditary, but sometimes elected.

The Venezuelan Indians were tenacious adversaries. Unlike the Incas and Aztecs who reigned over many subjects, the tribes in Venezuela were all independent. Thus, the Spanish Conquistadores had to fight a multitude of different tribes in Venezuela. This tradition of independence carries through to the present and contributes to making Venezuela difficult to govern. Early in the conquest, the Indian tribes tolerated the Spaniards. It was only after slaving activities began on a large scale and after the Spaniards started to <u>settle</u> that the Indians realized their danger.

In Venezuela, the more advanced tribes (Timotes, Quiriquire and Caracas) suffered to the point of extermination under the Spaniards, partly by disease (small pox and the plague). The backward and nomadic peoples that could retreat into the jungles and plains, which the Spaniards were not interested in settling, were preserved to the present.

Hugo Chavez claims part of his heritage from the Llanos nomad Indians – the Yaruro – some living in Amazonas and Apure States. The other part of his heritage, Chavez acknowledges as black. The Spanish Court agreed in 1560 to allow 200 Negro slaves to enter the colony duty free, and the Spanish <u>encomendero</u> began to buy African slaves. The Spanish settlers could control African slaves, whereas the Indians were adverse to Spanish domination.

Baseball

Baseball – a wonderful gringo sport, much loved by Chavez and Castro, and the national sport in both Venezuela and Cuba. It was US American oilmen who introduced Venezuelans to the US American sport in the 1920s. It was a sport played in the oil fields where there was no entertainment. And Venezuelans took to baseball, as did the Cubans, when they were introduced to baseball by the U.S. Marines, about the same time. In Venezuela, it is not soccer that dominates Venezuelan sports as in other Latin American countries. Venezuelan boys start playing baseball very young, and join the Little League, and some teams even make it to the Little League World Series. Poor boys in Venezuela dream of becoming professional baseball players in the United States! Some have made it to the Major League like Luis Aparicio, Andres Galarraga, and Bob Abreu. Hugo Chavez dreamed of becoming a Major League pitcher. He says he joined Venezuela's Military Academy because it had the best coaches in the country at the time. What a pity for Venezuela that he never made the cut to play professional baseball. In his so-called governing of Venezuela, he identifies every situation in baseball terms. When he reshuffled his 14 member Cabinet in August 2000, e.g. he said, "Just like in a baseball game changes are made – the shortstop is moved to second base, or one runner is changed for another – but the game strategy remains the same." (Alo Presidente, 27-8-00)

Travel

Boys who love baseball often love to travel. Since becoming President, Chavez has traveled the world, more than making up for his lack of travel before 1999. Chavez racked up foreign travel miles faster than the man he tried to overthrow in 1992, when he was returning from Davos, Switzerland. Carlos Andres Perez traveled so much that one Caracas newspaper had a banner headline welcoming him back to Venezuela. "He traveled and traveled and does not care about us." Chavez acquired the nickname of Marco Polo. Much was written about his trips. For example, his love of summits, any excuse to make another trip anywhere: the Middle East, Africa, Asia, South America, Central America and the Caribbean (particularly Cuba), to the United Nations in New York, to the Andean Community, and even the United States (Houston, to introduce his new president of Citgo, a general, and swear him in).

He sees himself as the leader of the so-called Third World, of OPEC, and of the Sao Paolo Forum. Chavez travels because he loves to get on his plane and be attended in all these countries. But there is an underlying reason for most of his trips, i.e., to show the United States how *sovereign* Venezuela is, and to create a multi-polar world with Chavez leading the opposition to the United States. He simply is following Fidel's attempts in the 1970s and 1980s, at gaining world power and prestige. Chavez does not miss any opportunity to refer to the "savage neo-liberalism" of the United States, and has called for a multinational Latin American force (like NATO) to exclude the United States.

His almost weekly foreign trips are the subject in the Venezuelan newspapers of ironic humour and careful note is taken as to which government officials he takes on these trips, besides his family members. Chavez takes his favorite officials with him, and those left in charge are blamed for problems that occur during his absence.

One of the most humorous articles was written by Milagros Socorro, "Presidente exilado," in *El Universal* (2 September 2000). She concludes that Venezuela makes Chavez sick, that he cannot stand being President of Venezuela, does not want to govern, detests his office in Miraflores, is not comfortable in La Casona; and the rich, the experts, the other presidents, the generals all intimidate him. Chavez has exiled himself! And in another article in *El Universal* (16-9-00), "The Traveling President," Adolfo P. Salgueiro, says there are trips yet to come: to Greenland, Moldavia, Estonia, and "other countries whose friendship and commerce are priorities for a Venezuela that has dignity, is sovereign, and has thrown off the Yankee yoke."

In addition, Chavez goes to places like La Paz, Bolivia and tells the Chileans that they should return Bolivia's access to the Pacific Ocean, which they took in the 19th century. The Bolivians applaud and the Chileans are furious. Chavez's response, "I will say it as many times as I want to" (tantas veces como me da la gana). And then there was his famous trip to the Middle East, to invite the heads of state to his OPEC Summit meeting in September 2000, when he visited Saddam Hussein in Iraq. This was a great victory for Chavez, because he defied the United States of America, and the United Nations' sanctions.

His three week trip around the world in May 2001: to Russia, where he signed a military technical cooperation agreement, then on to Iran, India, Bangladesh, China, Malaysia, and Indonesia, ended in San Antonio, Texas, before returning to Venezuela. Chavez, the "Marco Polo of Sabaneta," travels and travels, because the poor Venezuelans are financing his trips.

There is the serious question of how much these long trips cost Venezuela, a country where 80% of the people are now poor. After numerous trips, he found his presidential plane old and inadequate for his long trips, therefore, a new $54 million Airbus 319 Corporate Jetliner was ordered in Europe, in October 2000.

Two months later, in December, the order was changed to *two* Airbuses. Chavez has stated that he will not fly in a U.S. made airplane, and what he had was a Boeing 737, purchased 10 years earlier by Carlos Andres Perez. His government budget for 2001 included Bs 38 billion ($60 million) for 10 overseas trips, i.e., $6 million per trip. These are trips fit for an Emperor! After his worldwide May trip, Chavez must have surpassed the $60 million for 2001.

And, as Chavez travels the world, so do the Venezuelans – emigrating. Sammy Eppel has suggested that in comparing the Cuban exodus [2 million], the number of Venezuelans departing could be 8 million (*El Universal*, 13-10-00). Those departing were called "traitors" by Blancanieves [Snow White] Portocarrero, who subsequently was named Minister of Labor. "Traitor" is now a common threat by the Chavistas.

Castro's Visits to Venezuela

Fidel Castro did not return to Venezuela for 30 years after his first trip in 1959. In 1989, Castro was invited by Carlos Andres Perez to come to his February 2 inauguration, along with 21 other heads of state, like Daniel Ortega of Nicaragua. Perez's inauguration was called a coronation, so much money was spent, and it was held in the Teresa Carreno Theater, and not at the Congress as is traditional. The Caracas Hilton, across the street from the Theater, was rented out by the government for the invited heads of state. I was staying at the Hilton for two weeks just before the arrival of the heads of state and witnessed some of the preparations. It was not considered safe for Castro to stay with the other visiting dignitaries, as there was a great deal of opposition by the Venezuelans, who remembered that hundreds had lost their lives in Venezuela because of Castro's attempt to take over the country in the 1960s. Thus, Castro and 80 members of his delegation, complete with arms including machine guns, were housed in the new Eurobuilding Hotel, hurriedly finished to receive Castro and his party. The Cubans were given two floors of the hotel and while they were there no Venezuelans were allowed in. One of my cousins was in a group that inspected the two floors after the Cubans left: they had trashed the rooms and the halls, causing thousands of dollars of damage.

Carlos Andres Perez's second administration was certainly eventful. Not only did he re-establish ties with Castro; the worst rioting in Caracas broke out several weeks after he was inaugurated. Known as El Saqueo, for the extensive rioting and looting, and large packs of motorcyclists, it caused 380 deaths and billions of bolivars in damage. (The bolivar was then worth Bs 38 to the dollar, and WTI oil was $19/barrel.) Perez also proposed a summit of OPEC leaders, and he too made a swing through the Middle East. He also had grandiose ideas, thought he could bring peace between Iraq and Iran (interrupted by the 1990 Gulf War); traveled the world endlessly; and had two coup attempts against his government, the first one by Hugo Chavez, in February 1992. In 1993, he was impeached on corruption charges and spent 28 months in jail or under house arrest.

When Carlos Andres Perez became president in 1989, the country had food shortages because Venezuela had run through its foreign financial reserves, which were needed to pay for its large food imports. Perez tried to institute free-market reforms but the sudden rise in prices caused disastrous riots. That was the end of free market reforms in Venezuela!

Castro's 3rd trip to Venezuela, and the second during Perez's administration, was a quick trip to La Orchila Island. Castro's 4th trip was to Margarita Island for the IberoAmerican Summit when Rafael Caldera was president, and his 5th trip was for Chavez's inauguration in February 1999. His 6th trip was to La Orchila to celebrate Chavez's new Constitution during the December 1999 deluge. But there was no visit ever before like the October 2000 welcome, on his 7th trip.

Bienvenido Fidel! Venezuela's Foreign Minister, Jose Vicente Rangel announced on October 7 that Fidel Castro would visit Venezuela. On October 26, 2000, Castro arrived in Venezuela for a red carpet state visit with full military honors hosted by his greatest admirer, Hugo Chavez Frias. Castro came to be honored by Chavez, and to get 53,000 b/d of oil, at generous discount prices and for barter, from Venezuela. At current rates the oil was worth $1 billion annually. Venezuela would finance up to 25% and this financing can be repaid with: *Cuban doctors, treatment for Venezuelans in Cuba, education, cultural and social work*, greatly reducing the cost.

Rodolfo Schmidt asked in his news column in Venezuela Analitica whether Castro was bringing a check for $69 million owed to Venezuela since the first government of Carlos Andres Perez, in the 1970s. Mr. Schmidt also wondered if it would rain and rain, and mud slides would destroy Venezuelan towns, as happened the last time Castro came to celebrate with Chavez in December 1999. [October is in the rainy season.] He reminded his readers of what Venezuela had suffered when Castro tried to conquer Venezuela, and asked the question whether Castro would apologize to the surviving 30,000 mothers, wives, and orphans of his victims in the 1960s and 1970s?

There were organized protests against Fidel Castro's 5-day visit. Francisco Arias Cardenas, former candidate for the presidency and fellow golpista of Chavez in the February 1992 attempt to overthrow Carlos Andres Perez, now organized the response to Fidel Castro's trip to Venezuela. Arias called for a cacerolazo (pot banging) and "car lights on," to protest Castro's visit. And the Internet circulated e-mails calling for dressing in black to declare Castro's arrival as a "Day of National Sadness." A group of military officers (Frente Institucional Militar) repudiated the visit and said they would support those opposing Castro's visit.

On the day of Castro's arrival, Thursday, October 26, thousands took to the streets and marched in Caracas. The marchers included laborers and teachers denouncing Chavez's failure to pay overdue raises and pensions. They demanded that Venezuelan aid for Cuba go to underpaid workers. "Out with Fidel, We're dying of hunger," read one banner. A group of mothers dressed in black protested the deaths of Cuban women trying to flee Cuba. But Chavez avoided the demonstrations by taking Castro, after his arrival, to visit the towns in Vargas where the Cuban "doctors" were working, and here Castro received a Cuban flag waving welcome by the young people.

The two of them, Chavez and Castro, dressed in combat fatigues professed a shared faith in revolution. *We are you, and you are us*," Castro told a cheering crowd in La Guaira. And, Chavez told the crowd how he met Castro in Cuba shortly after his release from prison in 1994. "I told you then that one day I hoped to welcome you with the Venezuelan people in the way you deserve – and here we are." Chavez said cultivating Venezuelan ties with Cuba was part of an effort to counter-balance the economic clout of the United States and the European Union, in Latin America. "We have no alternative but to form an axis of power."

Venezuelan members of the National Assembly that oppose Chavez and Castro boycotted the Castro speech before the Assembly on Friday October 27. After speaking to the Assembly where he praised Chavez for an hour, and warned him of conspiracies to assassinate him, and the U.S. backlash against him, Chavez took him on a fun trip around Venezuela. On Monday, **October 30**, Fidel Castro got his oil accord from Chavez.

Caracas Energy Cooperation Accord

Named the Caracas Energy Cooperation Accord, Chavez will supply 53,000 b/d of crude and products to Cuba, and thus, relieve Cuba of the high prices it was forced to spend (an additional $500 million) on its oil imports from third parties, in 2000. Venezuela will finance up to 25% and Cuba can repay in trade. Cuban payment will be difficult to monitor, for it supposedly will be by sending more "doctors" to Venezuela, sending sick patients to Cuba, providing *expertise* in the sugar industry, and helping develop tourism.

Chavez used clever subterfuge to sell this Energy Accord to the Venezuelan people. He first said it was the Caracas Energy Accord, which would not supplant the 1980 San Jose Pact with Mexico, under which the two countries sold 160,000 b/d of oil to 11 Central American and Caribbean countries under special contracts. Chavez wanted Cuba included in the San Jose Pact, but Mexico said **no**. So Chavez came up with this subterfuge of another **80,000** b/d to the same countries, but including Cuba. When I added up the barrels going to each country, it was clear that 78,400 b/d in the Caracas Accord were taken, without Cuba. A signing ceremony with the Presidents of the countries took place in Caracas on Thursday, October 19, without Cuba. And the signing took place at the Circulo Militar, the luxurious military club built by President Marcos Perez Jimenez, in the early 1950s. There was no mention of PDVSA officials being present at the Energy Accord signing. The 10 countries that signed the October 19 Accord were Belize, Costa Rica, El Salvador, Guatemala, Haiti,

Honduras, Jamaica, Nicaragua, Panama and the Dominican Republic. The Dominican Republic got 20,000 b/d, the most, with Belize receiving 600 b/d, the least amount.

A week later when Castro went to Venezuela it came out that Cuba had a separate Accord, and would be getting a total 53,000 barrels per day. Chavez and Castro signed the Caracas Energy Accord in Miraflores Palace, with Guaicaipuro Lameda, the new president of PDVSA in attendance. The 15-year repayment terms carries a 2% interest rate, and has a two-year grace period. Repayment can be in sugar shipments, as well as the previously mentioned health services, and agricultural projects.

Cuba came out ahead of the other Caribbean and Central American countries. The Cuban contract runs for five years, plus a 6-month phase out period if not renewed, whereas the other countries have annual renewals. The other countries have only a one-year grace period and have no barter deal. The Cubans are not restricted from re-selling to third parties at a profit. And Cuba can opt for more than the 53,000 b/d face value of the contract, bartering goods and services for oil. Furthermore, the agreement with Cuba does not specify whether the oil's price is CIF or FOB, nor does it say who is to provide the financing.

It is the sending of sick Venezuelan patients to Cuba that also caused agitation in Venezuela. Chavez said he was going to use his new presidential plane to fly the Venezuelan patients to Cuba, every month. "There they will operate on them and it will not cost us anything." Well maybe a percentage of oil, after all operations in Cuba cost nearly twice as much as in Venezuela, according to Jesus Mendez Quijada, president of the Venezuelan Medical Federation. "If President Chavez wants to **give** petroleum to foreign countries he has to ask our permission, and it can be done in a referendum, to consult whether the owners want to give the crude away, or donate to our hospitals."

This Chavez plan raised several questions. First, what about the families of the patients who always accompany the patients in the hospital; and second, Venezuelans have competent doctors and good to fair hospitals, certainly much better than in Cuba. When Chavez's father got sick he was treated in Caracas, Chavez's wife went to Boston for her hypertension, government officials go to the United States if they need operations or special treatment, none go to Cuba! Furthermore, Chavez travels so much, that it would be very difficult to schedule operations in Cuba around the availability of the presidential plane. But it sounds good – Chavez deflects criticism of his expensive new plane, while finding an imaginary way for Cuba to repay Venezuela for its subsidized oil. (Actually, Chavez decided to order a second plane, for his $54 million Airbus 319 Corporate Jetliner would not be appropriate for a lot of sick people.)

It appears that Cuba's oil demand is under 150,000 b/d, with domestic production around 50,000 b/d of heavy oil (8-14 degrees with about 8% sulfur). Cuba's major oil producer is Sherritt International Corp. of Canada. In January 2001, Repsol YPF signed an agreement with Cuba on oil exploration off the Cuban coast. The Cienfuegos refinery would also be overhauled as part of the agreement. Cuba's oil imports are mostly refined products. It is thus evident that Venezuela will supply most of Cuba's oil imports, and a major part of its oil consumption.

Chavez needs to keep the world price of oil high to balance the Venezuelan subsidized oil for Cuba. Under the Caracas Energy Accord with Cuba, Chavez can use the increase in oil revenues earned in the United States to subsidize consumption in Cuba. The question, however, is what will Cuba do with all this Venezuelan crude, since she does not have the needed refining capacity. Cuba will resell some of the oil for higher prices, as she has done with earlier sales by Chavez. This is a unique arrangement, because PDVSA's three operating companies, for 20 years, sold oil only to the end user refinery. The destination of the oil was restricted, and not to be resold to third parties, as Cuba obviously is doing.

Venezuela is now the principal supplier of oil to the Caribbean area. Some Venezuelans wonder if Venezuela could now be viewed in the Caribbean as a sub-imperialist country to these debtor nations. It is not good business to sell oil on credit to poor countries! Furthermore, Venezuela is undercutting Trinidad and Tobago, which is the Caribbean's leading island energy producer. The Caracas Energy Accord is perceived as a serious threat in Trinidad, since Jamaica and Barbados are its two principal Caribbean customers. Trinidad's' Petrotrin supplies some 45,000 barrels/day to San Jose Pact countries, thus more low-cost oil from

Venezuela under the new Caracas Accord, was so worrisome to Trinidad that she called a meeting of Caribbean energy ministers in Port of Spain, on November 14. Since 1998, these countries cooperate under the Caribbean Energy Action Plan (CEAP). Trinidad hopes to keep further Venezuelan energy incursions at bay.

San Jose Pact

With the San Jose Pact of 1980, Venezuela relinquished hundreds of millions of dollars in oil revenues. Furthermore, the Central American countries have found curious ways of repaying Venezuela, e.g. in 1991, President Perez accepted Nicaragua's payment in government bonds then worth only 5%, but Venezuela accepted the Nicaraguan bonds at face value. In Costa Rica's case, Venezuela was paid with Venezuelan public debt bonds that Costa Rica had purchased at a discount, and now repaid at par. Besides a poor repayment record, the 11 Central American and Caribbean countries have failed to support Venezuela in important international matters. When Miguel Angel Burrelli left Rafael Caldera's service as Foreign Minister with the intent of becoming Secretary General of the Organization of American States, 10 of the 11 countries voted for ex-president of Colombia, Cesar Gaviria. Thus, Chavez may not get the support he expects from these countries in the Caracas Accord.

The San Jose Pact was a program of energy assistance to Central American and Caribbean nations, signed in August 1980, in Costa Rica, by Venezuelan President Luis Herrera Campins, and Mexican President Jose Lopez Portillo. The two oil producing countries jointly would supply up to 160,000 b/d at current prices, but only 70% paid immediately, with the remainder considered as soft loans. The oil was provided through commercial agreements established independently by Venezuela and Mexico with each participating country. Venezuela financed credits through the Venezuelan Investment Fund, but in 1986, it stopped granting development loans due to the financial crisis caused by the oil price collapse. In mid-1986, Venezuela was owed around $521 million borrowed under the Pact's terms to finance energy development and basic infrastructure projects in the Central American and Caribbean countries.

When Luis Herrera became President in 1980, he not only inherited a bankrupted country from Carlos Andres Perez, he was concerned about the situation in Central America, particularly that of Napoleon Duarte in El Salvador, following the takeover of neighboring Nicaragua by the Sandinistas, in 1979. Military support from Communist nations (Soviet Union and Cuba) had transformed the struggle in El Salvador into a major East-West conflict.

Each year the San Jose Pact was evaluated and some countries were added or dropped, and credit terms modified with 6 to 8% interest. The number of countries ranged from nine to 11. Nicaragua was dropped in 1982 and the Soviet Union became its supplier. Haiti was dropped in 1988, after its June 19 coup. Furthermore in 1984, Mexico and Venezuela, who were members of the Contadora group seeking a negotiated peace settlement in Central America, specified they would suspend oil supplies for any warlike actions against a neighbor. Also for the first time, the oil purchasing nations were encouraged to buy goods and services from Venezuela and Mexico with their oil-related credits.

What irony: the San Jose Pact was conceived to save the Central American and Caribbean countries from communism, and the Chavez Caracas Energy Accord was created specifically to bolster up the last Communist regime in the area – Cuba!

It was clear to many like Humberto Calderon Berti and Alberto Quiros Corradi that Chavez's real intention of this grand gesture toward the small countries around the Caribbean was to sell oil to Cuba on very generous terms. But there seems to be another important reason, i.e., to give Chavez economic and political power in the Caribbean, as he tries to organize his confederation of Latin American states, **against** the United States.

United: Chavez and Castro

Fidel Castro's trip to Venezuela served Chavez's purpose: to rouse up his boinas rojas (Red Berets) and rally his youthful followers (reminds one of the Chinese Red Guard); to show the United States (hago lo que me da la gana); and use the Roman Circus atmosphere to play to the poor, and inflate his own ego. The two boys romped across Venezuela having a barrel of fun, playing baseball and feasting, and distracting the people by making more empty promises to help the poor. But while Chavez shouts his continental plans, and preaches hatred, he neglects simple duties, like paying teachers' salaries on time, and organize his chaotic government. The hatred is becoming clearer every day – it is directed against foreigners, first Europeans, but deepest against US-Americans – and his Red Berets are already marching down this road spreading his hatred.

The expressions of love, admiration and awe from Hugo Chavez for Fidel Castro were embarrassing for educated Venezuelans. It is unseemly for a man to speak of another man in the ways that Chavez unabashedly spoke of Castro in praising him; and defending this dictator, who had caused so much misery to his people for over 40 years, as well as Venezuelans and all the citizens of the other countries that Castro tried to take over with the help of Che Guevara. On Venezuelan television and radio, Chavez said, "Hurt whom it will hurt," Castro is a man of history, and "when you give your hand to Fidel Castro, you are giving your hand to history." "Fidel is not a tyrant." Of course, many have called him this, and a Venezuelan President, Luis Herrera Campins called Castro "Dictator of the Caribbean." In praising Castro, Hugo Chavez criticizes the Venezuelan doctors and says that they should follow the example of the Cuban "doctors." And to the Medical Federation that have criticized Chavez for bringing Cuban "doctors" to Venezuela, he responds: meteme preso si pueden, vayan al Tribunal de Justicia y que me encarcelen si quieren y si pueden." (Put me in jail if you can, go to the Supreme Court and have me jailed if you want and if you can.)

The joining of forces with Fidel Castro was always Chavez's intent, but he had to proceed with a bit of caution until he had won his last election, July 30, 2000. Once that was behind him, he could invite Fidel to Venezuela and seal the marriage. This is a dangerous union!

These two countries are going to be closely tied from now on. It started out timidly, e.g. with Cuba exporting 15,000 bicycles to Venezuela, in 2000, for $570 million, to give to the best public rural students. Venezuelan bicycle companies can produce 600,000 bicycles a year, but in 1999 only sold 100,000, because of imports of cheaper Asian bicycles, forcing the layoffs of 80% of their workers. The Cuban bicycles, of an ancient model (Ring 26"), were questioned and objected to by the Venezuelan manufacturers. The most important part of this union between Chavez and Castro is that the *torch has been passed*. Castro said as much in Venezuela, on October 29, when he said he sees Chavez as a possible successor to his role as Latin America's most visible leftist. And in his speech before the Venezuelan National Assembly, on Friday (27th), he said he regards Chavez as his ideological or spiritual [?] heir. Hugo Chavez now rules, no one is above him, he answers to no one, no one is his equal. He is the new Conquistador of the world! This is the creation of the Anti-imperialist Front of the South with, he hopes, the support of Central America and the Caribbean. Now you understand why the Caracas Energy Accord, followed by Fidel Castro's trip to Venezuela in October 2000, occurred.

For those of us who knew Romulo Betancourt, the father of Venezuela's constitutional government, and who defended Venezuela against Fidel Castro's invasion of Cuban guerrillas in the 1960s, the adulation by Chavez of Castro, giving Venezuela's oil to Castro, along with his resurrection of Che Guevara, is a tragic disgrace. Betancourt's efforts gave Venezuelans 40 years of a free society, allowed Chavez to win power through a democratic process, and now gives the Chavistas the freedom to speak badly of him.

Che Guevara

Rather than honor Betancourt for his contributions to Venezuela, Chavez honors Ernesto "Che" Guevara as the *example for Venezuelan youth*, holding writing competitions about him, with orders that Che's picture be prominently displayed in the schools. Che Guevara, who wrote the manual for guerrilla warfare; assassinated hundreds of Cuban prisoners; as Minister of the Economy and head of the Central Bank ran the Cuban economy into the ground; cut a destructive swath across Africa and South America; was finally turned in by campesinos to Bolivian soldiers, and was shot; is Chavez's idea of a model for the youth of Venezuela. As "the most influential personality in the world during the 20th century," the Ernesto Che Guevara scholarship contest in 2000, was open to youths 14 to 24 years old.

Since Hugo Chavez has resurrected the Che Guevara aberration, more about "el Che". First, the "Che" is an Argentine informal way of greeting someone. Guevara was born in Rosario,

Argentina in 1927, but spent most of his early years in Buenos Aires. He attended but never finished medical school, and took part in leftist student demonstrations at the University of Buenos Aires. When he was called into the Argentine military service, he deserted and went to Peru. He married a Peruvian radical, Hilda Gadea, had a daughter, and abandoned them both. He served in the Guatemalan Communist government of Jacobo Arbenz. It was in Mexico that Guevara made contact with Fidel Castro and landed in Cuba with the Castro brothers, in December 1956.

Guevara in his book Guerra de Guerrillas, elaborated on his revolutionary theory, which departed from the traditional Marxist/Leninist views of the conditions necessary for revolution. Guevara advocated creating a revolutionary situation by its own momentum, i.e., a small band of armed revolutionaries, by gaining popular support, could grow in numbers and strength and defeat a national army. What Guevara did not comprehend was that his theory would work only if the United States interfered and supported his efforts, as the U.S. did in Cuba. On his own, he and this theory failed.

After Castro's revolutionary failure in Venezuela, Guevara slipped into Bolivia to try and establish a center (foco) of an insurgency for the whole region, i.e., a "second Vietnam," as Guevara described it in a manifesto to his followers, in April 1967. However, in Bolivia, Guevara alienated the Communist party; chose as his zone of operations both tropical jungles and arid mountain areas, cut off from contact with the outside world once fighting started; and the campesinos in the area owned their own land and were unwilling to cooperate with the guerrilleros. Moreover, President Rene Barrientos was well liked by the farmers. The small Cuban guerrillero force called itself Ejercito de Liberacion Nacional (ELN), just as in Colombia. Their movements over less than one year, until Che Guevara was killed by Bolivian "Rangers," on October 8, 1967, was enhanced by Castroite supporters around the world with exaggerated stories that substituted imagination for information.

During this period, Guevara only managed to smuggle out five communiqués. Also involved in Guevara's Bolivian venture was the Frenchman, Regis Debray, who preached the "third phase of Castroism," and who was captured and got worldwide press, too. To conclude, Guevara was never able to gain any active political support in Bolivia for his "second Vietnam," and at no time did the mere 50 armed foreign guerrillero campaign seriously threaten the political power of the regime.

Fidel Castro owed a great deal of his success in the 1950s to his falsehoods and disingenuousness concerning his communist ideological convictions, thus gaining the support of Cuban democrats and the United States left. It is no wonder Castro failed to export his model for revolution to other Latin American countries. He could no longer hood wink and mislead new potential supporters to his cause. However, the Left worldwide, and Hugo Chavez continue to praise and spin imaginary exploits of an imaginary hero, Che Guevara.

Grenada

Grenada was granted its independence from Britain on February 7, 1974. The island is only 21 miles long, with a population of 98,000. The little island of Grenada about 60 miles off the northeast coast of Venezuela was important to Cuba and the Soviet Union because it is strategically located in a region where sea lanes converge. Choke points that could hinder re-supplying of North Atlantic Treaty Organization forces from ports in the Gulf of Mexico are: the 90-mile stretch of water between Key West and Cuba; the 100-mile stretch between the tip of the Yucatan Peninsula and Cuba; and 60-mile passage between Venezuela and Grenada. The latter could prevent re-supply from Venezuela. Besides the importance of the sea lanes, Cuba wanted an airport, to use in re-supplying its 50,000 troops and personnel in Angola. Grenada was more than 1,000 miles southeast of Cuba – and on the route to Africa.

The 9,800-foot runway Castro's Cubans were building at Point Salines on the southwest peninsula of Grenade would enable a MiG-23 with its 500-mile plus range to carry a full payload of bombs, from Grenada to Puerto Rico, or cover Venezuela, Aruba and Curacao. The British-backed government of Eric Gairy, was overthrown on March 13, 1979, by Maurice Bishop, and Bishop's communist government informed the world that the new airport would be available for Russian and Cuban military use. This announcement was made by Grenada's minister of national mobilization, on December 19, 1981. By 1982, the Cuban air force consisted of more than 200 fighter-type aircraft, including 100 MiG-21s and a force of MiG-23 Flogger F ground attack versions, according to *Aviation Week and Space Technology*, May 3, 1982.

Because of the Cuban construction of the large airfield at Point Salines that clearly had military potential, as well as the Cuban involvement in an island so close to Venezuela, the Venezuelan government sought a means of protecting the country. The government of Luis Herrera Campins discussed with the Reagan Administration the purchase of 24 General Dynamics F-16 fighter aircraft, at a total cost of $615 million. President Herrera on a trip to Washington in November 1981, made it clear that Venezuela did not want "war surplus." "We aren't a market for scrap." If Venezuela might have to contend with Soviet MiG-23s based in Grenada, which could cover all of Venezuela, then Venezuela would find a means to defend her oilfields, refineries and oil installations. Grenada was joining Nicaragua as a Communist satellite of Cuba. In plain words, Cuba a Soviet satellite was developing satellites of its own, and this one was too close to Venezuela. Grenada had signed an economic and technical cooperation agreement with Cuba, which included aid for completion of the new airstrip at Point Salinas.

The plan to subvert the elected governments of the Eastern Caribbean, and replace them with Communist revolutionary governments, was worked out in 1976, on Rat Island, off the western coast of St. Lucia. Maurice Bishop and Bernard Coard of Grenada, George Odlum of St. Lucia, Tim Hector of Antigua and some lesser known Communist sympathizers met in secret conference to plan the political future of the Caribbean islands.

The blueprint for the plan of Grenada was then prepared in Trinidad at the University of the West Indies. In March 1979, as the Russian tourist liner Taras Schenensko steamed into the port of St. George's Prime Minister Sir Eric Gairy was removed (he was actually visiting the U.S.) and Maurice Bishop accomplished his coup d'etat and gained control of Grenada.

The next part of the plan was to select another Eastern Caribbean Government to overthrow. In the November 1979 meeting that Mr. Bishop called, the conferees signed "the St. George's Accord." Violence was now triggered on several islands:

first, St. Vincent whose rioting was put down by the by the intervention of the Barbados regiment, next St. Lucia, and Dominica, where Prime Minister Eugenia Charles displayed her remarkable talents in preventing a coup with a minimum of violence. All of this was coordinated by Fidel Castro.

Only President Reagan's action on October 23-25, 1983, by joining the other Caribbean forces to rescue Grenada, perverted the St. George's Accord from being carried out. Some tragic mistakes were made because of dreadful tourist maps, antique British charts, and troops lacking radio communications and assigned polyester uniforms, and overburdened with 120 lbs. of equipment. (They were like slow moving turtles.)

Grenada was an economic disaster after 4 and half years of socialist mismanagement. Maurice Bishop poured daily tirades on the U.S. and held endless propaganda rallies, while Grenadines were tortured in Richmond Hill prison. It ended with the brutal murder of Maurice Bishop and members of his cabinet, on October 20, 1983, carried out by members of his own government, who then set themselves up as a Revolutionary Military Council. People who ventured out of their homes were massacred in the streets, and on October 21, a *24 hour kill-on-sight curfew* was declared. This was an island with little refrigeration and almost no indoor plumbing! And there was the plight of the 600 US-American medical students at St. George's Medical School. When I was in Grenada in 1997, my driver on a previous trip gave me some horrifying accounts of these events as we drove around the island, as well as accounts by old friends still on the island.

It was this anarchy and violence that so frightened the other members of the Organization of Eastern Caribbean States (OECS), they appealed to the United States for assistance, after they had called on Britain. The five prime ministers of these Commonwealth countries called on Britain for help, but British Prime Minister Margaret Thatcher refused help. The OECS Prime Ministers than called on the U.S. under Article 22 of the OAS Charter, which covers collective security. The Queen's Governor General of Grenada, Sir Paul Scoon, also appealed to President Reagan, under the international principle of "friendly invitation."

The British Parliament and Mrs. Thatcher reacted rather strangely in attacking the U.S.'s action in Grenada. A Grenada under the boot of General Hudson Austin (and a Cuban/Soviet airport in Grenada) would have been far worse than the Falkland Islands (April 1982) under the Argentines. In the latter warfare, the U.S. came out on the side of Britain, just 48 hours after the OAS resolution supporting the Argentine. The United States support of Britain caused great anger in the rest of Latin America, as these countries united against two NATO countries (the U.S. and Britain). Mrs. Thatcher how could you forget – in just a year?

Some U.S. members of Congress and U.S. citizens may have questioned why the U.S. "invaded" Grenada in October 1983. In Grenada most of the people rejoiced at being "saved" by the Reagan effort. And in Venezuela there also was rejoicing that such a potential danger to Venezuela had been eliminated. To make sure that the point was not missed some Venezuelans took out ads in the Venezuelan newspapers, distinguished citizens like Nicomendes Zuloaga, as well as others sent letters to the editors.

The sea lanes north of Venezuela are heavily used by both crude and product tankers. Venezuela has always been Fidel Castro's primary target – not Angola or Nicaragua. Venezuela has the oil reserves and production to wage or prevent war in the Western Hemisphere. The United States and its Allies defeated Hitler in World War II with Venezuela's oil production, and it is this strategic resource that the Russians and Cuba sought. And now, we must add China to countries seeking Venezuela's oil reserves and production.

Angola

In 1977, Cuban military and advisers were assigned to some *24* foreign countries, mostly in Africa. In Africa's smaller countries, Cuban teams were often made up of medical personnel to treat the local citizenry, and serve as bodyguards to protect the local dictator. In return, Cuba was repaid by the country's anti-U.S. vote in the United Nations, or other international forums.

This occurred while Cubans in Cuba had to stand in line for two days to see a doctor. And the Havana bus service deteriorated because so many drivers had been sent to Angola, where Castro had his largest African army fighting against Jonas Savimbi's UNITA force. When the Portuguese finally withdrew from Angola in November 1975, they left a country divided by civil war.

Che Guevara and other Cuban officials met with Agostinho Neto, leader of the MPLA in 1965, and a few months later Cuban troops started to train MPLA guerrillas, and send them weapons. Ten years later with the departure of the Portuguese, Cuban soldiers and Soviet arms began to pour into Angola, in support of the MPLA, which held the capital, Luanda, and its port. The Cuban forces were engaged in battle upon arrival, and by the end of January 1976, there were between 6,000 and 7,000 troops in Angola, reaching 36,000 in the next ten years. Castro stated in 1985, that over 200,000 Cubans had served in Angola.

This protracted warfare destroyed much of Angola's economy and displaced large segments of its population. Without the support Castro's troops, and military advisers from the Soviet Union, the MPLA Angolan government could not have retained power. The Cubans had complete autonomy over their forces in Angola.

Angola was the major combat area, with the largest number of combat soldiers and pilots, and biggest battles that Castro's forces ever fought. There also were some 18,500 Cubans in defensive roles, protecting key infrastructure: rail lines, oil wells (Cabinda), important industrial areas such as those in Luanda, medical aid, construction of roads and bridges etc.

The Angolans grew to resent these Cubans and began to feel oppressed by their role as the new occupiers. The Cubans were better fed; the Cubans took diamonds and wood without payment. The other benefits to Cubans in Angola included: the large force in Angola kept unemployment low in Cuba; the Soviets paid the logistical cost of stationing the Cubans, and the Angolans contributed some $43 million monthly.

If the Russians had gained control of Angola, it would have been an ideal base from where to operate and control Central Africa. They also would have gotten Angola's oil reserves and production, which in 2001 is in the 800,000 b/d range. Offshore Cabinda was discovered by Gulf Oil (now Chevron) that first started seismic surveys in Angola in 1960.

However, Cuba, the Russian surrogate, found Angola to be its Vietnam. With a peace agreement signed between Luanda and UNITA in May 1991, the South Africans and then the Cubans withdrew their forces. The Cuban forces had been in Angola for 15 years!

Cubans did not want to serve in this mercenary army, particularly when the sons of the members of the Politburo or the sons of the principal government leaders did not go to Angola. There were over 50,000 deserters, and Cuban casualties (missing, wounded or dead) rose to over 10,000.

The price that Cubans paid for this mercenary force was exceedingly high. Besides the high combat losses, tropical diseases previously unheard of in Cuba were imported from Africa. These diseases caused problems in the general population, i.e., AIDS, dengue, conjunctivitis or red eye, rare strains of VD; problems in agriculture such as swine fever, etc. All this for Fidel Castro's revolutions!

DGI – Espionage

Castro's Direccion General de Inteligencia (DGI) was the largest most modern, and most aggressive intelligence organization in Latin America. In the 1960s and 1970s, the DGI was the main focus and instrument of espionage, subversion, terrorism aimed directly at the U.S. Government and people. Cuban funds supported the Weathermen, Students for Democratic Society (SDS), Black Panthers, Puerto Rican revolutionaries, American Indian subversive movements, and guerrilla Chicanos. The "Venceremos Brigades" of volunteer U.S. cane cutters traveling to Cuba formed an extensive network of recruits for Cuban subversion and intelligence activities. "The hub of Castro's American operations is the Cuban Mission to the United Nations." (Col. Robert D. Heinl Jr., "Cuba's DGI: Surrogate for Russia's KGB," Detroit News, January 4, 1975) This office served as the headquarters for the DGI. It was all financed by the KGB from the Kremlin.

In 2001, the Venezuelans became aware that Chavez had a new secret police operating out of the Government Palace, managed and trained by the Cuban intelligence service.

There is also electronic eavesdropping on communications which the Chinese are now using Cuba as a good base for spying on the United States. Western intelligence sources say that China has put money into Cuban military telecommunications. With the release of the Cox Committee Report it is clear that the Chinese are operating an extensive spy network in the Western Hemisphere.

In June 2001, Bill Gertz reported in the *Washington Times* that China was shipping arms to Cuba – at least three arms shipments to the Cuban port of Mariel.

China

The Communist Party of China was formed in 1921, and gained control of China on October 1, 1949, and named it the People's Republic of China. It is the world's most populous country with 1.3 billion people, of which 93 percent are Han Chinese.

An old Chinese saying: "When the finger points at the moon the Chinese say, the idiot looks at the finger." And when someone reveals the truth about Chavez's abuses of power, rather than look at the facts, the messenger is attacked.

Chavez said that his revolution is following Mao's -- and although Chavez's education in history is tepid at best, what should Venezuelans expect if he really does intend to follow the Chinese Communist revolution. The most horrendous part of Mao Zedong's revolution were the estimated **65 million** slaughtered or starved since 1949. There were the estimated 20 million to 43 million Chinese who died in the 1959-61 famine caused by Mao's Great Leap Forward, according to the 1997 French book, The Black Book of Communism, and the chapter contributed by Jean-Louis Margolin. "In the 20th century, more citizens were killed by their own governments than by foreign enemies," says Arnold Beichman, research fellow at the Hoover Institution at Stanford University. *"Totalitarianism first of all regards its own people as the enemy."*

And in Jasper Becker's book, Hungry Ghosts: Mao's Secret Famine (also published in 1997), the author attempts the first detailed treatment of the world's most nightmarish man made disaster, Mao's Great Leap Forward. Mao attempted to collectivize Chinese agriculture, abolish all private property, and launch China into the industrialized age overnight. China was propelled into an abyss of horror and hunger whose depths are beyond description. The government went about requisitioning grain in record amounts, leaving little for the rural people. Mass starvation followed in 1959 and 1960. Hunger drove many to *cannibalism*, to eat their own children, as *30 million people starved to death*. Empty stomachs distorted minds to evil. Mr. Becker points out the final inhumanity, as the Communist Party's successful effort to cover up this horrendous debacle. The greatest famine in history never happened. The Chinese Communists are superb dissemblers. Is Mao really the man that Hugo Chavez would follow? Is Mao "the great strategist, the great soldier, the great statesman, the great revolutionary," as Chavez wrote in the guest book at Mao's tomb when he visited China, in October 1999. Is Chavez planning a Great Leap Forward for the Venezuelans? And, seldom remembered was the *"Great Exodus of the Refugees"* to Hong Kong and Macao, in 1961.

Chavez and Mao

If Chavez follows the Chinese revolution then the following is to be expected:

Hunger is already apparent in Venezuela. Poor people are now going through garbage bags. The economic figures for food purchases were the first to drop, between 10% and 12%, in the first quarter of 1999.

Families once so close will be broken-up, a chasm between generations will grow, just as in China under Mao. Many of the young have left or are planning to leave. Soon, Chavez may banish the prodigal sons like lepers, as Mao did. Those who studied and traveled in the West will not be trusted, being suspect of being influenced by foreign ideas. And like the Chinese, Venezuelans will go through life wearing masks, the ones Chavez decrees. Instinctively they will suspect one another. The masses are pictured as idolizing the leaders unquestioningly. And the Young Pioneers (Red Berets) will be marching, and all will suspect all. People will feel unclean and powerless. There will be a scarcity of good will. When will there be a people's barricade, as the Chinese attempted in 1989 in Tiananmen Square, to protect the students on their march and hunger strike.

Old-fashioned envy and injustice is already infecting and fostering incivility in Venezuela, as it did in China under Mao? As in China, all Venezuelans will be in pain. Their traditional optimism will disappear. There will be no way for Venezuelans to provide for the future, to plan.

In October 1949, Mao takes power in China, and ten years later, in January 1959, Castro takes power in Cuba, and in February 1999, Chavez becomes President in Venezuela.

Chavez has closely followed the steps of Mao and Castro in gaining complete political and economic control of Venezuela. Ultimately, the Chavezlandia socialist society which was to better the lives of the poor majority will cause these Venezuelans to wonder why they were born. The 32 Venezuelan prisons, the most violent in the world according to Freedom House, will be bursting with increasing arrests of political offenders, or reflecting personal grudges.

Accounts of Chinese Terror

Bette Bao Lord in her book, Legacies, A Chinese Mosaic (Knopf 1990), writes: "There are no words to describe to innocents the mysterious density of terror," the inhuman tactics that the Maoists name "exhaustive bombardment," that reduces the victim to physical collapse and mental confusion, truly degrading. (p239)   Chavez has made good use of the Chinese Party technique of spreading vehement denunciations prior to a political move.

Another book about Chinese atrocities is Nien Cheng's Life and Death in Shanghai (1987), whose husband had worked for Shell International Petroleum. For 17 years, some foreigners and foreign companies, like Shell, had remained in Shanghai, staying even through the Great Leap Forward. But with the arrival of the Cultural Revolution and the Red Guards in 1966, they left. Almost all the senior members of foreign firms in China were locked up in detention houses during the Cultural Revolution, and endured reeducation punishment. Their Chinese employees were believed to have been contaminated, therefore, had to be reeducated and reformed! Self-criticism and confession were first steps! You could not have served the interests of the British firm and remained a good Chinese citizen under socialism. The Red Guards were formed by Mao's wife, Jiang Qing, in 1966, to carry the torch for the Cultural Revolution across China. Their attack was first on the "capitalists class;" to rid the country of the "Four Olds": old culture, old customs, old habits, and old ways of thinking. The definition of *Old* was left to the Red Guards as to what they would destroy.

Shell International Petroleum Company was the only major oil company that wanted to remain in mainland China in 1949. Mrs. Cheng's husband who was the general manager of Shell, died in 1957, and she became adviser to the new British manager of Shell. After Shell closed its Chinese office in Shanghai in 1966, at the start of the Cultural Revolution, Mrs. Cheng was imprisoned for nearly seven years in solitary confinement. Nien Cheng was an obvious target for the xenophobic and culture-hating Cultural Revolution. The relentless interrogations designed to extract the false confession that she had been a "spy of the imperialists," and the inhuman treatment never broke her will or spirit.

Chairman Mao said "everybody in China must take part in the Cultural Revolution," i.e., "The Great Proletarian Cultural Revolution," directed by their "Great Helmsman." *Proletariat* is a man with no property. Factions, not laws, rule under a Communist system; there are always dangers of a life subject to the vagaries of a system that in reality is no system. Fear will undermine progress in such an evil system.

During Mao Zedong's era, one of the most ugly aspects of life in China was the Party's demand that people inform on each other routinely, and denounce each other. It effectively destroyed human relationships. Parents were alienated from their children. Husbands and wives were guarded with each other. It inhibited all forms of human contact. Without friends, people became secretive and hypocritical. And, then there are the Residents' Committee of each district, which are an extension of the police department. They are responsible for weekly political indoctrination of the residents.

There are "the needs of socialism." China sent many young people far away from their parents to work in other parts of the country, and allowed short "marital leave" visits, only once a year. (Cheng, p418) Children grew up barely knowing their fathers, while women brought up children and held demanding jobs. This mindless cruelty was not imposed on Party officials and their children. They received "special consideration," and given jobs in the city. In this and all phases of their lives, the use of the "back door," bribery, and corruption were practiced in all parts of China among the lower-ranking Party officials.

The Cultural Revolution to purify the Chinese was simply an opportunity for personal advancement and ambition by the Revolutionaries. For every power struggle at the top, the people paid. There was no way to get ahead in China except through taking part in political struggles. The object is *revolutionary movement*, i.e., keep the pot boiling! The clumsy non-cooperative bureaucracy becomes utterly unwieldy. (This is what is happening in Venezuela under Chavez.) Better to have socialism's lower production figures than capitalism's higher production figures, or, "rather have socialism's poor harvest than capitalism's abundance." (p459) The conclusion: workers become fearful of doing too much work!

How many of the Chinese slogans will pop up in the Chavista language? The following are some of the favorite Chinese attack words. *Capitalist-roader,* was one of the most common, and the so-called *conspiracy of foreign companies and government departments*, along with *imperialist spy*, and *running dog of the imperialists. To serve the people* was the most publicized slogan of the Chinese Communist Party, used whenever the Party wanted a man to do something he did not want to do. And *internal, internal,* for goods and services reserved for very senior officials, especially military.

U.S. Abandonment of Nationalist China

The first book on Mao's Chinese Revolution that I read many years ago, was Freda Utley's The China Story, published in 1951, by Henry Regnery Company. It is an incredible documentation of how we lost China to the Communists, how the U.S. would not sell arms to the Chinese National Government of Chiang Kai-shek (our ally in winning World War II), just as later we would not sell needed arms to Batista's government in Cuba.

President Franklin Roosevelt and General George Marshall apparently decided that the military situation demanded the abandonment of the principles of the Atlantic Charter, which promised liberty and opportunity, freedom and self-determination, to all nations, including the vanquished. They sacrificed principle for immediate gain, as well as friendliness toward Communism by those who directed U.S. foreign policy during and after the war. They decided to demand unconditional surrender, realizing that this policy must lead to the Soviet domination over Europe.

Freda Utley's book is an analysis of Communist influence in U.S. policy in the Far East, first in China, which led us down the path to war in Korea. Roosevelt started the U.S. abandonment of China at Yalta, in February 1945, when the "pre-eminent rights" in Manchuria promised to Russia were Chinese rights, which were not ours to give away. Millions of Chinese had died in the Sino-Japanese War (began in 1937) to deny Japan the "pre-eminent rights" on their soil, which the U.S. awarded to the Soviet Union at Yalta. The great irony here is that Roosevelt did this to get Russia into the War, when instead it would have been to our advantage to keep Russia out, for Japan was ready to surrender before the Yalta Conference.

United States abandonment of Nationalist China continued with Russia's looting Manchuria of $800 million worth of industrial equipment, and handing over huge supplies of captured Japanese arms to the Chinese Communists whom they allowed to enter Manchuria. (Utley, p7) The United States accepted this violation of the Sino-Soviet Treaty of August 1945, and thus began the Chinese Communist march to victory in 1949.

General Marshall was specifically instructed by President Harry Truman, to exert pressure on the National Government to come to terms with the Chinese Communists. Unless the National Government made peace with the Communists, there was to be no aid. And more important, in Truman's instructions: "United States support will not extend to United States military intervention to influence the course of any Chinese internal strife." Thus, Truman barred China from U.S. aid until Chinese Communist ceased fighting the National Government. What the U.S. was asking for was a coalition government with the Communists. The unrealistic U.S. policy ignored the Soviet's policy of expansion by revolution.

Tragically, U.S. compulsion could be and was exerted only against Chiang Kai-shek and his National Government. Thus, the United States put the Communists in a position where they could blackmail the National Government and thus take over China. Chou En-lai charmed General Marshall and U.S. journalists into believing Mao's Communists were simple "agrarian reformers," fighting against a despotic Chiang Kai-shek.

Each time the Nationalists had the Communist in retreat, General Marshall would step in and persuade Chiang Kai-shek to accept another truce. The U.S. took steps to prevent the Nationalist forces from rearming by clamping an embargo on the sale of arms and ammunition to China. Truman even issued an Executive Order to this effect. Of course, the Communists received not only arms but expert military advice and training from Russia. It seems unbelievable, but the U.S. in the summer of 1946 even assigned officers to train the Chinese Communist armies and sent 400 tons of U.S. equipment for this training program. (Utley, p14) The Nationalist kept winning and General Marshall kept saving the Communists, by forcing the Nationalists to accept one truce after another. It was all so bizarre! The Truman Administration wanted a coalition Chinese government with the Communists, and went so far as to threaten complete withdrawal of U.S. interests, if the Generalissimo did not acquiesce.

South Korea

The United States and its allies would pay dearly for its efforts to install the Mao Communists in China. After Chiang Kai-shek's retirement to Formosa (Taiwan), the Chinese Communists and Russian trained North Korean Army of 500,000 were ready to fight the US Americans. The North Koreans would thus fight *alongside the Chinese Communists* that Truman had supported in achieving power. Unfortunately, the United States Government had not changed, the arrogant stupidity continued. Effective military aid was denied to the South Korean Republic and government of Syngman Rhee. As in the case of China, "the deficiencies of our friends were given as a reason for leaving them defenseless before our enemies." (Utley, p87) Little South Korea was urged to show evidence of its democratic aims by coming to terms with the Communists. It was the same Truman-Marshall-Dean Acheson breathtaking stupidity. "Having abandoned China to the Communists, it seemed only logical that we should let South Korea fall," (p89) and so the Administration refused to let the South Koreans acquire arms for defense – even thwarting the intent of Congress.

Thus, South Korea was invaded from the North, in June 1950, after being given the green light, and the United States became engaged in the Korean War where we lost 34,000 Americans, 1 million Koreans, and 250,000 Chinese. And the U.S. still has a military force on the Demilitarized Zone. The war achieved no purpose! Truman had no need to invoke the United Nations. The reason he did was that he took the United States into the war without Congressional approval first, and wanted the U.N.'s "moral authority." The consequences of this war were enormous. Joseph Stalin polarized the Cold War. China became a nuclear power with the help of the Russians. China under cover of the crisis grabbed Tibet, on October 21, 1950. Korea revolutionized the U.S. public and Congressional attitude toward defense. As for South Korea, it became one of the fastest growing economies in the world, averaging around 9% GDP growth for most of the last 30 years. And North Korea, is ranked last in a list of 161 countries, next to Cuba, as the most economically repressed country in the world, by the 1999 Index of Economic Freedom, published by The Heritage Foundation and the *Wall Street Journal*.

Taiwan

Just before the war, the Communists were almost invited to attack Formosa, since President Truman, on January 5, 1950, announced that "no military aid or advice" would be given to the Chinese Nationalists to defend Formosa. Fortunately the Communists were too busy on the mainland to do so. Today, Taiwan ranks No.7 in the 1999 Index, below the United States, which is No. 6, in the Free category. Taiwan became one of Asia's famous "tigers" in the industrialized world, has a functioning democracy, holds multi-party elections, and has a population of 22 million.

It became obvious to this U.S. citizen while living overseas, that if a country is a reliable ally of the United States, it will be treated badly, because so many U.S. Administrations treat enemy nations better than friendly nations. The United States directly caused the downfall of an ally and friendly government in China in 1949, and in Cuba 10 years later. In both these cases, the U.S. State Department had influential Communist sympathizers working to overthrow friendly governments and install Communists in their place. In China's case, it was known as the

China Lobby, and it now exists in a new form, filled with company executives with or intending to have business operations in China. They see a billion new customers!

The United States fought against China on the Korean Peninsula in the early 1950s; and through the late 1960s, the U.S. tried to isolate and contain China. With President Richard Nixon's visit to Beijing in 1972, the United States developed a strategic alliance with China to contain the Soviet Union. The March 1996 confrontation between the U.S. and China in the Taiwan Strait illustrates the limits of Beijing's understanding of U.S. interests in Asia. Furthermore, the Chinese have now stated in a October 16, 2000 policy paper, that because the foundation for a peaceful reunification of China and Taiwan "is seriously imperiled" by the "hegemonism and power politics" (code words for U.S. meddling), *China was being forced to arm.* It is doing this by purchasing sophisticated Russian made weapons. The People's Liberation Army of 2.5 million troops is still the world's largest army. China has made it clear that it views the United States as its potential enemy, and war with Taiwan is inevitable. Weren't we assured that trade would open up China and make it a friendly and freer country? In 1999, U.S.-China trade was worth nearly **$95 billion**!

Chinese Ballistic Missiles

Modern China – the People's Republic of China (for a long time known as Red China) has a population of 1.3 billion people. It has tried to control its population growth by forced abortion, infanticide and sterilization. The current Chinese President, Jiang Zemin, has sought admission to the World Trade Organization, while trying to prevent Taiwan's admission. In Steven W. Mosher's latest book on China, Hegemon: China's Plan to Dominate Asia and the World (Encounter, 2000), he argues that China's present leaders want to get the U.S. out of Asia. Young Chinese have been trained as xenophobes: to hate the U.S.; and that China is the victim of great historical wrongs that should be avenged. This is particularly worrisome because of China's ongoing ballistic missile buildup.

China is increasing the size and capacity of the People's Liberation Army's ballistic missile and strategic nuclear forces. China already has deployed over 250 short-range ballistic missiles (SRBM), a number expected to grow to over 650 missiles in the next five years, according to the Pentagon. These missiles are undermining the stability in the region, for they pose a threat not only to Taiwan, but also to South Korea, and Japan and the U.S. forces stationed there. As for the United States, the Cox Committee report estimates that China will deploy over 100 ICBMs with over 1,000 warheads by 2015 that can reach the United States!

In Bill Gertz's new book, The China Threat (Regnery, 2000), he reveals the tragic consequences of the U.S.'s foreign policy, which under the Clinton Administration was outright appeasement, and helped to create a new superpower threat to world peace. "China's government and its military poses the most serious internal threat to the United States today." (p.xii) China has targeted the U.S. with an aggressive espionage campaign, while the Clinton Administration determinedly stripped away national security *export controls*. Clinton started with the dismantling of the Coordinating Committee for Multilateral Export Controls, known as COCOM. With the election of Clinton and Gore, "the floodgates opened." "Everything and anything was for sale."(p62) As to the Chinese missile buildup, Clinton did not demand that China stop the destabilizing deployments.

Panama Canal

The Chinese are already close by: in the Panama Canal, in Cuba, and in Venezuela. As the U.S. moved out of the Panama Canal in December 1999, the Chinese moved in, through a company called Hutchison Whampoa Ltd. that got a 25-year concession to operate the Canal's Atlantic and Pacific entrances. (Hutchison also has a port facility in the Bahamas.) Hutchison was given the right to build transshipment seaports on both sides of the Panama Canal: Balboa, next to Panama City on the Pacific, and Cristobal, next to Colon on the Atlantic approach to the Canal. They also got first refusal for control over the former U.S. military bases throughout Panama. U.S. concern is that U.S. Navy ships will be at the mercy of Chinese-controlled pilots, and could even be denied passage through the Canal by Hutchison.

But the greatest concern for the U.S. is the possibility that "China could secretly infiltrate missiles into its leased ports," according to Bill Gertz (p97). They could easily conceal in shipping containers mobile medium-range ballistic missiles that could reach U.S. East Coast cities in times of crisis. "A nuclear war with China over its dispute with Taiwan is a real danger." (p172) Cuba and Venezuela would be the destination for those shipping containers with mobile ballistic missiles.

The Canal was always run as a nonprofit enterprise. Now, Panama wants to become a center for transshipment, especially container transshipment.

However, all of these plans depend on enough rainwater. In 1998, the Canal suffered from its worst drought in 84 years, lowering the fresh water lakes that feed the Canal's locks. The levels of Madden Lake, a major reservoir for the Canal, dropped more than 23 feet, in February 1998. Uncontrolled development of the Canal's watershed is causing massive deforestation and greater water contamination from sewage and industrial waste. As sediment levels rise, the storage capacity of these bodies of water falls, reducing normal operations during a serious drought. There is no system in place to pump from the ocean the 52 million gallons of water needed for the transit of each ship through the locks, which happens an average 35 times a day. Ship size is restricted to 50,000 dwt, depending on length.

Chavez's Protector

For years, the United States and the North Atlantic Treaty Organization (NATO) have conducted annual military aviation training exercises, named Red Flag. Venezuela has been included in these training exercises, but in April 2000, Hugo Chavez said that Venezuela would no longer participate. Nor would Venezuela's Navy participate in the Unitas exercise with the U.S. Navy. He went even further, to attack the School of the Americas, a U.S. warfare-training center, formerly in Panama, where some 5,000 Venezuelan military had been trained. (Obviously, he was not one of them.)

What Chavez had in mind was to substitute the "imperialist of the North," for Chinese ships armed with ballistic missiles. He offered the Chinese a Venezuelan Caribbean naval base! As Carlos Savelli Maldonado, points out in his April 16, 2000 article, "Maniobras Chinas en Venezuela," in El Nacional, the purpose of this is to provoke the U.S. and permit the Chinese Communists to retaliate for the U.S.'s Seventh Fleet that protects the island of Taiwan. 1) This action follows Chavez's refusal to allow the U.S.

ships to land carrying aid and equipment for the Vargas flood victims in January; 2) after refusing to allow U.S.-DEA airplanes to overfly Venezuela in their counter-drug shipments effort; 3) and, Chavez's amazing efforts to mount a Latin American military organization to counter NATO and the United States!

Hugo Chavez is not a friend of the United States. His every effort is anti-Yankee, and he chose China as his support system, and Cuba as his guide. Everyone of his foreign moves has been *toward* the Communists, and "in your face" attacks on the United States. It is not only his rhetorical attacks, but the countries he visits *and* the persons he invites to Venezuela. Fidel Castro leads Chavez's list of honored guests, which include Chinese President Jiang Zemin (April 2001).

Chavez is also attempting to divide Latin America between the Indians and the Whites: thus, the visit of Rigoberta Manchu of Guatemala, and the enormous preferential treatment of Venezuelan Indians in the Bolivarian Constitution.

But to do all of these things, Chavez had to have a "godfather." Therefore, he took his longest trip to China to offer Venezuela as the Cuba of China. A country of 1.3 billion people with the third largest economy, a nuclear power, with $154 billion in foreign reserves, and 20 years with a 10% annual growth, *what a great market for Venezuelan oil*! What could possibly be better in your efforts to separate Venezuela from the United States – Chavez gets a protector and a customer, too. His calculations could not be clearer. He will no longer need the U.S. market for Venezuela's oil exports, and he can do as he pleases ("lo que me da la gana") because China is his protector. There is just one small problem for Venezuela, if China joins the World Trade Organization with the U.S.'s help, what then?

China entered Venezuelan oil production through bidding in the Operating Agreement round, in June 1997. Out of a total bidding of $2.19 billion for the right to operate 18 fields, the Chinese National Petroleum Corp. (CNPC) were high bidders on two fields. The Chinese got <u>Caracoles</u> for $240.7 million and <u>Intercampo</u> for $118 million. PDVSA in this round of bidding added some new terms that limit a company's rate of return. The major oil companies were absent from the winning list. Shell and Exxon did not bid. Shell said they could not see making money under the terms. Most oil companies realized that it was questionable whether a company would make any money on these high bids. Therefore, why did the Chinese bid so high to get into Venezuela? For example, the <u>Caracoles</u> site that the Chinese paid $240.7 million for was only producing 2,700 b/d, which they planned to increase to 10,500 b/d, but on which they have tax rates up to 90 percent. In early 1999, when oil prices were low, CNPC began negotiating with Norway's Statoil to sell them 50% of Intercampo Norte, in Lake Maracaibo.

The Chinese interest in Venezuela is long term. They expressed an interest in joining PDVSA in investing in the construction of one of the two additional modules for the export of Orimulsion to Chinese markets. The Chinese began testing Orimulsion in several power plants in 1997, with the intention of importing 5 million metric tons/year. In 2000, they imported around 400,000 metric tons.

If the purpose of the Chinese is to purchase large volumes of Venezuelan crude oil, as well as Orimulsion, there is the problem of transportation. When it comes to shipping oil long distance, the oil industry use VLCC tankers, in order to reduce the costs. Very large crude carriers of 250,000 dwt, or larger, cannot go through the Panama Canal, which is limited to ships of 50,000 dwt. Therefore, Venezuelan oil headed for China is going to be expensive oil. In 2000, Orimulsion in 100,000 dwt tankers was going around South Africa.

Because of their boundary dispute with Guyana, Venezuela has asked the Chinese to cancel their timber contract for logging in the Esequibo, which Venezuela claims. The Jilin Guyana, Inc. has a license to log in a region between the Rivers Barima and Guainia, or Region 1, the same one where Beal Aerospace Technologies was going to build its satellite launching site. The Chinese have been informed that Venezuela does not recognize concessions granted by Guyana in this region. The question was "is this a government or private Chinese company" – and which party will blink?

Finally, what Venezuelans may have most to fear from Chavez's revolution, modeling itself on Mao's revolution, is the savagery of the Cultural Revolution. Mao's anti-teachers campaign started in the "Red August" of 1966. Teachers were called "class enemies," which students then began to torture and murder. According to Dr. Youqin Wang of the University of Chicago, who has been documenting this depravity of the Cultural Revolution, "the sheer invention of torture . . .: nail-spiked clubs, boiling water, hot cinders, drowning in fountains, the forced swallowing of chemicals, and nails, and excrement, and always the beatings." The students were cheered on by their government, and were sent from Beijing into the countryside, to instruct other students in the brutalization of their teachers. "The students killed not only their principal targets, but their families, too." (*The Weekly Standard*, August 20-27, 2001, pp.18-19)

There is no doctrine for totalitarianism, no dictator admits to the label of modern totalitarian, and there is no argument for totalitarianism. It is a concept developed by political scientists in order to understand unfamiliar political systems. Tyrants focus attention on past frustrations and future perfections. But the question of totalitarian government is how much power the government has over the lives and fortunes of its citizens, and can the citizens protect themselves against the arbitrary use of power? The Nazi and Soviet regimes, with slave labor and extermination camps, propaganda and hostility to human freedom, shared the drive to establish political control over the lives of the people. Mao Zedong and Fidel Castro achieved modern totalitarian governments, i.e., total power over their people. Where is Hugo Chavez heading with all the power he now controls over the Venezuelans, and will they retain any liberty?

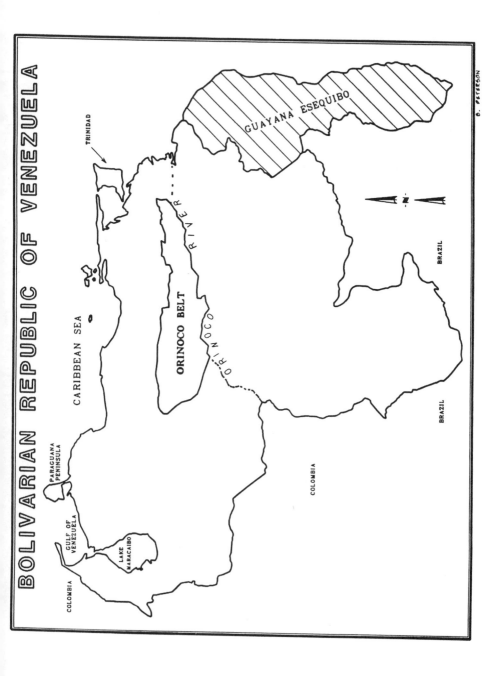

BOLIVARIAN REPUBLIC OF VENEZUELA

CHAPTER VII

VENEZUELA's POPULATION and BOUNDARY PROBLEM

"Governments derive their just powers from the consent of equals who join in civil society to secure their inherent rights to life and liberty." Harry V. Jaffa, Equality and Liberty, 1965.

Venezuelan political history must be understood through its immigration. In the 1920s and 1930s immigration was mostly from the United States, i.e., oilmen working in the new oil industry. During World War II, President Medina in 1944, began to offer advance loans to Spanish, Portuguese and Italian immigrants. These were artisans. The postwar plan called for bringing large numbers of European immigrants to set up agricultural communities. The Europeans came after the War, but they staid in the cities. It should be noted that Venezuela's oil royalties made possible Venezuela's balanced budget and a surplus in the treasury during this period.

Unfortunately, Venezuela's highest income per capita in Latin America began to attract a flood of immigration from the Andean countries, mostly poor Indians. By 1985, the presence of so many illegal undocumented aliens in Venezuela became overwhelming. A Caracas *Daily Journal* editorial (September 4, 1985) stated: "There is no marginal area in any part of Venezuela where the majority of inhabitants is not made up of illegal aliens." They "abuse Venezuelan hospitality, overloading our hospitals and aid stations and thus making public medical care even less competent." They brought contagious diseases that had been eradicated in Venezuela, e.g. tuberculosis and venereal diseases. These illegal aliens greatly increased the numbers of the unemployed both in rural and urban areas. The Minister of the Interior made a request to Venezuelan businessmen in August 1985, "do not employ illegal aliens," which was not heeded. This invasion of illegals greatly increased the population of Venezuela,

195

from a population of 4 million people in 1944, to 17 million in 1984, to 23 million in 2000.

Many in the early groups of legal immigrants returned to their own countries after 5 or 20 years of working in Venezuela. Most of the 75,000 Americans returned to the United States after their contracts were up, and many of the remaining Americans in the oil industry left after nationalization of the industry in 1975. The "Gallegos" returned to Spain after they had saved their nest egg, as did many Portuguese and Italians. The northern Europeans, who because of their education and background entered established companies or started businesses, became wealthy, and joined the upper classes. It was this latter group of Europeans who also benefited during the good times of Carlos Andres Perez's first government, for they were the beneficiaries of lucrative contracts and loans. Venezuela was one of the few countries that welcomed the displaced Jews of World War II.

But it was the illegal immigration from the Andean countries that added to Venezuela's population problem after the 1970s, first from Colombia, then Ecuador, Peru and Bolivia. Not only did many come to Venezuela, they have high birth rates. A large number were Indians, easily spotted because their facial characteristics are different than the few Indian tribes in Venezuela.

The Colombians

The Colombian immigrants are a special case. It is not generally known how the Colombian immigration to Venezuela got started in such large numbers. Colombians and Venezuelans for generations considered themselves sister republics, for they fought together for independence and were part of the Gran Colombia. Colombian schools were considered first rate, and many young women in the western states of Venezuela, like Tachira, went to boarding schools in Bogota (including some of my cousins). Colombians have immigrated to Venezuela for a hundred years, but slowly. And some Europeans, like my Danish grandfather, Julius Jacobsen, living in Colombia and selling his cattle in Venezuela, decided to move to Venezuela.

In the 1950s, as Venezuela's economy grew with increased U.S. investments, Colombian women came to work as maids in the large cities. They filled a new need, because Venezuelan women in the lower class could now get jobs in factories. Even today, most maids are illegal Colombians. But it was the Colombian men who swelled the illegal numbers **after 1970**, and it was not over the narco-traffic in the beginning – it was over emeralds!

Colombia was the major producer of gem emeralds. The Colombian Government owns the mineral rights to the mining and sale of emeralds, and the Central Bank had the concession to the Muzo and Coscuez mines in the Boyaca Department, northeast of Bogota. The Bank has designated certain companies to run these mines, e.g. Colombian Emerald Syndicate, Ltd., which had the Muzo mine, and my father was in charge of from 1919 to 1921, when the government closed the mine. (This was the period before my father went to graduate school, and then to Venezuela in 1923.) The following is a description of life in Colombia in the 1920s from one of my father's letters in August 1920.

"The people down here are gloomy. They don't respond to lighthearted things, nor can they amuse themselves. The lower class dress in black all of the time, and one can read in their faces the lack of fun that should have a definite part in everyone's makeup."

Colombia, before it became known as a source of marijuana, and then cocaine and heroin, was known as the country of beautiful emeralds. But in 1970, mining emeralds became a dangerous job when some 40,000 decided to join in the hunt for emeralds in the Boyaca Department, in the Muzo and Coscuez mining area. Enter the guerrilleros and the numbers of dead start to increase. The government moved in a garrison of soldiers to protect the miners. This provoked an exodus of Colombians to the United States and Venezuela, the wealthier to the U.S., and the poor to Venezuela.

A wave of Cuban Communist-backed violence was sweeping Colombia in 1965. The pro-Castro National Liberation Army (ELN) founded after Castro's 1959 victory in Cuba became financially self-supporting through revenue from kidnappings, extortion, and bank robberies. These Communist guerrilleros were using the threat of kidnapping in the hope that panic-stricken

Colombians would leave the country. Wealthy Colombians, as well as foreigners, received letters from the ELN advising them to leave the country or end up in a guerrilla concentration camp. The ELN, following the Castro-trained guerrilla force in Venezuela, also had a program of attacks on rural towns.

The ELN in the next decades went on to unleash a scorched earth campaign against the oil companies in the Eastern Plains of Colombia. The ELN's prime target has been Occidental, which discovered the giant Cano Limon field in July 1983, and later built the $500 million Cano Limon-Covenas 500-mile crude export pipeline to the Caribbean. The ELN also launches raids on the Caribbean oil-export port. Ecopetrol, the Colombian national petroleum company is the operator of all new pipelines, therefore this is their ongoing problem.

The ELN and the other guerrillero groups have caused through dynamiting of oil and gas pipelines, together with their destruction of pumping stations, exploration camps, and drilling rigs, some of he worst oil contamination in the world, in the Colombian waters. By leaking of oil into marshes, rivers and lakes, the livelihood of thousands of fishermen was threatened, and the costs of the destruction of wildlife and the contamination of agricultural land cannot be calculated.

In early March 1971, the new President, Pastrana Borrero, was forced to order a *state of siege* because of a week of turmoil in several Colombian cities, with many dead, scores injured, and arrested. However, there was so much more to come! And today, Pastrana's son, Andres, is President of Colombia and faces a country so badly divided that he decided to cede 40,000 square kilometers of national territory to the largest group of guerrilleros, the FARC (Revolutionary Armed Forces of Colombia). Now known as Farclandia or Marulandia in an "obstacle-free area," the guerrilleros are in control of about 90,000 people. The five municipalities in the region are still governed by the elected mayors. A fourth of the cocaine was cultivated in Marulandia. Andres Pastrana made his deal with FARC leader, Manuel Marulanda, age 72, in 1998, giving up control of an irregular rectangle of a jungle-like territory at the foot of the central mountain range. However, this does not mean the guerrilleros have given up their terrorism in other areas of Colombia. The slaughter goes on!

Of all the countries in Latin America, it would be hard to find a country that has been at war with itself more than Colombia has during the past two hundred years, particularly the last hundred. One has to wonder how so many Colombians are left to immigrate to Venezuela and the United States when the population is diminished with such wanton killings.

1) In the 19th Century many Colombians lost their lives fighting for independence with Bolivar against the Spanish.

2) Then there was the 1,000 days war between 1899 and 1903, when 100,000 lost their lives.

3) Next was *La Violencia* that was touched off by the Bogotazo, April 9, 1948, led by Fidel Castro, whereby over 300,000 Colombians died in the 1940s and 1950s.

4) In 1970, the Marxist guerrilleros commenced their escalating terrorists activities. Now with nearly 30,000 violent deaths per year, Colombia has become the world's most violent country.

The Communists and the Nazis in Colombia

In the 20th Century, it was Colombia that Moscow first tried to subvert and gain control of in their efforts to stifle U.S. prestige in Latin America. First, Maxim Litvinov arrived in Havana, on April 7, 1943, to be replaced by Andrei A. Gromiko a few months later. The Soviet Embassy in Havana became the center of Communist operations in Latin America. Moscow was able to get 150 Soviet officials accredited in Havana. The Soviet officials first recruited Cuban youths for the USSR in 1943, among them Fidel Castro. These trained Cubans were then sent to Mexico, Colombia, Venezuela and Guatemala. Some of these youths were reserved for the future.

With the announcement that a Pan American Conference would take place in Bogota, Colombia, to adopt resolutions against Communist activities in the Western Hemisphere, Moscow went into action to thwart the Bogota Conference. Moscow sent Lazaro Pena, a Communist union leader, to Bogota to organize workers to promote strikes, demonstrations, conduct sabotage and foment disruptions in order to prevent the international conference from occurring on April 9, 1948. Fidel Castro and Alfredo Valdes traveled as students to subvert Colombian students. They were to attack priests, nuns, and churches, to get Catholics to take to the streets in protest of those attacks.

Besides Moscow's interest in Colombia, Berlin and Hitler had been very interested in Colombia. It was here that U.S. Ambassador Spruille Braden turned back the Nazi air threat against the Panama Canal. The German airline SCADTA in Colombia was a potential menace to the Canal, but oh so curiously, it was 84% owned by Pan American Airways. In 1939, Colombia swarmed with Nazi spies and a Nazi Fifth Column, as well as over 5,000 German settlers. After World War I, the German Government saw its future in the air, first in a fleet of commercial planes (easily converted to military operations), along with a military air force.

German prestige rose with SCADTA, possibly the first airline in the Western Hemisphere developed after World War I, by Peter Paul von Bauer.

It was an ingenious way of circumventing the Treaty of Versailles and train flying officers.

The Communist penetration of Colombia had an early ally: anti-American Nazi propaganda, brought in and distributed by the Communists. The Nazi had a strong organization in Colombia, therefore they didn't need the Communists to distribute their anti-US material. However, one has to remember that this was the period of the Nazi-Soviet Pact of 1939-1941. The Ribbentrop-Molotov Pact (non-aggression) between Hitler and Stalin arranged to divide up Poland, and granted Russia eventual sovereignty over the Baltic states, etc.

The Guerrilleros

Within Colombia there are more than a million people who live in a perpetual exodus, running away from one gang or another. And there is a virtual bidding war in the schools for recruits, between the guerrilleros and the paramilitary. A weak military means a stronger paramilitary presence. "We live in the Wild West, there are many bandits but no sheriff." It is the paramilitary that hold the guerrilleros at bay. The paramilitary organizations were legal in until 1989. They were formed by large landowners in the Middle Magdalena Valley, in conjunction with the Army, to combat the guerrilleros.

The population has been sustained because Colombians have very large families and those who get out often help maintain those who stay. Colombia, which in the past was the most Catholic country in the Hemisphere, initiated a _sterilization_ program. Colombia received the most generous grants for its family planning program in 1970, from Planned Parenthood Association. With former Colombian President Alberto Lleras Carmargo's support, and then under President Carlos Lleras Restrepo (became President in 1966), the U.S. Government and various foundations carried out the most extensive birth control campaign on the continent. The campaign in government medical centers was stepped up under Lleras' successor, President Pastrana. This effort at controlling population was viewed by some as not coming from the undeveloped world, but rather as the efforts of progressive industrialized countries to the north. The utterance of President Lyndon Johnson on the convenience of investing $5 in birth control, instead of $100 in economic development, was widely quoted in the whole Hemisphere.

In their early years, the two Colombian guerrillero armies, the **FARC** (Fuerzas Armadas Revolucionarias de Colombia), and the **ELN** (Ejercito de Liberacion Nacional) financed their warfare by kidnappings and ransoms, and bank robberies, some carried out in Venezuela, in Tachira and Zulia, along the border. FARC is a Marxist insurgency group founded by Manuel Marulanda in 1965, as the military wing of the Colombian Communist Party. Today, their numbers are about 12,000 and they control a wide corridor of Colombia, officially called the Distention Zone, ceded by the Pastrana government, in 1998. _FARC's mission is to conquer all of Colombia_! The ELN was founded in 1964, by Fabio Vasquez Castano, with the help of Cuban advisers and supplies. In the beginning, its followers came from the urban middle class. It remains the smaller of the two Marxist rebel groups. The ELN finances its activities by extorting over $300 million/year from foreign oil companies operating in Colombia.

Security is a major expense and concern for foreign oil companies operating in Colombia. Some companies have to invest as much as 10% of their budgets to protect against attacks and kidnappings. The oil companies pay the Colombian Government a special $1 per barrel "war tax" on oil production, to cover the costs of defending oil field sites; and the companies pick up many of the living expenses incurred by local patrols. In 1996, the war tax amounted to around $250 million. Unfortunately, the government forces give only marginal protection to the oil field sites and the guerrilleros continue to create havoc. How ironic that more oil companies have operated in Colombia in the last three decades than the rest of South America – all the majors and many of the independents. In 1985, there were 61 companies! British Petroleum in 1991, discovered Colombia's biggest field, the Cusiana 2A, in the Llanos foothills of the Eastern Cordillera. Including Cupiagua, BP's reserves in this area are estimated at 2 billion barrels. BP also made a giant gas discovery, called Volcanera, in 1994.

FARC, on the other hand, earns hundreds of millions of dollars a year protecting the illegal drug crops of the narcos, which provides the bulk of an estimated $1 billion per year collected by this guerrillero group. FARC has come up with a novel way of raising funds: imposing a **10% tax** on anyone whose net worth was $1 million or more! The penalty for nonpayment was kidnapping, something they are expert in performing.

Both the FARC and ELN enter Venezuelan territory to evade the pursuit of the Colombian army; as well as to grow drug crops, kidnap and murder Venezuelan citizens. A recently famous case of kidnapping was that of Richard Boulton, member of a prominent Venezuelan family, who was visiting friends in the state of Carabobo, and was forced to fly off in his Beechcraft King 90 with his kidnapers, on July 15, 2000. After 5 months of searching for Boulton, a ransom of $30 million was demanded by the ELN. At this writing he still has not been released. The audacity of the Colombian guerrilleros knows no limits, for they have even assaulted Venezuelan military guard posts along the frontier. Brazil and Panama are also under frequent assault by the FARC and ELN.

The Colombian experience illustrates the impossibility of negotiating peace with Marxists bent on imposing a Cuban-style dictatorship. Each newly elected president would vow to find a way to make peace with the insurgents. Colombians were weary of the guerrillero war. In 1982, President Belisario Betancur tried to fulfill his campaign pledge, when he offered six guerrillero groups amnesty, which was so generous that the terms provoked disquiet in the army ranks and the ruling Conservative Party. About 1,500 rebels accepted his amnesty, which included pardons and government loans to buy farms. Betancur's amnesty allowed insurgents to regroup and the number of armed guerrilleros increased by **65 percent.** The festering Colombian Marxist guerrilleros reached a new level of assaults in 1984.

Cuba has trained both the M-19 and the ELN, but the FARC has obtained its funds from kidnappings, extortionist levies, cocaine trade, and is the much larger of the Colombian guerrilleros. After 1984, it was apparent that the guerrilleros and narco-traffickers had joined forces and had a common benefactor, Fidel Castro. It should now be clear how Hugo Chavez fits into this operation.

Cuban Protection and Aid

In 1979, the United States and Colombia signed an extradition treaty, in an effort to suppress the smuggling of cocaine and marijuana from Colombia to the United States. Colombians were having a hard time bringing drug lords to justice with so many judges under death threats by the narco-guerrilleros. Colombia (Turbay Administration) broke diplomatic relations with Cuba in 1981, following the capture of some M-19 terrorists who admitted they had been trained and outfitted in Cuba. Cuba was not only training and supplying arms to the Colombian guerrilleros, the Cubans after 1980 were also aiding Colombian drug smugglers, allowing large shipments into Cuban waters to be transferred to smaller boats. By some estimates, Castro was getting as much as $50,000 per shipment. Cuba thus got hard currency to buy arms that were then secretly ferried by the drug smugglers to guerrilleros in Latin America.

The Colombian government began to crackdown on the powerful drug industry—*narcotraficantes* – after the April 30, 1984 assassination of Justice Minister, Rodrigo Lara, 38, on a Bogota street. Minister Lara was the leading opponent of the drug trade and after his death, President Belisario Betancur declared a *state of siege*, whereby the President could rule by decree. The government started raiding major cocaine processing laboratories, arrested 600 suspected drug figures, and Pablo Escobar Gaviria who was an alternate member of the House of Representatives. President Betancur went even further and agreed to extradite Colombians indicted on drug charges in the United States. (Under Article 69 of the Bolivarian Constitution, the extradition of Venezuelans is prohibited.)

The Cuban connection to both the Colombian drug trade and the guerrilleros became tragically evident in November 1985, when the M-19 guerrilleros captured the Palace of Justice, i.e., the Supreme Court in Bogota. The M-19 *destroyed files* relating to Colombians that the U.S. was seeking to *extradite* on narcotic charges, <u>and</u> they *murdered* four Supreme Court Judges who had heard, or were about to hear cases involving drug smugglers. More than 90 people died during the battle to recapture the building.

Colombian Penetration of Venezuela

In the early 1980s, I had a graduate student from the Venezuelan Air Force, a Lt. Colonel, who told me that all of the military bases in Venezuela were surrounded by illegal Colombians living in shacks. He saw this as a Fifth Column in Venezuela. During the government of Venezuelan President Herrera, in an effort to encourage patriotism they ordered the playing of the national anthem, <u>Gloria al Bravo Pueblo</u>, several times a day, including at noon, over the radio and television. In the Colombian barrios they played the Colombian anthem.

Colombians have used Venezuela with impunity since the advent of the marijuana/cocaine drug trade and guerrillero war with: illegal aliens; kidnappings; land invasion to grow their drug crops; attacks on bordering Venezuelan oil fields; and the occupation of the Guajira Peninsula, and their claims on the Gulf of Venezuela, at the entrance to Lake Maracaibo.

The zone in dispute since 1830 (when the Gran Colombia split apart, i.e., Venezuela and Colombia), is the large peninsula north of Lake Maracaibo, and the seacoast and underwater areas in the Gulf of Venezuela. A November 1952 diplomatic note, in which Colombia recognized Venezuela's sovereignty over the Los Monjes archipelago near the mouth of the Gulf of Venezuela, would seem to give Venezuela exclusive rights to the entire Gulf. However, any proposed agreement encounters virulent opposition from Venezuelans and Colombians. And when the Colombians came out with a 1995 official map of its frontiers and coastlines it ignored the existence of the Monjes islands in the Venezuelan zone north of the Gulf of Venezuela. It was one more burr in the frontier war! It is contended that President Carlos Andres Perez in 1978 *ceded* to Colombia the Montes de Oca Range's western slopes, when he ordered the boundary marks to be placed along the watershed instead of along the western spurs. However, President Herrera refused to sign the corresponding minutes and the territory was not lost to Venezuela. Ironically, it was on the Guajira Peninsula that Colombia mostly controls, where marijuana was first grown, and the 150 dirt airstrips were built to supply U.S. marijuana smokers with Santa Marta Gold. The traffickers operated with impunity, for the Colombian army did not venture into the Peninsula, except in force.

Venezuela has refrained from exploratory activities in the Gulf out of concern that it would inflame public opinion in Colombia. Venezuela has many areas to explore for petroleum in the years ahead, but there will come a time when Venezuela will pursue its right to explore its Gulf for needed new petroleum reserves.

For many years, i.e., prior to Hugo Chavez, it was believed by some in Venezuela, that one day these two countries would go to war over their border problems. If these countries were in Europe with the problems that Venezuela and Colombia have faced, a war would probably have occurred long ago. Their 1,300-mile border has offered many opportunities for Colombian incursions, since the Venezuelan population is scant along the border. Colombian incursions have also occurred in the Gulf, e.g. in 1987, a Colombian ship, the Caldas, entered Venezuelan waters and stayed from August 9 –12. The incident occurred in waters at the mouth of the Gulf, which are claimed by both countries. Venezuela closed part of the border, informed Venezuelans in Colombia to return to Venezuela, and filed a formal protest. Both countries' armed forces were put on a *state of alert*.

There has also been violence and piracy in the Gulf, particularly around Los Monjes, which is located 44 miles from Macolla Point on the Paraguana Peninsula, and 41 miles west from Castilleles on the Guajira Peninsula. The exit from Lake

Maracaibo through the Gulf of Venezuela to the Caribbean is strategically important to Venezuela. Annually several thousand oil tankers and cargo ships carrying tons of seafood and other products pass through this waterway. The Venezuelans also have constant patrols against Colombian drug traffic in the area.

Chavez versus Pastrana

In 1999, with the new Chavez government, relations between Venezuela and Colombia became even more strained. Colombian President Andres Pastrana opposed Chavez's meddling in Colombian domestic issues, i.e., Chavez's attempts to seek a high profile role in Colombia's fragile peace process. "I'm asking Chavez, please stay in your own land and we'll manage our own problems," Pastrana said, according to the *Washington Post* (24-9-00) ("Lo que estoy pidiendo a Chavez es que se mantenga en su proprio terreno.")

The two Presidents are the same age, but world's apart in background. Andres Pastrana's father was President of Colombia, and Andres has a Harvard degree, speaks English, is white, was a former mayor of Bogota and belongs to the Conservative Party of Colombia. Chavez, on the other hand, comes from the lower class and spent his life in the military, does not speak English, is zambo, had no experience in governing, and gained his fame staging a coup against a democratically elected President, and spent two years in jail for the deed. Pastrana became President of Colombia in August 1998, and Chavez became President of Venezuela in February 1999.

Colombia suffered a devastating *earthquake* in January 1999, which left more than 1,000 dead, and 200,000 homeless in the northern coffee region. The quake caused more than $1 billion in damage. Venezuela suffered devastating *floods* in December 1999, in Vargas state, with around 30,000 deaths and 240,000 homeless. The floods effected 70% of the population of the small state of Vargas, and left a rebuilding bill estimated at $10 billion. Chavez welcomed the "Cuban doctors," and turned away the U.S. Navy that was coming to build roads and destroyed infra-structure, for the devastated survivors. Colombia is a country of 38 million and Venezuela 23 million (of this number there must be at least 4 million illegal Colombians).

Chavez's answer to the Colombian problem was to get closer to the guerrilleros. Both the FARC and ELN have representatives living in Caracas that serve as contacts with the Chavez Government. Raul Reyes, chief FARC negotiator, has stated that they are "the same as Chavez." The Chavez Government never denied this statement. Some Venezuelans wonder, **if** the FARC is the same as Chavez will they one day be fighting **in** Venezuela for Chavez?

Chavez is believed to have been in contact with the Colombian guerrilleros since 1991. They would figure in his plans for a Gran Colombia. But what can Chavez offer these terrorists? First, Chavez on October 2, 1999, declared that the guerrilleros were not the enemy of Colombia or Venezuela. Later that month the FARC said Chavez was the leader to follow. And on November 17, Pablo Beltran, the ELN leader, told Globovision that Chavez and the ELN were part of the *Sao Paulo Forum* and they got together to exchange ideas. The purpose of the Sao Paulo Forum is to extend the Cuban Revolution. Through Chavez, the Forum has been successful in Venezuela, and the next Andean country to take over is Colombia. The Gran Colombia is a perfect subterfuge. To accomplish this Chavez has been accused of supplying both money and arms.

Pastrana asked the United States in 1999, under his Plan Colombia, for $500 million in military aid to fight the drug lords and the guerrilleros, and rebuild the country. The Colombian army is poorly trained, equipped, and led. In August 2000, Colombia was accorded $1.3 billion, more than double Pastrana's request. Pastrana pledged to bring peace to Colombia where roughly half of the country is controlled by the guerrilleros, in a conflict that costs 30,000 lives per year. President Clinton visited Cartagena, Colombia for a few hours on August 30, to avow the U.S. military aid that includes U.S. attack helicopters, advisers and trainers (Green Berets) for the "war on drugs," and to deal with FARC. However, the rebels have no real incentive to negotiate peace. The guerrilleros are not yet strong enough in military terms to capture Colombia's urban centers and topple the government. But they have defeated the Colombian Army and now shape the political agenda, and with Hugo Chavez's military they may soon accomplish the final takeover of Colombia.

President Pastrana faces the most daunting tasks. First, fight a war against two drug-rich rebel groups; second, battle drug cartels; third, deal with the right wing militias (United Self Defense Forces of Colombia); and fourth, improve a troubled economy; and at the same time improve the human rights record of the country's security forces. He's pressured by the United States on one side and his Latin American colleagues on the other. Panama does not want to get involved in Colombia's problems, while Ecuador borders Colombia's rebel-dominated Puntumaya Province and is seen as very vulnerable. The overthrow of President Jamil Mahuad in January 2000, is believed to have had the support of Chavez. President Noboa's Foreign Minister, Heinz Moeller, made this accusation to Jose Vicente Rangel when he was still Chavez's Foreign Minister.

Chavez points out that Venezuela also pays a heavy price for this guerrillero war, by heavy border security and unused agricultural lands due to frequent incursions by Colombian guerrilleros. In October 2000, Jose Luis Betancourt, president of the Cattlemen's Federation, stated that the guerrilleros have a presence in 11 Venezuelan states. Chavez could also mention the multitude of criminal attacks in Caracas led by Colombian gangs, resulting in daily deaths in the streets and in homes. Then there is the drug traffic through Venezuela – down the Meta River in Colombia, to the Orinoco; or through Lake Maracaibo. For years, Colombian narcos have used Venezuelan real estate for their drug laundering, greatly raising the price of Venezuelan property, beyond the reach of most Venezuelans. Finally, there is the problem of hundreds of thousands of stolen Venezuelan automobiles that wind up in Colombia, never to return to their owners. There simply is no solution to Venezuela's problems as long as its neighbor is Colombia. But these are not the problems in Venezuela that concern Chavez about Colombia. What is of course of concern to Chavez and his Marxist advisers is Pastrana's Plan Colombia and the U.S. military aid – and they have stated their objection, calling it another Vietnam.

Panama

Then there is the curious problem of Panama for Colombia and Venezuela in Hugo Chavez's grand scheme for his Gran Colombia. Theodore Roosevelt, in 1903, decided to complete the

Panama Canal. The Canal, started by Ferdinand de Lesseps, was abandoned because of yellow fever and malaria. This province of Colombia was separated from the southern continent by an impenetrable, malaria-infested tropical jungle. The Colombian Congress rejected the treaty that Roosevelt proposed, but days later Panama declared itself an independent republic and accepted the treaty. The United States recognized Panama, and Panama reciprocated by ceding the United States a strip of land ten miles wide. Panama received $10 million and an annual rent of $250,000. The first ship passed through the Canal from the Atlantic to the Pacific Ocean on August 15, **1914**. It took ten years to build and cost $340 million.

The whole affair was a momentous accomplishment. Such raw power by the United States, in the end was of immense benefit to the international community. And, since December 31, 1999, the deadline President Jimmy Carter negotiated in 1977, Panama is running the Canal, and the U.S. has moved out! Ironically, it is now Colombia that needs U.S. help against the narco/guerrilleros in this area (which the Cuban trained M-19 used, to infiltrate into Colombia). It is only a matter of time before the guerrilleros move into undefended Panama, which has no army. And who will then protect the Canal? The Chinese?

A prime objective of the Communists was always to ease the United States out of control of the Canal Zone. In this the Communists had their man, Alger Hiss, in place in the State Department, in the Office of Special Political Affairs, in the 1940s. "If he could put over the fiction that the Zone was 'occupied territory,' the Russians would be able to demand that the UN have a voice in the operation of the Canal." (Braden, Diplomats and Demagogues, p354) But instead of the Russians, it is the Chinese who made it in after the United States moved out.

The Flight of Colombians

Colombians of means during unsettled times have traditionally immigrated to the United States, just like the Cubans. In the early 1960s, when I was living in California, in the San Francisco area, there were a number of Colombian families from Medellin and Bogota. The husbands were going back and forth for a month at a time, to run their businesses in Colombia, leaving their families safe in California. The reason for their departure from Colombia was fear of kidnapping. During my 18 years of teaching in U.S. universities, I had many college students from Colombia, in similar circumstances. This was not the case with Venezuelans, who always planned to return to Venezuela after their U.S. studies were concluded. Venezuela had very little brain drain until recent years. Now its departure of its foreign educated young professionals is a river flow.

The following are quotes about Colombians from a front page article in the *Wall Street Journal*, (8-30-00) by Jose de Cordoba, with the title "Executive Retreat."

"The flight from Colombia comes amid a wave of emigration from its neighbor Venezuela, spurred by President Hugo Chavez's heated rhetoric of class warfare and his erratic economic policies. The timing of the brain drain is terrible: As more and more entrepreneurs liquidate their businesses, lay off workers and sell their houses to raise capital for their exodus, the legions of unemployed swell, feeding the cycle of violence and poverty that is badly damaging both countries."

"The Colombian government estimates that 800,000 people have left during the past four years. Last year, about 366,000 applied for nonimmigrant U.S. visas, more than double the number that applied in 1997."

"Now a different type of refugee can be found on the streets of Miami: "airplane people," middle and upper-class Colombian professionals desperate to stay in the U.S. on their tourist visas."

"Colombian kidnappings have been particularly rampant in the past 18 months. In April last year, guerrillas seized a domestic Avianca airline flight with 46 passengers aboard and held them for ransom."

"Armed with automatic rifles and <u>personal computers</u>, guerrillas often stop traffic, check motorists' bank records, then detain anyone whose family might be able to afford a lucrative ransom."

Once again, another group of Latin Americans are escaping their insecure countries, Colombia and Venezuela, and going to Miami, and making financial and cultural contributions. While there are many reasons concerning personal security for leaving, the basic reason is to save the children!

Xenophobes in Venezuela

There are some xenophobes in Venezuela who are encouraging others to leave the country. A group calling itself the "Simon Bolivar Front of Sovereign People of Venezuela" in August 2000, started handing out pamphlets in Caracas and other cities, and using the Internet. They were demanding the departure of Venezuelan citizens of Spanish, Italian and Portuguese heritage, and calling for popular courts to judge these people and to freeze their bank accounts and investments. It is a Pandora's box that could easily attack other nationalities from sister republics, *and U.S. citizens.* Just who are the members of the "Simon Bolivar Front? And why didn't Chavez condemn this xenophobia and put a stop to it? Is he behind it, as a distraction from his government's failures to fulfill his countless promises to improve the lives of the poor, and end corruption?

Since Chavez started defending every action with the Liberator's name, the name of Simon Bolivar is regularly abused. Whatever you want to do in Venezuela now that is questionable, or cruel, or unworthy of Venezuelans, just tack on the great name of Simon Bolivar.

Simon Bolivar and Gran Colombia

In Jose Gil Fortoul' classic and superb three volume, Historia Constitucional de Venezuela (1930), there is much that can give insight into Chavez's grandiose thinking. The following paragraph I translated from Vol. I, p.476, covers Bolivar's aspirations for liberating the countries of Latin America, following the liberation of Venezuela, Colombia, Ecuador, Peru and Bolivia.

"Other grandiose projects had also seduced, during this time, the genius creator: declare war against Paraguay, where the eccentric Dr. Francia governed, and annex it to the Confederation of Plata; invade Brazil, to substitute the Imperial Republic; take part of the Colombian army to gain Cuba and Puerto Rico's independence; unite in a grand Confederation all of the Republics of Spanish origin and crown his [Bolivar's] career by disembarking with his army in Spain (romantic after the conquest) to transform it also, into a modern democracy. A vast ideal, that if realized would have changed the destiny of the world."

If his hero, Bolivar, could think so grandly, then Chavez thinks he could fulfill Bolivar's grandiose dream. Bolivar, spent the last years of his life (died at age 47, on December 17, 1830) without funds. trying to prevent the dissolution of his Gran Colombia, and consumed with tuberculosis. Unlike Chavez, Bolivar had a revulsion for dictatorship. Acting only for the welfare of his countrymen, he encouraged them to wage a war that left the nation in ruins and committed to tyranny.

Simon Bolivar was born July 24, 1783, in Caracas, to one of the noblest and wealthiest families among the Creole aristocracy. The Bolivar family, from Basque, Spain, had first settled in the West Indies, in Santo Domingo between 1550 and 1560. Simon de Bolivar was assigned to high government positions. After going to Venezuela, the Bolivar family intermarried with aristocratic families of Caracas; and the San Mateo, an <u>encomienda</u> worked by Indians, remained in the Bolivar family for 200 years. The life and deeds of Simon Bolivar were unlike any other in South America. He successfully led his men to free five countries from Spanish rule.

Gran Colombia was established by Bolivar in 1819; and its Constitution in August 30, 1821. The war with Spain was still engaged in Venezuela, Nueva Granada (present Colombia) and Ecuador. Bolivar was named President and Francisco Santander, Vice-President.

Never before has a general covered so much territory on horseback, and over such mountains as the high Andes, as Bolivar. His Llanero horsemen called Bolivar "<u>culo de hierro</u>." Bolivar had the iron determination of the Spanish conqueror and his tough Basque heritage. Bolivar built his army out of nothing. It was his unshakable belief in freedom, and in himself as its instrument, that made it possible for him to defeat the army of the greatest military power, Spain. In 1817, after escaping a Spanish ambush he stated his plans: "I shall liberate New Granada and create a Greater Colombia. I shall carry the banner of liberty to Lima and Potosi." And he did! But, oh the price he paid, and others, too.

Bolivar's dream of Colombia was proposed in his report on December 14, 1818, to the Congress (of Angostura). The name **Colombia** was Bolivar's from Columbus (<u>Colon</u>). The boundaries included the former Captaincy-General of Venezuela, and the former Viceroyalty [higher than Captaincy] of New Granada, whose public debts were to be consolidated. The executive would be a president and there would be three Departments, each governed by a vice-president. The Departments would be: Venezuela with Caracas its capital; Quito (today Ecuador) with Quito its capital; and Cundinamarca (today Colombia) with Bogota its capital. For the new Republic, there would be a new capital city called Bolivar, to be selected by the Congress. Bolivar states in this report: "The union of New Granada and Venezuela is the sole aim I have entertained since I took up arms." Venezuela gained its independence after Bolivar's victory at the battle of Carabobo, June 24, 1821, and was incorporated into the Gran Colombia. (However, Spain did not recognize Venezuela's independence, until March 30, 1845.)

The very formation of the Gran Colombia in 1821 was cause for suspicions and hostility between the various parts of the new Republic, therefore, the cause of Colombia's eventual disintegration, in 1830. In Venezuela, there were important men who opposed being ruled from Cucuta, and later from Bogota, and in 1826 brought about a separatist revolution.

In 1830, Bolivar had planned to go to live in Europe, but he became too ill and died. He was to depart from Cartagena on an English ship. The state of anarchy that Bolivar had prophesized arrived and his Gran Colombia was falling apart. On May 13, Ecuador severed from Gran Colombia; and on June 4, Antonio Jose de Sucre was murdered in the mountains on his way to Quito from Bogota. General Sucre was a generous and good man who was hated and pursued only because of his virtues. His talents were exceptional, his merits so undeniable, some day he would be chosen President, a post he did not seek. Sucre became Bolivar's commander-in-chief of the army, his most trusted deputy, and after winning the battle of Ayacucho in Peru, Bolivar appointed Sucre Marshal of Ayacucho, for liberating Peru. With Peru, South America was liberated from Spain, and the Liberator had reached his goal. Bolivar continued to be President of Gran Colombia and now Dictator of Peru, and his desperate problems now centered on his enemies, the very people he had fought and sacrificed his worldly possessions to free. "All my reasoning comes to the same conclusion; I have no hope of saving the fatherland." "I am of the opinion that everything is lost forever."

The tragedy of these independence leaders came in their bitter final days: Francisco de Miranda, the precursor to the Wars for Independence, died in a Spanish prison; Jose de San Martin, who liberated Argentina, and helped to liberate Chile, was in exile in Europe and died there, in 1850; Sucre was murdered; and Bolivar was outlawed from Venezuela and awaiting death, in 1830. What had 20 years of war and revolution brought? Bolivar's often quoted bitter answer: **"We have plowed the sea."**

Bolivar's mistake was not stopping after he had freed his own country from Spain in 1821, and governing it as his countrymen wanted him to do. Once he went on to free the rest of the continent, his countrymen turned against him, and his enemies accused him of treason. Colombia, his creation, began to disintegrate. When news of his death reached Venezuela there was rejoicing. Today, he is entombed in Caracas in the Panteon with the statues of the Founders. And the name "Bolivar" is ever present in every speech of Hugo Chavez. What crass irony!

The best biography of Simon Bolivar in English is by Gerhard Masur, 1969, and he ends this book with a quote by Bolivar in his last year of life.

"I love my country, and I think I understand it. . . . When Colombia was the prey of Spanish despotism, I ventured my life and my fortune for the victory of independence. I have gone even further. I have led the name of Colombia to the slopes of the Chimborazo and the Pichincha. . . . The dictatorship which I hold has not the omnipotence of tyranny which I abhor; it is the sacrifice which I offer to the public order. . .

"This country will pass through all forms of government until the day dawns when the Anglo-Saxon race invades Hispano-America in a democratic fashion and one immense nation is formed that one day will conquer the American sea, and will bring the wealth and civilization of Europe to this great continent. . . .

"I have achieved no other good than independence. That was my mission. The nations I have founded will, after prolonged and bitter agonies, go into an eclipse, but will later emerge as states of the one great republic, AMERICA."

This statement by Bolivar is not quoted by Chavez, for obvious reasons!

Bolivar had a unique education through exceptional tutors, starting with Miguel Jose Sanz; Andres Bello, Venezuela's gifted poet and scholar; and the longest one was Simon Rodriguez, who had studied Rousseau. Rodriguez followed Rousseau's teaching of the fictional student Emile with Bolivar. After Rodriguez had to flee from Venezuela, Bolivar went to Europe and continued his education, more formally, under the guidance of his uncle Esteban Palacio. He had contact with the Spanish court and the atmosphere of a great European capital. And, he met his future wife, Maria Teresa de Toro y Alaysa, who unfortunately died of yellow fever, six months after Bolivar took her to Venezuela in June 1802. He was only 21, and returned to Europe. He was in Paris when Napoleon crowned himself Emperor of France in 1804. This made him think of his own country's enslavement and the fame that would accrue to him who would liberate it. He met up with Simon Rodriguez again and took a walking tour of Europe. On top of Monte Sacro in Rome, Bolivar made his famous oath not to rest until he had freed his country from Spain. Bolivar returned to Venezuela in 1807.

Venezuela's Declaration of Independence came on **July 5, 1811**, and after the fall of the First Republic, Bolivar became the personification of Venezuelan liberty. After Bolivar entered Merida in May 1813, he was hailed as El Libertador, the only title he aspired to, and for which he is remembered in Venezuela and South America.

Bolivar's great battles would not have been won without the help of the soldiers from Nueva Granada, and his brave British and Irish legionnaires. The experienced European soldiers trained his inexperienced American brothers-in-arms, and became a vital element in the melting pot of the American future. One Irishman in particular, General Daniel O'Leary, became Bolivar's Adjunct and one of his closest confidants. O'Leary's careful written accounts of Bolivar's exploits, published in 32 volumes, 1879-1888, gave us the history record we otherwise might never have had, of Bolivar and the Wars for Independence.

Venezuela in the Colonial period existed as an integral unit for only 36 years (1777-1811) under the central political power of the **Captain-General**, whose capital was Caracas. Prior to this there were only three provinces: Caracas (1577), Cumana (1658), and La Grita (1622). Venezuela had separatist tendencies not only from Spain, but *between* provinces, as well. Indeed, the War of Independence was noted for its lack of unity among the rebels! And, thereafter! Captain Guillermo Hernandez Jacobsen, a medical doctor and pilot in the Venezuelan Air Force, said to me in 1958, "Any Venezuelan campesino with a machete in hand thinks he's a leader."

Venezuela's Boundaries

Amazonas

The Federal Territory of Amazonas (now a state), was once the entire Southern part of the Captaincy-General of Venezuela. This large zone was bounded to the north by the 1st parallel, and bordered by the Piedra del Cocui and the Essequibo springs on the other side. During the Captaincy the area looked like a perfect square reaching as far as the equator. The delimitation of the Amazon began with a series of misunderstandings between the Spanish and the Portuguese empires. Pope Alexander's papal decision, Inter Caetera of 1493, divided the world between Castille and Portugal in such a way that Portugal was not given any part of the New World. The following year, the Treaty of Tordesillas pushed back the dividing line from 100 to 370 leagues giving Portugal a foothold on the subcontinent and enough to settle in Brazil.

After Venezuela seceded from Gran Colombia in 1830, the battle for lands continued, and Venezuela and Brazil began to dispute borders. The first border treaty between Venezuela and Brazil was signed on May 5, 1859, giving the Guainia waters to Brazil. However, the tributaries of the Guainia that were recognized as Venezuelan were later lost to Colombia. The border with Colombia was negotiated for nearly 100 years, and finally on April 5, 1941, under President Lopez Contreras, the "Treaty for demarcation of frontiers and navigation of rivers common to Venezuela and Colombia," was signed. Venezuela lost almost one-third of the Federal Territory of Amazonas. With Brazil the border went better for Venezuela. Under the Caracas Act of 1873, Venezuela was granted a major part of the Amazon, some 3,700 square kilometers.

The Amazonas was where the Europeans searched for El Dorado, and was the home of the great Cacique, Arichuna. In 1800, Baron von Humboldt and Bonpland made their famous voyage through the Amazon region.

In 1971, there were between 75,000 and 100,000 Indians in Venezuela. President Rafael Caldera launched a Conquest of the South in an area of southern Venezuela, comprising of 242,000 square kilometers, more than one-fourth of Venezuela's territory. This southern area is composed of the Cedeno District of Bolivar State, the Amazonas Federal Territory (now a state), and the greater part of Apure State. The largest population of Indians lived in this area, though widely dispersed, 2 inhabitants per 100 square kilometers. Approximately 40% of these Indians were not included in any of the country's cultural, or economic activities, had no ties with the government, and did not speak Spanish. In other words, Venezuela has a huge undeveloped land area, rich in natural resources, agricultural land, forests suitable for harvesting, minerals, and a considerable hydro-electric potential, inhabited only by scattered Indian tribes.

Three New States

Venezuela for many years had 20 States with Legislative Assemblies. In the previous Constitution of 1961, they were all named. They are Anzoategui, Apure, Aragua, Barinas, Bolivar, Carabobo, Cojedes, Falcon, Guarico, Lara, Merida, Miranda, Monagas, Nueva Esparta (Margarita Island), Portuguesa, Sucre, Tachira, Trujillo, Yaracuy, and Zulia. Besides the States, the national territory was composed of the Federal District, two Federal Territories (Amazonas and Delta Amacuro), and the Federal Dependencies, which include the archipelagos and a number of individual islands.

A curious thing happened when the December 1999 deluge hit Caracas and its coastal mountains. Suddenly all news articles reported on the disasters occurring in the State of Vargas. And when did this area become a state? This question turned into an inquiry to find out when Venezuela got **three** new states, which was finally answered by a longtime friend, former president of one of PDVSA's operating companies, who went to great effort to find out the dates. The difficulty he had in obtaining this simple information, demonstrates how frustrating it is to get any

217

information in Venezuela that is connected in any way to the inefficient government. The attitude of government employees is *please do not bother me.* This says so much about doing business in Venezuela. It truly boggles the mind!

I now reveal the formerly unavailable information, which took *9 months to obtain.* The two Territories were made into states, first, <u>Delta Amacuro</u>, on August 3, 1991, and <u>Amazonas</u> on December 31, 1992, when Carlos Andres Perez was President. The newest state, <u>Vargas</u>, was formerly the District of Vargas, and was carved out of the Federal District (where the capital, Caracas, is located). It became a state July 3, 1998, when Rafael Caldera was President, and just months before the December 1998 presidential elections.

One might ponder why no one knows when these new political states were formed, and conclude that the Federal system in Venezuela is irrelevant. All power is concentrated in the hands of the President – Chavez! The 1961 Constitution mentions the 20 States by name, the 1999 Constitution does **not** mention their names or number, however it does name all of the islands in the Federal Dependencies. In Chavez's new Constitution he not only changed the name of the country, but also the Federal District to Capital District.

Trinidad -Tobago

Then there is Trinidad, only about seven miles from Venezuela at the nearest point in the Gulf of Paria, which should have been a Venezuelan island like Margarita. Columbus discovered the island in 1498, and in 1530, the Province of Trinidad was created. Spanish settlers arrived in 1532, and named the capital Port of Spain (<u>Puerto Espana</u>). Columbus discovered Venezuela the same year, 1498, and this resulted in one Spanish colony. In 1777, Spain made Venezuela a Captaincy-General, which included Caracas, Cumana, <u>Guiana</u>, Maracaibo, Margarita, and <u>Trinidad</u>. However, the British gained control of Trinidad in 1802, and when Venezuela gained its independence from Spain in 1821, Trinidad was a new British colony.

In the future, Venezuela will probably be challenging Trinidad over the drilling and production of natural gas in the Gulf of Paria. Trinidad produces approximately 120,000 b/d of crude, but recent natural gas discoveries have turned Trinidad into a gas producing country, shifting its dependence from oil to gas. Trinidad is producing natural gas for liquid natural gas (LNG) for export, and would also like to attract gas-to-liquids (GTL), ammonia, ethylene, and methanol plants. Venezuela has made two LNG attempts (Cristobal Colon in 1990, and Sucre Gas in 1994), and now is on its third attempt in the last 10 years, to develop its gas discoveries north of the Gulf of Paria. Both Venezuela and Trinidad have large gas discoveries north of the Gulf of Paria, while Trinidad has commercial discoveries in the Gulf of Paria.

Amoco made giant gas discoveries in the 1980s and 1990s on Trinidad's east coast, which led to their large investments in natural gas and LNG infrastructure. Atlantic LNG's newly built $1 billion LNG single-train plant, at Point Fortin on the Gulf of Paria, started operations in January 1999. Atlantic LNG project was a joint venture of Amoco (now BP) LNG, 34%, British Gas Trinidad LNG, 26%, Repsol International Finance (now Repsol-YPF) 20%, Cabot Trinidad (now Tractebel), 10%, and NGC Trinidad and Tobago LNG, 10%. More natural gas was discovered in August 1997, by a British Gas consortium off the north coast of Trinidad. Most major foreign oil companies are active off the north coast. British Gas and other companies have a stake in blocks off the east coast, where most production is now occurring. BP through its acquisition of Amoco has an estimated 70% of gas production offshore. The government is encouraging an aggressive expansion program.

Eco Electrica L.P., a joint venture between Enron and Edison Mission Energy, began importing LNG from Trinidad for its new 507-megawatt power plant in southern Puerto Rico, in July 2000. Before this in May 1999, Atlantic LNG began exporting LNG to the Distrigas import terminal in Everett, Massachusetts. Trinidad can supply the most competitively priced LNG to southeastern U.S. markets. Its liquefaction facilities are economical and efficient, and its proximity to the United States is most advantageous. And, it may be the only LNG that meets current U.S. natural gas pipeline specifications for heat value, 1070 maximum, on the east coast. Furthermore, Trinidad's proven natural gas reserves of 21 trillion cubic feet are expected to grow with more exploration.

With Trinidad now prepared to expand its LNG exports to the United States and Europe, and construct two new LNG trains, one for 2002 and another for 2003, increasing their total exports to 10 million metric tons/year in 2000-05, they will need to produce gas from the Gulf of Paria. Thus, a new Venezuelan boundary dispute is about to get under way, with Venezuela disputing with Trinidad the flow of gas under the Gulf of Paria!

The Guayana Esequibo (Essequibo)

First the confusing spellings: Venezuela spells this river and the land area it borders, the Esequibo, and has its own **Guayana** region nearby. **Guyana** was first used by Sir Walter Raleigh, in 1595, to describe the "Wild Coast," which today is the country of Guyana. And, Guyana's spelling for the river and the land in dispute is Essequibo. It originally was part of a British colony called British Guiana (1831). [There were originally three Guiana colonies side by side, British Guiana, Dutch Guiana (now Suriname), and French Guiana. French Guiana is now the only remaining European colony in South America, and is where France launches its Ariane rockets from the European Space Agency Centre, in Kourou.]

In March 2000, Hugo Chavez said the Esequibo was back on the negotiating table. Chavez said the decision of the International Tribunal of Arbitration in 1899 in Paris was null and had stripped Venezuela of the Esequibo. Romulo Betancourt's government in 1962, pulled this dead carcass out of its grave when they raised the question at the United Nations, regarding the validity of the 1899 accord. The reason Betancourt did this was because the British Government was about to grant independence to British Guiana, which became Guyana in May 1966. Curiously, it was after this that Venezuela started to add this area to the Venezuelan map, as the Zona en Reclamacion with Venezuela's border at the Esequibo River. The first map I have with this Zona added on is a Creole Petroleum map.

Venezuela and the British signed an accord in Geneva, February 17, 1966, which provided for the creation of a Mixed Commission formed by two representatives of Venezuela and two from British Guiana (Guyana).

Should the Commission fail (and they did) to reach a settlement after four years, the governments of Venezuela and Guyana were to, as a last resort, call on the Secretary General of the U.N. under Article 33 of the Charter. Venezuela proposed a plan for the joint development of the remaining disputed 45,000 square mile area. The size of present day Guyana is 83,000 square miles, and Venezuela's claim would amount to more than half of Guyana, which is the better half. On the other border to the east, Suriname, a former Dutch colony, is also claiming some of Guyana's land. Again, the border question dates back to colonial times when the Dutch territory was ceded to Britain. Britain claimed Demarara, Essequibo and Berbice, by conquest, in 1814, from the Dutch, whose rights in turn rested on their occupation of Spanish territory.

The Esequibo was the largest tract of land that Venezuela lost after gaining its independence in 1821. The surge of revolutionary feeling and the passion for politics occupied the Venezuelans from one government to another for the rest of the 19th Century. They simply were not protecting their borders, which were so distant from Caracas. The British claimed the territory by conquest from the Dutch in 1814; and the British government in 1834 sent Robert H. Schomburgh to explore Guiana, and in 1840, to make a survey of the country. Without consulting the Venezuelan authorities, Schomburgh set up boundary marks as far north as the mouth of the Orinoco River. Although Great Britain did agree to remove the boundary marks when Venezuela protested, Britain nevertheless went right on publishing maps including this huge tract.

In 1887, Venezuela demanded the evacuation of the territory held by Britain, from a point east of the Moruca River, and broke off diplomatic relations with Britain when the demand was rejected. From 1876 on, Venezuela repeatedly tried to get the United States involved, citing Britain as violating the Monroe Doctrine of 1823. Finally, in 1895, President Grover Cleveland, worried over British expansion of power in the Caribbean, got involved in Venezuela's boundary dispute with Britain, and demanded Britain accept arbitration. There was the additional concern that Britain was trying to re-establish the monarchy in Brazil. Britain's position was that it would settle the dispute whenever Venezuela renounced her unreasonable claims to lands east of the Schomburgh line.

The United States now became very much involved in this issue. Congress in February 1895, unanimously acceded to Cleveland's request to appoint a commission so that the U.S. might determine the true boundary line – and the Commission of distinguished Americans was appointed in January 1896. Civil War veterans rushed to offer their services. Theodore Roosevelt wrote: "I earnestly hope our government do'n't (sic) back down. If there is a muss I shall try to have a hand in it myself." The U.S. press was on the subject. Finding themselves at odds with Germany's Kaiser Wilhelm, with the French and the Russians, the British could not risk war with the United States over a Venezuelan boundary dispute over uninhabited land. Furthermore, all the United States was asking was that the matter be arbitrated. Thus, Britain accepted the U.S. as surrogate for Venezuela and agreed to arbitration in principle, just as William McKinley became U.S. President, in 1897.

The problem for Venezuela over the Arbitration Tribunal was Britain's insistence on Britain having two members of Britain's highest Court, two members of the U.S., and a neutral European jurist – a Russian. The two British judges and the Russian supposedly made a deal to vote for the line already claimed by Britain. On **October** 4, **1899**, the Arbitration Tribunal handed down a unanimous award – and gave no reasons. The award granted Great Britain almost 90 percent of the territory in dispute, with the exception of the mouth of the Orinoco River and a region of about 5,000 square miles on the southeastern headwaters of the Orinoco. This decision remained a mystery as to how it was decided, until 1949.

Mr. Severo Mallet-Prevost, one of four distinguished American counsel representing Venezuela before the Arbitration Tribunal, upon his death in 1949, left a Memorandum addressed to Judge Schoenrich. [Others representing Venezuela were: ex-U.S. President Benjamin Harrison; ex-Secretary of War, General Benjamin S. Tracy; and Mr. James Russell Soley]

Mr. Mallet-Prevost revealed the pressure brought upon the American members representing Venezuela. The Russian President of the Tribunal, Professor Martens, had called on the two

American members to say that the two British members wanted a unanimous award, and if the Americans did not agree to it, he would vote with the two British judges for the line claimed by Britain, thus a majority vote. The two American judges, Justice Brewer and Justice Fuller were greatly disturbed by the proposal for they thought the evidence (later printed in 11 volumes) clearly showed Venezuela's right to considerable territory east of the Orinoco. However, if the two Americans rejected the Russian judge's offer then Venezuela would lose an even more valuable piece of territory – the control of the Orinoco River Delta.

Mr. Mallet-Prevost concludes his Memorandum, "The decision . . . while it gave Venezuela the most important strategic point at issue it was unjust to Venezuela and deprived her of very extensive and important territory to which, in my opinion, Great Britain had not the shadow of a right." (dictated on February 8, 1944)

On January 10, 1905, representatives of Venezuela and Great Britain met in Georgetown and formally declared that the demarcation had been completed in keeping with the dictates of the October 3, 1899 Award. Actually, if it had not been for Mr. Mallet-Prevost and his Memorandum this whole matter would have been concluded in 1899. Instead, today, it is a kicking corpse!

While the American efforts in Paris in 1899 failed to achieve the desired goal of all of Venezuela's claim, it achieved more than Venezuela had been able to accomplish in 50 years of protests to Britain. One might ask if the U.S. Judges had not accepted "the British deal," would we have then gone to war with Britain? Curiously, by accepting, U.S. relations with Britain began to improve. Prior to 1895, Britain paid little attention to U.S. wishes in world affairs, and Americans continued to see Britain as their ancient foe, ever threatening. This change in relations was fortunate because the Spanish–American War was in progress in 1898. Ironically, therefore, the two great English speaking powers for the first time grew closer – and it came about because the U.S. Government stood up for Venezuela.

Regardless of past just claims by Venezuela, the fact remains that Guyana is an English speaking country of East Indian and Negro citizens, freely conducting its affairs since independence, in 1966. The formerly "Wild Coast" as it was known to European explorers in search of El Dorado is a land of hot tropical jungles, swamps, mud flats and sand bars. Ten major rivers pouring to the coast cause flooding. Guyana is rich in bauxite deposits, gold, diamonds, molybdenum and manganese, and timberlands. Its main crop for export has been rice and sugar. The most serious internal problem it has is the violent racial feud between Negroes and the East Indians. The East Indians were brought to the colony to work the rice and sugar plantations. The Negroes are descendents of African slaves, with their numbers increasing more slowly than the East Indians. The rest of the population is made up of Amerindians, **Chinese**, Portuguese, and Northern Europeans.

The most famous East Indian was Dr. Chedi Jagan, a dentist, and professed Marxist, who rose to power in 1953, as leader of the People's Progressive Party (PPP), and an admirer of Fidel Castro. The leader of the Negroes was Forbes Burnham, of the People's National Congress (PNC), which split from the PPP in 1955. Burnham became Prime Minister of British Guiana, in December 1964. Curiously, the Esequibo dispute has provided the only subject that binds East Indian and black men. The Venezuelans are the feared menace, so much so that the Guyanese are welcoming the Chinese and their investments, particularly timber logging in the Esequibo. The Guyanese signed a contract with the Chinese company, Jilin Company Guyana Inc., to cut timber in the same region where Beal Technologies planed to build its satellite launch site. Venezuela has protested both of these concessions, as being on their territory.

With Hugo Chavez now rejecting the 1899 border demarcation with Guyana, the latter cannot achieve any progress in its efforts to move from one of the poorest countries in the Hemisphere, to a self-sustaining country utilizing its rich natural resources. In other words, Venezuela may have lost this vast territory through arbitration in 1899, however, it now has Guyana *boxed-in*! Venezuela is now the giant facing a small poor neighbor and preventing it from developing. For example:

In May 2000, the Guyana Government of Prime Minister Samuel Hinds signed a contract for a $100 million commercial satellite launch project with the Dallas company, Beal Aerospace

Technologies. The country would benefit from 500 construction jobs and some 200 permanent jobs in what is a swampland. It would hopefully also attract other high-tech investors. Beal got a 99-year agreement for 25,000 acres as a primary site, and restricted development on another 75,000 surrounding acres. Beal's location on the northern coast is ideally close to the equator to send big commercial satellites into space. It would be the world's first site to be privately financed (100% by Andrew Beal), owned, and operated.

But Hugo Chavez said no deal! "We will not permit that." Chavez claims he is defending Venezuela's honour and sovereignty! In July 2000, he called upon Venezuelan public opinion and retired military to support the Armed Forces, to prevent the installation of a base to launch U.S. satellites on "Venezuelan soil." Chavez won! And, on October 23, Andrew Beal announced he would desist in building his company's satellite launch site in Guyana.

There is another little known historical fact, regarding Guyana, i.e., its close relations with **Moscow**, **Havana** and **Beijing**. Guyana is a strategic budge between Latin America and the Caribbean, easily a threat to its neighbors Venezuela and Brazil, allowing easy infiltration for subversives and drug traffickers. Guyana could have provided the Soviet Union with a base of operations against U.S. strategic missile submarines and interdicting the Middle and South Atlantic sea lines of communication. Thus, while Guyana had a nearly continual negative GNP after independence in 1966, and unemployment averaging about 35%, the Soviet bloc upgraded Guyana's Defense Force.

In the 1970s, most major foreign economic holdings were nationalized, bringing more than 80% of Guyana's goods and services under government control. After 1970, the Burnham government established close ties with the Communist bloc. Burnham applied for membership in COMECON (Soviet bloc's economic community), but was not accepted. Guyanese students were sent to the Soviet Union for "post graduate training." **And**, the Soviet Union and Cuba supported Guyana's claim to the Esequibo.

225

Diplomatic relations with Cuba were established, in 1972. Burnham supported Castro's African guerrilla activities. Chedi Jagan encouraged Burnham to "invite" Cuban soldiers to Guyana to guard against Venezuelan aggression. Cuban advisors shared office space with Guyanese bureaucrats in the Ministries of Finance, Agriculture, Planning, Manpower, and Cooperatives. (Then there is the question of President Burnham, dying August 6, 1985, while undergoing surgery by a team of Cuban "doctors" for a throat ailment.)

Cuban military advisors (400) provided training and technical support to all branches of the Guyanese armed forces in the 1980s, and the Soviets sent arms shipments. Besides Soviet artillery pieces, mortars and SAM-7 anti-aircraft missiles, Guyana received armed North Korean patrol boats, and Soviet Mi-8 Hip helicopters and purchased three TU-154 aircraft from the Soviet bloc. What the Venezuelans also had to be concerned with, during the 1980s, were the 11 new airfields under construction in the Esequibo. This increased military activity occurred after the U.S. invasion of Grenada in October 1983, and the expulsion of the Cubans from this island. Burnham was responsible for alerting the Revolutionary Military Council of Grenada of the impending arrival of the U.S. and Caribbean forces, and he later offered haven to some of Grenada's most militant Marxists.

This problem with Guyana becomes more curious when you consider the two Marxist leaders, Chedi Jagan and Forbes Burnham (both deceased) and their close ties to Fidel Castro, to the Soviets, and China. Burnham received aid from China throughout his governing period.

We, therefore, have an interesting dilemma! The Cubans and the Guyanese have been "Marxist brothers," both running their economies into the ground for decades, and now Hugo Chavez is rattling sabers against Fidel Castro's old friends. But probably there is no dilemma, Guyana has no oil production and is so poor.

Not to be forgotten, if Chavez thinks of sending in the Armed Forces, particularly the Navy to remove offshore oil exploration rigs, he should be aware that Guyana is a member of the British Commonwealth of Nations. And this time, Venezuela would not have the United States on its side, nor the Soviet Union. Since Guyana's independence in May 1966, Venezuela has had the upper hand – possessing the most warships, armored cars and helicopters, etc. The veiled threats and occasional forceful gestures have kept petroleum companies out of the Esequibo, and now, offshore, too. Exchanged insults describe relations between Venezuela and Guyana, but in 1969, new heights of acrimony increased with Venezuela (Andres Aguilar) denouncing the Guyanese government for racial discrimination against Amerindians, concluding that its racial problem was the residue of British imperialism. This was done at the U.N. Security Council, on October 7, with the Guyanese response on October 8, by Sir John Carter. Venezuela's problem was that it resented "the emergence of a predominantly black society on the borders of a predominantly white Venezuela." That was in 1969, before the illegal immigrants arrived in Venezuela en masse.

As one studies this issue, one is reminded of the Balkans, or Israel/Palestine. There is so much unresolved history and hatred between these two countries, that one should not be surprised if Chavez finds an excuse to invade and capture the long lost Esequibo!

How can Venezuela continue to claim land they lost nearly 200 years ago, claiming a border that is within 30 miles of Georgetown, Guyana's capital **and** strip this nation, with a population of 856,000 people, of its richest territory. Guyana needs to develop its petroleum potential so that it does not need to import all of its fuel oil (from Venezuela and Trinidad), most of which goes to generate electric power, because Venezuela objects to their upper Mazaruni River hydroelectric dam project. It can not produce its bauxite into aluminum because they lack the needed power generation. Guyana calls this "economic aggression." And how unseemly this is, with Venezuela's own utilization of its vast oil resources, and its own development of its Guayana region with the Guri Dam and all the power it has for its own "Ruhr" of South America. The Corporacion Venezolana de Guayana (CVG) not only developed hydroelectric power and industries, but fomented agriculture and built a model city for the region. Yes, Venezuela was so rich, and Guyana is so poor.

Therefore, in South America, Bolivia and Ecuador are not the only countries that Simon Bolivar freed from Spain that after independence lost large tracts of their territory to their neighbors. Ironically, it is some of these same people, whom Bolivar helped to gain their country's independence, that are now in Venezuela, uninvited, undocumented!

In 1777, when Spain established the Captaincy-General of Venezuela it included most of present day Venezuela. Venezuela's population in 1800, may have totaled around 700,000. By race the population was roughly: 140,000 whites, 100,000 negro slaves, 70,000 Indians, and 400,000 pardos (mixed blood) and free Negroes. The white minority dominated this society. Under colonial law, only Spanish gentlemen, whose racial backgrounds contained no Jewish, Moorish or Negro antecedents, could join the royal army, attend the university, or take religious orders. The criollo class could use the partitive "Don" or "Dona" in front of their Christian names. The criollo class did not do manual work. (Even 40 years ago, one would not go out and wash one's car, which was considered work for the maid or gardener, or chofer if you had one.)

Looking at this illegal immigration problem, **and** these boundary problems that commenced in the 19th Century, one can see how Venezuela has turned into a country that is ungovernable! With the use of the ballot, 80% of the population, which is now poor, can vote for a demagogue who promises nirvana. Through the ballot, a democracy can vote to destroy itself by voting for a tyrant.

Leo Strauss, the scholar (and my teacher at Claremont) and author most responsible for the revival in the United States of the serious study of ancient political thought, wrote a book On Tyranny (1963). Why was Mr. Strauss concerned with modern tyranny? It was his conviction that thanks to the modern "conquest of nature" and of human nature in particular, tyranny threatens for the first time to become universal and perpetual. Therefore, man must reconsider the conditions of human freedom.

EPILOGUE

World War I caused great demands on U.S. petroleum resources, resulting in an increase of 60% in domestic production between 1912 – 1918, from 609,000 b/d to over 1 million barrels per day. By the mid-1920s, U.S. geologists were active on every continent. Large oil reserves were developed abroad by U.S. oilmen during the intensive search. In 1923, U.S. oil companies owned share of all foreign production, excluding the Soviet Union, was 46 percent. However, many large fields were soon discovered in the United States, including the giant East Texas field in 1930, and U.S. interest in foreign development was dampened for the next 10 years, except for Venezuela. By 1943, the U.S. overseas share had declined to 30% (440,000 b/d out of 1.53 million b/d) and most of this production was in Venezuela. During World War II it was Venezuelan oil from these fields that greatly contributed to the Allies winning the War.

Venezuela leaped into petroleum production in the 1920s under foreign direct investment, and by 1928 was the largest exporter of crude oil in the world. Foreign direct oil investments were the best investments the U.S. ever made abroad, having an average annual return of $2 for every dollar invested. U.S. oil companies invested over $3.5 billion in their operations in Venezuela, in the 55 years they operated in Venezuela.

My father, Gene Brossard, landed in Maracaibo on August 17, 1923. He was hired by Andrew Mellon (who at the time was U.S. Secretary of the Treasury), to go to Venezuela as one of the first geologists that Gulf Oil sent to Venezuela. The first year he worked on both sides of Lake Maracaibo. These young geologists mapped from Altagracia, east to La Victoria and south including El Cansejo, Cabimas, Quiros, El Merito, and Lagunillas.

"The big discovery well La Rosa had already been drilled. We began a camp at Cabimas, and the wells began. The influx of drillers, tank builders, and pipe liners was rapid. Crebbs [Chester] moved from Caracas to Maracaibo and Boylan [E. E.] was sent to open up the work in Eastern Venezuela.

229

I and about a dozen geologists and engineers followed. We had a set up like the first days in Maracaibo. Every night we moved back the drawing tables and put up the cots that were personal equipment used in both town and bush. Each time we left for the job we were taken 28 kilometers to Carataquiche where we found our not so "beloved" mules and pack burros. Our work consisted of measuring section, and reconnaissance mapping. The engineers were surveying district and state lines to find out how much area our concessions encompassed. Then too, there were private concessions to survey. We worked the northern half of Anzoategui [state] and I got a three months trip examining some claims we had options on in the state of Sucre.

After several years of this we moved to Ciudad Bolivar [on the Orinoco River] because it was closer to our work, which was now in central and southern Anzoategui, as well as part of Monagas.

We had a fast change of bosses. After Boylan, came Shorty Martin, and then after Avery Turner, I took over very soon after our arrival in C.B. There I remained 12 years, enjoying the work, which expanded most rapidly my last three years there. In that time was built two large terminals at San Tome and Puerto la Cruz, and a 98 mile, 16 inch pipeline connecting the two. I had the honor of opening the gate valve [and I was there, too] that loaded the first tankers [December 4, 1939].

The set up for loading tankers at Puerto la Cruz is the finest I have ever seen, and I have heard the same from others who have seen many installations for handling oil from shore to ship. The Puerto la Cruz tank farm has the discharge tanks at an elevation of 300 feet higher than the tankers that load through 24-inch discharge lines. The individual tanks hold 134,000 barrels and have pantoon roofs that float on the oil inside the tanks, raising and falling according to the amount of oil in the tanks.

The last three years were spent in Caracas.

In all, I had 19 years in Venezuela and took in most of it the hard way—most of it on a hay burner [mule]. I was Representative of the company [Gulf Oil]. There were 3,000 on the payroll including all departments that make up a production outfit. We were heavy on geophysical work the last ten years in exploration work."

Written to me by Gene (Eugene Edward) Brossard on April 25, 1949, in San Jose, Costa Rica, where he had started the first airlines in Central America (Transportes Aereos Nacionales, S.A.) with Jimmy Angel, in 1946. Jimmy Angel discovered Angel Falls in Venezuela, in 1936. Jimmy and his wife, Marie, used to stay in our home in Ciudad Bolivar. Jimmy gave me my first airplane ride (in the co-pilot's seat) when he flew me to Caracas to visit my grandmother, Ana Julia Gandica de Jacobsen.

When I was studying at the University of Wisconsin, I wrote the first thesis on the Venezuelan oil industry, and the above letter from my father answered some of my questions. My father left Venezuela at the height of World War II in 1942, to serve his country, again. He had been a pilot in World War I, was a University of Wisconsin graduate in geology, and had a Masters in petroleum engineering. He was in Colombia for four years, in charge of the Muso emerald mines, before he went to Venezuela. In addition to his oil exploration work in Venezuela, and the building of San Tome oil camp and the Puerto la Cruz terminal, Gene Brossard discovered Cerro Bolivar, the great iron mountain, in **1928**, while flying his company's Ford Tri-Motor south of the Orinoco River. Unfortunately, he never received credit for this discovery, although it is well documented, and I have a copy of his geological report, dated May 31, 1928. Thanks to Dr. Hollis Hedberg's insistence that I locate this report, and Juan Chacin who was President of Meneven, I poured through their geological files for two weeks and located it – under file 193-A:8, in the old Mene Grande files. This discovery of Cerro Bolivar also resulted in the discovery of the great Guayana Shield, proving there was no oil to be discovered south of the Orinoco River in Venezuela.

At Louisiana State University, I established the Hollis D. Hedberg Award in Energy in 1983, and when I left, I gave it to the Institute for the Study of Earth and Man (ISEM) at Southern Methodist University (SMU), in Dallas. It seemed a logical choice at the time, since this was Juan Chacin's alma mater and he was President of PDVSA, and had been one of the many geologists who had trained and worked under Dr. Hedberg's guidance in Mene Grande (Gulf Oil). This award has honored some fine geologists, starting with the great man himself, who received the first award. In time, through a key member of the Board of PDVSA, I was able to get the Board of PDVSA to make a $150,000 endowment for a Hedberg Award and Fellowship Fund, in November 1990. The Agreement between CEPET (for PDVSA) and ISEM to sponsor a Venezuelan graduate student at SMU has never been acted upon. In spite of my efforts to get first CEPET and then Intevep to send someone, there has never been a Fellowship Award recipient. For some qualified PDVSA employees, this has been a missed opportunity to study for graduate degrees.

It has been a personal disappointment not to be able to help a few capable Venezuelans that would have benefited and honored to receive a Hedberg Fellowship. Hollis Hedberg arrived in Venezuela in 1926, and through his hard work made enormous contributions to Venezuela's subsurface and surface geology in both western and eastern Venezuela. No one else knew the geology of Venezuela like Dr. Hedberg. He was also a great admirer of its people. He was often at our home in Ciudad Bolivar, in the 1930s, when I was a child. He worked with my father for Mene Grande, and one can safely say, he was loved and respected by all who knew him, particularly by the many young Venezuelan geologists that he trained. Dr. Hedberg died in Princeton, New Jersey, on August 14, 1988.

Hollis Hedberg and Gene Brossard were part of a group of exceptional men who went to Venezuela in the early days of the oil industry, and made enormous contributions to this country's development. They were well educated at our best universities. Some married lovely Venezuelan women, among them, my mother. These men contributed with unstinting energy and endeavor to find and develop Venezuela's oil fields. And when they were able, they educated and trained the best Venezuelans. This was a good partnership between the foreign oilmen and the Venezuelans. And not to be overlooked, these foreign oilmen and their families grew to love Venezuela. Few ever wanted to leave the country. I used to say, "Venezuela gets a hook in you and never lets go." With a sad heart, now I have to say, "there is no hook," for Venezuelans have left or are leaving, seeking personal security and liberty!

SELECTED BIBLIOGRAPHY

Arrioja, Jose Enrique, <u>Clientes Negros</u>, Petroleos de Venezuela
    Bajo la Generacion Shell, Editorial Torino, Caracas 1998.

Becker, Jasper, <u>Hungry Ghosts: Mao's Secret Famine</u>. Free Press,
    1997.

Braden, Spruille, <u>Diplomats and Demagogues</u>, Arlington House,
    New Rochelle, N.Y., 1971.

Brossard, Emma Beatriz, "The Military Government of Marcos
    Perez Jimenez," MA thesis, Claremont Grad Univ., 1968.

Cheng, Nien, <u>Life and Death in Shanghai</u>, Grove Press, New York,
    1987.

Cordeiro, Jose Luis, <u>El Gran Tabu Venezolano</u>, Ediciones Cedice,
    Caracas, 1997.

Courtois, Stephane, et.al., <u>The Black Book of Communism</u>,
    Harvard University Press, 1999 (English).

Garrido, Alberto, <u>Guerrilla y Conspiracion Militar en Venezuela</u>,
    Fondo Editorial Nacional, Caracas, 1999.

Gertz, Bill, <u>The China Threat</u>, How the People's Republic Targets
    America, Regnery Publishing, Washington, D.C., 2000.

Gott, Richard, <u>In the Shadow of the Liberator, Hugo Chavez, and
    The Transformation of Venezuela</u>, Verso imprint of New
    Left Books, London, and New York, 2000.

Lazo, Mario, <u>Dagger in the Heart</u>, American Policy Failures in
    Cuba, Twin Circle, 1968.

Lizaso, Felix, <u>Marti, Martyr of Cuban Independence</u>, University of
    New Mexico Press, 1953.

Lord, Bette Bao, <u>Legacies, A Chinese Mosaic</u>, Alfred A. Knopf,
    New York, 1990.

Masur, Gerhard, <u>Simon Bolivar</u>, Univ. of New Mexico Press,
    Albuquerque, 1969.

Morin, Guillermo, <u>Los Presidentes de Venezuela</u>, 1811-1979,
    Meneven, 1981.

Olavarria, Jorge, <u>El Golfo de Venezuela</u>, Ernesto Armitano,
    Caracas, 1988.

Smith, Earl E. T., <u>The Fourth Floor, An Account of the Castro
    Communist Revolution</u>, Random House, New York, 1962.

Turchetti, Claudio, <u>El Informe Poseidon</u>, Editorial Bonfanti,
    Caracas, 1999.

Power and Petroleum

Utley, Freda, The China Story, Henry Regnery Co., Chicago, 1951.
Vallenilla, Luis, La Apertura Petrolera, Un Peligroso Retorno Al
    Pasado, Ediciones Porvenir, Caracas, 1995.
Velasquez, Ramon J., Los Libertadores de Venezuela, Meneven,
    1983.

General Publications:
Business Venezuela, VenAmCham monthly magazine, published
    in Caracas.

U.S. Cuba Policy Report, published monthly by the Institute for
    U. S. Cuba Relations, Washington, D.C.

PDVSA al Dia, published by PDVSA
PDVSA Contact Newsletter
PDVSA Annual Reports

Newspapers:
Houston Chronicle
New York Times
The Wall Street Journal
Washington Post
Washington Times

Hundreds of articles taken from major Venezuelan newspapers,
particularly those on the Internet:
El Nacional; *El Universal*; and *Tal Qual*.

The Daily Journal (Caracas)

INDEX

A

Accion Democratica (AD), 14, 22, 36, 56-57, 61, 98, 150, 152,

Acosta, Cecilio, 110

Acosta Carles, Felipe, 157

Acton, Lord, 60

Adams, John, vi-vii

Adams, John Quincy, 115, 136

Agrarian Reform Law (INRA) of 1959, 124-125

Airbus 319 Corporate Jetliner, 162, 168

Albright, Madeleine, 135

Alcock, Frank, 51, 53, 62, 77

Alfaro Ucero, Luis, 55

Allende, Salvador, 35, 125

Alliance for Progress, 130

"Alo Presidente," 17, 28, 103, 154, 161

Alvarez, Bernardo, 97

Alvarez Paz, Oswaldo, 26, 55

Amazonas, 216-217

Ameriven Hamaca, 63-64

Amoco, 54, 70, 88, 219

Amuay refinery, 81, 105

Andean Community of Nations (CAN), 18, 39, 162

Andean Pact of 1969, 39

Andersen Consulting (Accenture), 78

Anderson, Howard, 124

Angel, Jimmy, 231

Angola, 177-179

Angulo, Edgar, 43

Apertura (Opening), 51, 58, 60-75, 87, 92, 99

Aponte, Pedro, 58

Arab Oil Embargo, 1, 44, 57

Arbenz Guzman, 125

Archbishop Baltazar Porras, 44-45

Arco, 63, 72

Arias Cardenas, Francisco, 25, 157, 165

Arichuna, Cacique, 216

ARMA (Alianza Revolucionaria de Militares Activos), 32

Armas, Celestino, 64, 98
Armonicos de Oriente y Occidente, 55
Arrieta, Erwin, 52, 53, 55, 74
Atlantic LNG, 62, 219
Autentico party, 146
B
Bagehot, Walter, 25
Ball, George, 111
damnificados, 148
Bank of America, 58
Barreto, Aires, 95
Barrientos, Pres. Rene, 173
Batista, Fulgencio, 119-121, 127, 137, 145, 184
baseball, 160-161
Bastidas, Adina, 27
Bauer, Peter Paul von, 200
Bay of Pigs (Playa Giron), 112-115, 125, 130, 144
Beal Aerospace Technologies, 192, 224-225
Becker, Jasper, 180-181
Beichman, Arnold, 180
Bello, Andres, 110, 214
Beltran, Pablo, 207
Benacerraf, Baruj, 110
Benton Oil, 65
Benzo, Linares, 149
Betancourt, Jose Luis, 208
Betancourt, Romulo, 7, 19, 20, 22, 27, 31, 37, 39, 57, 111,
        121, 126-130, 140, 149-154, 172, 220
Betancur, Belisario, 203-204
Bishop, Maurice, 174-176
Black Friday 1983, the Bolivar, 40-42
Blanco Munoz, Agustin, 45
Bogotazo, 123, 199
boinas rojas (Red Berets), 170-171
Bolivarian Church, 45
Bolivarian Constitution (la bicha), 5,15-16, 25-26, 29, 164, 191, 204
Bolivarian Republic, 5, 18
Bolivariano Revolutionary Movement 200, 46

Bolivar, Simon, vii, 2, 11, 18-20, 45, 48-49, 90, 109, 115, 127, 131, 134, 146, 154-155, 158, 199, 211-215, 228

Boulton, Ricardo, 202

Boulton, Roger, 40

Boylon, E.E., 229-230

Braden, Ambassador Spruille, 200

C.F. Braun Engineering, 107

Bravo, Douglas, 31, 158

Brewer Carias, Allan, 15

British Gas, 219

British Petroleum, 65, 68, 70, 82, 105, 106, 202, 219

BPAmocoArco, 76, 90

Brossard, Eugene E. (Gene), 81, 197, 229-232

Burrelli, Miguel Angel, 169

Bukovsky, Vladimir, 123

buhoneros, 151

"Bullets and hate," 129

Burke, Edmund, 60, 148

Burnham, Forbes, 224-226

Bustillos, Silvino, 31,

Bush, President George, 144

Bush, President George W., vii, 50, 71

C

Caballero, Manuel, 158

Cabot Trinidad (Tractebel), 219

Cacerolazo, 144

Caldera, Juan Jose, 44

Caldera, Rafael, 20, 22, 29, 52-53, 56, 58, 60, 129-130, 134, 137, 146, 150, 154, 157, 169, 217-218

Calderon Berti, Humberto, 52, 55, 75, 99, 170

Caligula's horse, 15

Capital costs of producing oil, 82

Captaincy-General of Cuba, 136-137

Caracas Energy Accord of 2000, 74, 149, 166-169

Caracas Indian tribes, 159

Caribbean Community (Caricom), 11

Caribbean Energy Action (CEAP), 169

Carlos the Jackal, 1

Carter, Jimmy, 26, 41, 209

Casas, Bartolome de las, 115
Castillo, Carlos, 51
Castro, Cipriano, 35
Castro, Angel (y Lina Ruz), 155
Castro, Emma, 127, 155
Castro, Fidel, vi-vii, 1, 3, 7-8, 11-14, 16, 25, 28, 31-32, 35, 38, 44-
47, 49, 109, 110-147, 148-156, 160, 163-180, 193, 198-200
Castro, Juana, 145, 155
Castro, Raul, 120, 147, 155-156
Caterpillar bulldozers, 114
Catholic Church, 5, 9, 45, 124, 152
Causa Radical Party, 61
Central Bank, 15, 41-42, 57, 64
Central University (Universidad Central de Ven.), 20-21, 126, 148
Ceresole, Norberto, 32-35
Cerro Negro, 63-64
Chacin, Juan, 231
Chalmette Refining, 105
Champlin Petroleum Co., 102
Charles, Eugenia, 176
Chavez, Adan, 158
Chavez Frias, Hugo, vi-vii, 1-13, 14-50, 51, 56, 73-74, 85-109,
110, 125, 129-130, 132, 138, 146-147, 148-193, 205-208,
210-212, 213-214, 218, 220-226.
Chavez, Hugo de los Reyes, 156, 158
Chavez, Marisabel Rodriguez de, 158
Chavezuela (Chavezlandia), 25, 49, 158
"Chavista," 2, 26, 44, 94, 149,163, 184
Cheng, Nien, 182-183
Chevron, 54, 67, 72, 76, 82, 88, 91, 106, 179
Chiang Kai-sek, 184-186
China, 2, 7, 11-13, 28, 180-193
China Lobby, 188
China National Petroleum Corp., 72, 191
Chou En-lai, 186
Ciavaldini, Hector, 10, 28, 32, 48, 51, 88-94
Cienfuegos, Camilio, 123
Cienfuegos refinery, 168
Circulos Bolivarianos, 7

Cisneros, Diego, 145
Cities Service Co., 99-101
Citgo Petroleum Co., 2, 15, 29-30, 58, 88, 90, 94-95, 98-105
Citgo International Latin America (CILA), 104
Clean Air Act Amendments of 1991, 103
Cleveland, Grover, 221
Clinton, William, 54, 133-135, 139, 144, 189, 207
Clinton-Castro Agreement of 1994, 115-116, 126
Clinton's "wet foot-dry-foot" test," 116
COMACATE, 157
CMS Energy, 67
Columbus, 6, 115, 218
Conoco, 62-63, 70, 92
Constitutional Assembly (ANC), 3, 23-24, 47
Contreras Maza, General Oswaldo, 28, 95, 103-104
Control Committee (of CVP), 68
Convergencia party, 44
COPEI (Christian Dem.) party, 14, 22, 36, 55, 61, 98, 150
Cordeiro, Jose Luis, 74, 85
Cordoba, Jose de, 210
Corporacion Venezolana del Petroleo (CVP), 54, 58, 68, 77, 96
Corpoven, 51, 54-55, 77,
Cox Committee, 180, 189
Crebbs, Chester, 229
Creole Petroleum Corp., 21, 47, 54, 57, 81, 90, 220
Cristobal Colon LNG project, 60-64, 219
Cuban Adjustment Act of 1966, 132-133
Cuban Brigade's Air Squadron, 114
Cuban Communist Party, 46
Cuban Democracy Act of 1992, 138
Cuban doctors, 8, 179, 195, 296
Cuban Families Committee, 114
Cuban guerrillas, 150
"Cubanizar," 38
Cuban Refugee Emergency Center, 131
Cuban Revolution, 12, 46, 110, 207
Cuban Vigilance Committees, 7
Cultural Revolution, 183-184, 192-193
Cunningham, Ralph, 103

Curacao refinery, 81
Cusiana 2A, 175
CTV (Confederacion de Trabajadores Venezolanos), 29
CVG (Corp. Venezolana de Guayana), 30, 58, 227
D
Dallas Petroleum Club, 66
Da Silva, "Lula," 46
Davila, Luis Alfonzo, 27, 34
Debray, Regis, 123, 173
Declaration of Caracas, 144
de Gaulle, Charles, vi
DGI (Direccion General de Inteligencia), 179-180
Diaz Lanz, Major Pedro, 123
Diaz-Verson, Salvador, 125
DISIP (Direc. de los Servicios de Intelig.y Prevencion), 46
Distrigas terminal, 62
Doherty, Henry L., 99
Draper, Theodore, 147
drilled reserves, 81
DSMA Oil Belt project, 64
Duarte, Napoleon, 170
Dulles, John Foster, 119
Duvalier, Papa Doc, 16
E
Eastland, Sen. James O., 120
Education and Decree 1011, 9, 34-35, 146
Eisenhower, Dwight (Adm.), 60, 113, 119, 121, 125, 144
Eisenhower, Milton, 114, 119
ELPV (Ejercito de Liberacion del Pueblo de Ven.), 156-157
ELN (National Liberation Army), 1, 10, 47, 173, 197-199,
        201-203, 206-207
Enabling Law (Ley Habilitante), 23-24
"en cadena," 45
El Encanto train, 128
El Saqueo, 157, 164
El Silencio, 126
encomendero, 160
Enron, 70, 76, 219
Environmental Protection Administration (EPA), 103

Eppel, Sammy, 163
ERBZ (Ejercito Revolucionario Bolivariano Zamorano), 159
Escobar, Pablo, 204
Esso, 122
Estrada Palma, Tomas, 116, 118
Exploration Assoc. Contracts (Operating Agree.), 67-69, 70-73
ExxonMobil, 54, 62, 71-72, 76-77, 81-83, 91,105, 106, 140,191
EZLN (Zapatistas), 46
F
Factor de Valorizacion (FDV) or Bonus, 71
FALN (Fuerzas Armadas de Liberacion Nacional), 31-32, 36
FAN (National Armed Forces), 4, 27, 30-32, 36, 47
FARC (Rev.Armed Forces of Col.), 1, 10, 198, 201-207
Fedecamaras (Federation of Chambers of Commerce), 39
Fedepetrol union, 28, 152
Federal War (1858-1863), 19
Fernandez Moran, Dr. Humberto, 110
Fifth Republic, 2, 32, 49
Figueres, Jose (Pepe), 127-128
Floods of December 1999, 2-4, 27, 49, 164, 206
FMC (Frente Militar de Carrera), 31
Fondo Estabilizacion Macroeconomica (FEM), 88, 92
Fondo Unico Social (FUS), 30
Fox, Vicente, 95, 148
Fundamental Law of the Rev. Govt., (Cuba), 145
G
Gaceta Oficial, 3, 9, 15, 16, 91
Gallegos, Romulo, 150
Gairy, Eric, 174-175
Gaitan, Jorge, 123
Garcia Morales, Captain Luis, 31
Garrido, Alberto, 32
Gas Hydrocarbons Organic law of 1999, 96
Gaviria, Cesar, 147 169
General Electric Credit Co., 102
Gertz, Bill, 112, 180, 189
Gil Fortoul, Jose, 211
Gilman, Rep. Ben, 139
Giordani, Jorge, 32

Giusti Group, 59-60
Giusti, Luis, 51-56, 59-60, 70-75, 78, 90-91, 108
Giusti, Roberto, 23
Golden Goose, 60, 85-109
Gomez, General Juan Vicente, 16, 29, 35, 149-150
Gonzalez, Elian, 134
Gonzalez, Prime Minister Felipe, 143
Graf, Claus, 54, 55
Grafters, 118
Gramsci, Antonio, 32-33
Gran Colombia, vii, 10-11, 19, 109, 204, 207, 212-216
Grau San Martin, Ramon, 119, 146
Great Leap Forward, 16, 180-181
Grenada, 174-177, 226
Gromiko, Andrei A., 199
Grupo Garibaldi, 32
Guaicaipuro, Cacique, 159
Guantanamo Bay, 118
Guayana (Esequibo), 220-227
Guevara, Ernesto (Che), 1, 32, 129, 171-174, 178
Gulf Oil Corp. 77, 83, 99, 106-107, 178, 229-232
Gulf War of 1990, 164
Guri Dam, 227
Guzman Blanco, Antonio, 19, 110
H
Hall, Ron, 103
Halliburton, 107
Hammer, Dr. Armand, 99
Havana Rotary Club, 144
Hayek, Friedrich, 5
Hearst, Randolph, 117
Hedberg, Dr. Hollis D., 231-232
Helms-Burton Act of 1996, 139-140
Hernandez Grisanti, Arturo, 58
Hernandez Jacobsen, Guillermo, 216
Hernandez, Hugo, 151
Herrera Campins, Luis, 41-42, 57, 98, 170-171, 175, 205
Herrera-Vaillant, Antonio, 14
Hess Joint Venture, 104-105

Hinds, Samuel, 224
Hiss, Alger, 209
Houston InterAmerican Chamber of Commerce, 66
Hussein, Saddam, 1, 12, 109, 162
Hutchison Whampoa Ltd., 189
Hydrocarbon Nationalization Law of 1975, 57, 61, 88
I
Ibero-American Summit, 7, 143
Ibor City (Tampa cigars), 135
International Conference of American States, 123
International Confed. of Free Trade Unions (ICFTU), 28
International Labor Organization (ILO), 28
International Petroleum Exchange (IPE), 80
Interven, 102
J
Jacobsen, Ana Julia Gandica de, 231
Jacobsen, Julius, 196
Jaffa, Harry V., 14, 195
Jagan, Chedi, 224-226
Jantesa, 71
Jefferson, Thomas, 136
Jiang Zemin, 191
Johnson, Lyndon, 132, 144, 201
Jones Costigan Act (1934), 137
July 26, 1953 Movement, 145
K
Kamkoff, Jorge, 95
Kennedy, John F, 111-115, 144
Kennedy, Robert, 114
King John of England, 24
Kissinger, Henry, 59
Korean War, 1
Khrushchev, Nikita, 111-112, 128, 153
Kuwait Drilling Co., 106
Kuwait Petroleum International, 106-107
Kuwait Oil Company, 106
Kuwait Petroleum Corp. (KPC), 106-107
L
La Alquitrana, 83

Labor Law of 1936, 29, 69
La Casona, 162
Lagoven, 51, 54-55, 61-65,
Lake Maracaibo Bridge, 150
Lameda Montero, General Guaicaipuro, 10, 28, 94-95, 167
Land of Grace, 6
La Orchila island, 3, 164
La Petrolia, 83
Lara, Justice Minister Rodrigo, 203
Larrazabal, Wolfgang, 126
Latell, Brian, 154
La Violencia, 123, 199
Lazo, Mario, 114, 121, 155-156
Leoni, Raul, 121, 130, 150
Lleras Camargo, Alberto, 200
Lleras Restrepo, Carlos, 200
Lincoln, Abraham, 51
Lingoteras, 65
"Little Venice," 159
Lopez Contreras, Pres. Eleazar, 20, 146, 216
Lopez Michelsen, Pres. Alfonso, 47
Lopez Portillo, Pres. Jose, 147
Lopez Quevedo, Eduardo, 52, 67, 91
Lord, Bette Bao, 182
Louisiana Land and Exploration, 70
Lourdes operation (SIGINT), 138, 143
Lusinchi, Jaime, 58, 98
M
M-19, 203-204, 209
Machado, Gerardo, 102
Machado, Gustavo, 127
"Machine Gun Alley," 131
Madison, James, 21, 136
Magna Carta, 3, 5, 16, 24
Mahuad, Jamil, 40, 208
Mallet-Prevost, Severo, 222-223
Mandini, Roberto, 10, 48, 53, 79, 88-93, 157
Mao Zedong, 1, 7, 25, 32, 150, 180-186, 192-193
Marathon Oil, 99

Maraven, 51-52, 54-55, 62-63, 66-67, 77
March and Banging of the Empty Pots, 125
"Marco Polo of Sabaneta," 162
Margolin, Jean-Louis, 180
Marielito exodus in 1980, 132
Mariscobetre, Domingo, 95
Marshall, Gen. George, 184-186
Marti, Jose, 110, 116
Martin, Everett G., 56
Martin, Shorty, 230
Martinez, General Rafael, 95
Marulanda, Manuel, 198, 201
Marx, Karl, 125
Mas Canosa, Jorge, 154
Maso, Fausto, 30
Masur, Gerhard, 214
Mata Osorio, Andres, 154
Matos, Major Huber, 123
Matthews, Herbert, 120, 156
Maxus (YPF), 66, 70
May Day 1961, 125
Mayobre, Jose A., 60, 85
MBR-200, 7, 46, 157
McKinley, William, 117, 222
McCullough, David, vi
Medina Angarita, Pres. Isaias, 20-21, 146, 150, 195
Mellon, Andrew, 229
Mendez Quijada, Jesus, 167
Mene Grande Oil Co. (Gulf), 21, 54, 81, 231
Meneven, 52, 54, 77
Merriman, Gary, 92
Midwest Refining, 90
Mikoyan, Anastas, 125
Ministry of Energy and Mines, 10, 51-53, 59, 64, 97-98
Miquilena, Luis, 3, 26, 32, 48, 129
MIR (Movimiento Izquierda Revolucionaria), 152-153
Miraflores palace, 1, 5, 89, 91, 94, 102, 154, 162, 167
Miranda, Francisco, 48, 213
Missile Crisis of October 1962, 112-114, 128, 132

Mitsubishi, 61-62
Mobil Oil, 54, 63, 70, 82, 106
Montiel Ortega, Leonardo, 149
Morles, Colonel Arraez, 31
Mosbacker Oil, 66
Moscoso, Mireya, 48
Mosher, Steven W., 188
Munoz, George, 28
Munoz Marin, Gov. Luis, 127
Muso Emerald Mines, 197, 231
MVR (Movimiento Quinta Republica), 32, 157
N
Narco Traffic, 38, 225
Natera, Brigido, 54, 100, 102
National Assembly, 18, 23, 44, 48
Natural Gas Law of 1971, 83
New York Mercantile Exchange, 80
Nippon Oil, 70
Nixon, Richard (and Pat), 37, 113, 188
Noboa Government, 47, 208
Norcen, 70
North American Chamber of Commerce of Ven., 60
North Atlantic Treaty Organization, 166
North Korean Army, 186-187
O
OAS Foreign Ministers, 126, 128-129, 138, 177, 199
Occidental Petroleum, 66, 99-100
Ochoa, Orlando, 43, 54, 109, 151
October 27, 1982, 57
Office of Strategic Services (OSS), 121
Oil Entitlements Program of 1975, 101
Oil Investment Fund, 57
Oil in storage, 81
Oil traders, 79-83
Olavarria, Jorge, 34, 86, 88
O'Leary, General Daniel, 215
OPEC, 9, 12, 21, 39, 49-50, 54, 73, 79-80, 82-83, 87,
        96, 105-108, 161, 162 (Caracas Summit), 164
"Operation Caracas," 153

Operation Peter Pan, 114
OPIC (Overseas Private Investment Corp.), 28
Organization of Eastern Caribbean States (OECS), 176
Orimulsion, 192
Orinoco Oil Belt, 58, 63-64, 70, 72, 83
Ortega, Carlos, 28
Ortega, Daniel, 46, 163
P
Pact of Caracas, 127
Pacto de Punto Fijo, 22-23, 37, 158
Panama Canal, 109, 189, 192, 200, 208-209
Pan American Conference, 199
Paria North LNG, 62
Parra, Alirio, 66
Pastrana, Andres, 10, 46-47, 198, 201, 206-208
Pastrana Borrero, 198, 201
PDV America, Inc., 58, 105
PDVSA Board of Directors, 1, 28, 52-53, 56, 78, 89-91,
        95, 103, 108
PDVSA Oil and Gas, S.A., 78
PDVSA Gas, 96-97
PEG (Participacion del Estado en las Ganancias), 68-70
Pena, Alejandro, 47
"People's Balcony," 37-38
People's Liberation Army, 188
Pemex, 54-55, 57, 76, 95
Pequiven, 91
Perez Alfonso, Juan Pablo, 57
Perez, Carlos Andres (CAP), 9, 19-20, 30-32, 41, 52, 55, 58, 64,
        101-102, 142, 150, 154, 156, 161, 163-165, 169, 196, 205
Perez Companc, 66, 70-71, 97
Perez Jimenez, Marcos, 19-21, 37, 125, 166
Perez la Salvia, Hugo, 53
Peron, Juan and Eva, 25
Petkoff, Teodoro, 31, 129
Petrobras, 54-55
Petroleos de Chavez, 9, 50, 78, 108-109
Petroleos de Venezuela (PDVSA), 1-2, 10, 13, 28-29, 32, 48-50,
        51-84, 85-109, 191, 232

Petrozuata, 63-64
Plan Bolivar 2000, 30
Plan Colombia, 11, 207-208
Platt Amendment, 118
Pluspetrol, 97
Phillips, 63, 72
Pickens, T. Boone, 99
Pierce, Pres. Franklin, 115
Policia de Giusti, 59
Polo Patriotico coalition, 157
Portocarrero, Blancanieves, 163
Pradas, Francisco (Paco), 66
Praetorian Guard, 30
Praselj, Eduardo, 95
PRD (Democratic Revolutionary Party), 46
PriceWaterhouse, 54
Prio Socarras, Carlos, 119, 125, 146
Project Gas, 83
PRV (Party of the Venezuelan Revolution), 32
Pulido, Manuel, 83
Pulitzer, Joseph, 117
Putin, Vladimir, 143
Q
Qadhafi, Mu'amar, 1, 109
Quijada, Manuel, 34
Quiriquire tribe, 159
Quiros Corradi, Alberto, 86, 90, 92, 104, 170
"Q8" service stations, 107
R
Rangel, Jose Vicente, 4, 8, 26-27, 32-33, 46,129, 164, 208
Rangel, Domingo Alberto, 152
Reagan, Pres. Ronald, 79, 124, 144, 175-176
Recadi, 40-41
Red Guards, 182
Reed, Dr. Walter, 117
Referendum of December 3, 2000, 27-28
Refugee Act of 1980, 133-134
Reno, Janet, 133-135
Repsol YPF, 72, 97, 168, 219

Revel, Jean-Francois, 141
Revolutionary Front (led by Ciavaldini), 88
Revolutionary Law No. Two (Cuba), 120
Reyes, Raul, 207
Rhee, Syngman, 186
Ribbentrop-Molotov Pact of 1939, 200
Rio Pact, 112, 144
Rodriguez, Ali, 49, 77, 129
Rodriguez, Isaias, 23, 27
Rodriguez Ochoa, General Arnoldo, 95
Rodriguez, Simon, 158, 214-215
Rolando, Nicolas, 35
Roosen, Gustavo, 52, 55
Roosevelt, Eleanor, 114
Roosevelt, Franklin, 121, 184-185, 208
Roosevelt, Theodore, 222
Root, Elihu, 118
Rowan, Michael, 10, 47, 49
Royal Dutch Shell, 61, 64, 72, 76, 82, 91, 102, 122, 191
Rubottom, Roy (Dick), 119-121, 124
Ruhr Oel, 98
S
al Sabah, Ali Khalifa, 106
al Sabah, Jaber al-Ahmad, 101
Saez, Irene, 151
Salgueiro, Adolfo P., 162
Salomon Brothers, 58
Sanabria, Edgar, 126
Sandinistas, 46, 131
Santa Fe International, 106-107
Salazar, General Raul, 4, 27
San Carlos Cuartel, 37
San Jose Pact, 41, 154, 166, 169-170
San Martin, Jose de, 213
San Tome oil camp, 231
Saman de Guere, 157
Sao Paulo Forum (Foro de S P), 12, 26, 46-47, 161, 207
Saudi Aramco, 60, 76, 106
Savelli Maldonado, Carlos, 190

SCADTA German airline, 200
Schlesinger, Arthur, 114
Schmidt, Rodolfo, 30, 165
Schomburgh, Robert H., 221
School of the Americas, 190
Scoon, Sir Paul, 177
Seaview Petroleum Co. (asphalt refinery), 102
Senate Foreign Relations Committee, 124
Seven Sisters, 83
Seventh (7th) oil operation, 80
Shell International Petroleum, 182-183
Shell de Venezuela, 21, 52-55, 61, 91
Sherritt International Corp., 168
Simon Bolivar Front of Sovereign People of Venezuela, 183
Sino-Soviet Treaty of 1945, 185
Sincor, 63
Smith, Earl E. T., 119-121
Somoza, Anastasio, 130
Socorro, Milagros, 162
Southland Corporation, 99-101
Sosa Pietri, Andres, 55
Sosa Rodriguez, Julio, 53
South Atlantic Military Organization, 35, 161
Sovereignty, 38-39
Spanish American War (1898), 194
Spanish Conquistadores, 139
Stalin, Joseph, 187
Star Enterprise, 106
State Dept.'s Fourth Floor, 119-122
Statoil, 63, 72
Stevenson, Adlai, 114
St. George's Medical School, 176
Strategic Petroleum Reserve, 81
Strauss, Leo, 228
Sucre, Antonio Jose de, 213-214
Sucre Gas, S.A., 61, 219
Sweeney Joint Venture, 90
T
Tarbes, Jack, 51, 54, 93

Tauzin, Rep. Billy, 51
Teikoku Oil, 64-65
Tejera Paris, U.N. Ambassador, 56
Ten Years' War (Cuban), 116
Teques Indians, 139
Teresa Carreno Theater, 163
Texaco Corporation, 63, 76, 82, 106, 120, 122, 140
Thant, U, 112
Thatcher, Margaret, 176-177
Thompson, John P., 100
Timote Indians, 159
Tippeconnic, David, 103
Tocqueville, Alexis de, 5, 95
Total/Fina, 63-64, 66, 76, 97
Torres, Elroy, 31
Trade Embargo (1960), 137-138
Treaty of Madrid (1670), 136
Treaty with Spain (1819), 136
Treaty of 1977 with Panama, 33
Treaty to Avoid Double Taxation (1999), 105
Trinkunas, Julius, 53, 63
Truman, Harry, 121, 185-187
Turbay Administration, 176
Turner, Avery, 230
U
Unions, 10, 17, 27-30, 132
Union Pacific, 88
United Nations, 6, 75, 152, 162, 177, 227
URD party, 22
Urdaneta Hernandez, Col. Jesus, 46-47, 157
Urdaneta, Luis, 53
Urdaneta, Renato, 51, 61, 217
Uslar Pietri, Arturo, 6-7, 13, 23(death), 41, 84(Sowing), 86
U.S. Foreign Claims Settlement Commission, 122
U.S. Maine, 117
U.S. Mandatory Oil Import Program of 1959, 21, 60-61, 87
U.S. Maritime Administration, 138
"U.S. troops," 4
utilidades, 69

Utley, Freda, 184-185
V
Valle de los Caidos, 55
Vasquez Castano, Fabio, 201
Veba Oel, 63, 70, 97-98
Venezuelan Congress, 23, 33, 61, 63, 69-70, 148
Venezuelan Investment Fund, 169
Venezuelan Petroleum Chamber, 151
Vietnam War, 1
Vinccler Oil, 64
W
Wall Street, 7, 89
Walker III, Edward B., 106
Welles, Sumner, 118
Westin Galleria Hotel, 94
Westinghouse Audio Intelligence Devices, 59
Weyler, Valeriano (el Carnicero), 116
Wieland, William, 119
Wood, Dr. Leonard, 117-118
Workers Party (PT) of Brazil, 46
World Trade Organization, 164, 167
World War II, 1, 199, 200
X
Xenophobes in Venezuela, 211
Y
Yalta Conference, 185
Yamani, Sheikh Ahmed Zaki, 88
Yankee, vii, 191
Yare prison, 32-33, 37, 152
Yaruro Indian, 156, 159-160
Yeltsin, Boris, 138
Young Pioneers (Red Berets), 181
Dr. Youqin Wang, 193
Z
Zamora, Ezequiel, 158
Zapatistas, 46
Zuloaga Pocaterra, Nicomedes, 34, 177

Emma Brossard grew up and worked in the oil industry (Mene Grande/Gulf) in Venezuela. In 1983, her first book on the petroleum industry was published, <u>Petroleum Politics and Power</u>; followed in 1993 by <u>Petroleum Research and Venezuela's Intevep, The Clash of the Giants</u>. For 18 years, she taught political philosophy, Latin American politics, and energy politics, in several Midwest and Southern universities, and in 1979 was awarded the Distinguished Teaching Award. She was granted a BA in International Relations from the University of Wisconsin, Madison, and MA and Ph.D. in Government from Claremont Graduate University. She has testified before the energy and finance committees of the U.S. House of Representatives and the U.S. Senate. Between 1985 and 1994, Dr. Brossard was an adviser to the Presidency of PDVSA and its affiliates; and has been a consultant to U.S. oil companies.